Confessions
of a Boatbuilder

James D. Rosborough

SHERIDAN HOUSE

This edition published 2001 by
Sheridan House Inc.
145 Palisade Street
Dobbs Ferry, NY 10522

Library of Congress Cataloging-in-Publication Data

Rosborough, James Douglas, 1928–
    Confessions of a boatbuilder / James Douglas Rosborough
        p.cm.
    ISBN 1-57409-127-1
    1. Rosborough, James Douglas, 1928– 2. Naval architects—Nova
Scotia—Biography. 3. Boatbuilding—Nova Scotia—History—20th
century. I. Title.

    VM140.R67 A3 2001
    623.8'1'092—dc21
    [B]   00-047075

Design by Richard Cartledge

Printed in Canada
ISBN 1-57409-127-1

DEDICATION

DEDICATED TO ALL THOSE WONDERFUL, SINCERE, AND HARDWORKING
PEOPLE WHO MADE THE WORLD OF SAILING A BETTER PLACE.

TABLE OF CONTENTS

	Introduction vi
	Prologue ix
1	The Early Years—from Rowboats to Schooners 1
2	More Boats—More Hard Knocks 15
3	Atlantic Marine: A Business Disaster 21
4	Looking for Boats in Newfoundland................................. 29
5	Last of the Newfoundland Schooners................................ 35
6	*Lillian and Lizzie*: Traded for a Trailer 43
7	Back Again to Newfoundland.. 49
8	Gearing up in Nova Scotia 55
9	New Boats—New Ways—New Days 61
10	Dick Shaw Delivers 71
11	Business Expands—More New Yards 79
12	New Yards—New Boats 87
13	Bluewater Boats Busily Building—1966-1970 97
14	The Chester Boats 103
15	Simply Gorgeous Hal and the Magic Burning Boat 109
16	*Arctic Witch* 117
17	The Russells: Flying on their own 121
18	*Sea Chase – Trillium – Sea Trek II – Lesana* 131
19	The Admiral's Cannons 137
20	More 46-foot Yachts at Theriault's 147
21	Big, Medium, and Small at Theriault's 157
22	*Santa Maria* and Operation Sail 169
23	Custom Designs.. 173
24	A Final Trio From Bluewater Boats 181
25	A Quartet From Windjammer 189
26	Four Privateers From Theriault's 193
27	A Special Trio From Meteghan River 201
28	A Final Quartet of Privateers from A.F. Theriault's 209
29	The Last Days of Windjammer Yachts 217
30	Last of Our Wooden Boats at A.F. Theriault & Son 225
31	Some Last Boats With Donnie Russell 235
32	A Few More Before The End.. 243
	Appendix 253

INTRODUCTION

THIS IS A BOOK ABOUT WOODEN SAILING SHIPS. Not large ships as the world romanticizes them, but that great flotilla of small wooden vessels built in more honorable times, by men with heart and integrity.

In both design and construction, there was a good deal of tender loving care. In fact, it was the joy of the creativity that brought these craftsmen together. The designer had a dream; he could see the completed vessel on his drawing board; see it sailing away on a voyage of adventure and discovery. And he transmitted his vision to the builders, who worked with his plans to make the dream a reality.

In those days, wages were low, materials simple, strong, and inexpensive. Trees became sailing ships with the soul of the forest still in them. Coupled with sails, rigging, engines and equipment, each new vessel became a living thing, ready and eager to undertake its new life.

When Europeans first set foot in North America, they soon realized that here was a natural 'shipyard' ready to hand. Abundant forests provided the sturdy spruce, pine, hackmatack, oak and birch for timbers, plank and spar for their flotillas. The many snug harbours and inlets provided shelter while they gathered the plentiful harvest from sea and forest. Then, in order to market their products, they began to construct those sturdy and sea-proven vessels for which they became famous. Before roads crisscrossed the new colonies, builders turned out thousands of the smaller shallops, pinks, and schooners, which were principally used for in-shore fishing and coastal trading.

As trade expanded, east-coast yards and builders turned their talents to ever faster and taller ships both square-rigged and later fore-and-aft rigged. For more than a century these graceful, white-sailed merchantmen plied the ocean trade routes of the world and could be found in every port and harbour.

The three mast 'tern' schooners were a fine example of the builder's art, and from the 1850s to the 1920s were employed in exporting fish and timber cargoes to Europe and the West Indies, bringing home salt, sugar, and rum on the return voyage.

Gradually there developed a graceful and unique type of craft—a safe, dependable, sea-worthy fishing vessel which could be easily handled by two men, while the crew were off in dories, and yet could ride out the sometimes sudden and often vicious storms peculiar to the Atlantic Banks. As rugged and hardy as the men who sailed them, these vessels made their home ports in most of the small sheltered coves along the coast and sailed winter and summer in their hundreds, ranging in size from 30 feet to well over 100 feet in length.

With the advent of steam, these too all but passed from the scene, and there were all too few builders left who understood the materials and methods of their construction, and who had the inherited skill with broadaxe, adze and saw to 'put up' such vessels as proved themselves beyond equal during the Golden Age of Sail.

But this was not the end of the wooden schooners. A new affluent generation was drawn to the romance of the sea, and the builders, who are the heroes of this book, with salt-water in their veins and a proud maritime heritage behind them, set to reviving one last time the proud, romantic square-riggers which so gallantly filled their place in North America's history.

My purpose in writing this book is to recapture some of the maritime lore and romance during the last days of wooden boats and the craftsmen who built them. This was a time of adventure and adversity that shaped the destiny of both builders and sailors, and allowed progression to the sea-going vessels of today.

In it, I hope to show the integrity, humour and purpose of the characters involved. During 35 years, I designed and had built some 130 vessels at various sub-contracting boatyards in Atlantic Canada, delivered them to their owners and sent them sailing away over the oceans of the world. The colourful mix of owners, builders and suppliers provides the characters for the story of each vessel as it unfolds.

Most of the pictures, sketches and drawings included here were done by the author over a 35-year period. The reader's indulgence is begged in those where detail and clarity is lacking.

The story begins in the early 1950s when experienced, dedicated and hard-working boatbuilders, living and working in semi-isolation, might be paid little more than one dollar per hour, and ends in the 1980s, when a small shop of two to four men required $25 per man-hour, or more. Since wooden boatbuilding is labour intensive and requires skilled builders, eventually the cost of a completed vessel became prohibitively expensive. At the same time, investment income for the would-be buyer was affected by dropping interest rates ringing the death knell of small wooden boat building. But until then, it was a glorious, colourful and busy period, which this book attempts to portray.

Looking back over my years of association with boats and the marine scene, I can now say how grateful I am for having had the experience. All the wonderful, wise, and strange people who came along were a pleasure to observe and interact with. Some of the experiences were painful, some pleasurable, and all were very hard work, but they added up to a huge learning experience for which I am truly appreciative. I trust that all the characters involved, living or passed on, will allow me to share their stories in the spirit of gratitude in which this book is written. As the millennium closed, the days of wooden yachts and vessels passed into history as another of man's accomplishments. I felt that the story needed to be told for posterity.

DESTINED FOR BOAT DESIGN: JAMES DOUGLAS ROSBOROUGH, ONE–YEAR OLD.

IN ORDER TO BETTER UNDERSTAND the stories that follow, it might be useful to know a little of the author's background, and the culture and genealogy that shaped his mind, and personality.

I was born in Halifax, on May 13, 1928, as an only son to middle-class parents who had enjoyed a good social and economic life for ten years, before I arrived. Halifax was then a church-going, tea-drinking society that had been founded in 1749 as a military and naval base for British colonial forces. My father was a professional bass baritone and an accomplished figure skater, my mother a pianist. Social life largely centred around the churches, live theatre and gracious sports, such as snowshoeing, sleigh rides, tennis, quoits, amateur theatrical productions, musical evenings and bridge clubs. It was said that Halifax—the un-named East Coast port mentioned in war dispatches—simply slept between wars. The first between the English and French, then the U.S. War of Independence, and finally World Wars One and Two. During these exciting and dramatic periods, Halifax was a busy seaport with a rich and colourful mix of troops, seamen, merchants and all the hustle and bustle of the times.

My father, Ivan Halse Rosborough, the eldest of nine children, was born in Halifax. Back then, times were hard and money scarce. He was expected to help look after his eight younger siblings, including runny noses and all the other baby chores in days before the invention of Pampers. To make matters worse, his father liked to drink. He worked from 1875 to 1900 as a boss-carpenter with Brookfield's, a construction company based in south-end Halifax, and had to walk all the way across town to the house he had built for his family on Agricola Street in the north end. This necessitated passing by several pubs and taverns, which were just too tempting to ignore. On paydays, my grandmother, Tory (Victoria), sent my father, though only a young boy, from one drinking establishment to another to find his father and bring him home before all his money was gone. This chore was even more odious to my father than babysitting. He developed a strong resolve never to have anything to do with liquor or to have children. He was good at arithmetic, and after he trained himself in it, eventually became an actuary with the Workmen's Compensation Board. They gave him a new Model T Ford, and he cut a dashing figure in his grey pearl-buttoned spats, celluloid collar, and Homburg hat, when he presented himself as a suitor to my mother, five years his senior.

My mother, Grace Darling Bowser, was among the last in her family of a self-perceived post-Edwardian aristocracy. Her home was in south-end Halifax on Tower Road, a bastion of good breeding and civility, in her mind at least. Her father, Theophilus Smith Bowser (always referred to as T.S.) was a dignified gentleman resplendent in King Edward goatee, moustache, and ramrod military bearing. He had been a merchant and buyer for Halifax dry-goods establishments, including Webster and Smith, to whom he was related. His work took him away to England and Europe, first on sailing ships and then on steam powered carriers. He often brought home samples of furniture, china, and silverware, which my mother treasured as family heirlooms in later years. My maternal grandmother was Laura Tidmarsh, a granddaughter of James Heaton Tidmarsh, a well-known ship owner and master, merchant and adventurer.

My great-great-grandfather James Heaton Tidmarsh, born in Halifax, December 18, 1777, was the second son of Philip and Mary (Reynolds) Tidmarsh. He exemplified the adventurous life of his era. His father had left Boston the previous year as a pre-loyalist wishing to remain in a British colony. He was a merchant and took up residence at 15 Granville Street in Halifax.

James Heaton first went to sea in September 1797 in the schooner *York*, but it was a short voyage. A French privateer *L'Italie Conquise* captured the ship and he spent the winter in prison in Point Peter, Basseterre and Martinique. He arrived home in the schooner *William* on February 21, 1798. In 1799, he married Margaret King who was born in New York on June 7, 1781. Margaret was the daughter of the late commander of British troops in garrison at Boston. They had ten children.

Between 1802 and 1812 "grandfather Heaton" was on board a variety of vessels and captured and released by the French three more times.

During the War of Independence in the USA, James Heaton was a successful privateer before finally settling in Halifax in 1825 as an enterprising businessman. His many enterprises included a sugar refinery, a candle-making business and the importing of aromatic coffees.

After a long and colourful life, James Heaton Tidmarsh died on February 17, 1856, at the age of 78, and was buried in St. Georges Cemetery. His wife Margaret, died January 17, 1846, and was buried in St. Paul's cemetery.

My mother was keenly impressed by her lineage. In her day, Halifax was divided in half, north and south with east-west Quinpool Road the dividing line. In my mother's mind, this also defined the social classes. When I was a child, the tramcar system ran in a circle, through central and south-end Halifax with no service running north and south, and very little service at all to the north end. When I mentioned to my mother that it would be practical to run a line north and south, she looked aghast. Drawing herself up to her five-foot height she exclaimed, "Well! There would never be any need for a southender to go north, and we certainly wouldn't want those people down here!" It is therefore surprising that she married my father over several other south-end suitors, when he was poor Irish from the north end without, apparently, any noteworthy lineage at all.

I was not to find out about my Rosborough ancestry until many years after their deaths.

Apparently, the Rosborough clan originated around 1000 CE in a fortified town called the Borough of Roc in Scotland, just across the border from England. They were cleric advisors to the Scottish kings who often graced their castle during skirmishes and travels. This happy condition lasted until a great battle was fought with the English in the mid 1300s. They lost, and the Rosboroughs had to flee, making their way across the Irish Sea to County Antrim near Londonderry in the north of Ireland. In 1838, my paternal ancestor James and his brother Robert took ship for the Americas. At this point, it might be said that the Rosboroughs were Scottish steel, tempered in Irish fire. They landed at Saint John, New Brunswick, where James married Sarah Halse and moved to Halifax, eventually becoming a merchant. Robert emigrated to California taking up land to farm. One day, while plowing, black sticky stuff bubbled from the ground. He was the only Rosborough I ever heard of that made lots of money.

A BRIG OF THE TIMES

The Early Years—
From Rowboats to Schooners

Testing the water: with mother and father at Purcells Cove, 1930.

Chapter One

WHEN I WAS BORN IN 1928, I instinctively knew that it was my idea and not that of my parents. I may not have been part of their plan but they were part of mine. For one whole year, I enjoyed being the centre of attention in my little family. My father had established a moderately large real estate empire in houses, flats, and small apartment buildings. He had the latest car and the best clothes. My mother had designed a new and modern house, which they had contractor-built in the best new neighbourhood. I had a little fur coat and hat, and pure leather leggings. It could not have been better.

Then, one dark day in 1929 his bubble burst. The banks called in all the mortgages and loans, which my father, as a bookkeeper, had so carefully arranged. He had financed his empire by convincing my mother's family and their friends to mortgage their own homes and give him the money to manage. Now it was over, and everyone was literally out on the street; doors were barred and Sheriff's notices were on every door!

My wonderful, capable, and careful father was now the villain, the scapegoat for the whole stock market crash. That day, something in his mind snapped. He came in, went to the piano and started playing hymns! From then on, this careful, exact, responsible person never took responsibility for anything! My mother took over the reins of our domestic life. She became a seamstress, always saving a few dollars from her meagre earnings for the light or coal bills.

We moved 21 times in the next 20 years, always late at night and always down the back stairs. It was important to my mother that we find lodgings in her old family area. Her father and elder sister had lost their home as well, through my father's misadventures, a fact which we never heard the last of. We always had to have a bedroom for "Aunt Lou."

My father took a job selling life insurance in a world where no one had any money. His work kept him out late most nights and I was cautioned to play quietly and sleep late in the mornings so as not to disturb him.

Because of an ear infection resulting in an operation, my mother overprotected me; I couldn't play with other children, go swimming or engage in rough activities.

But I loved going out in the rain, and I always had my boats to play with. I would make them from chips of wood with little sticks for masts and a bit of paper for a sail. They would bounce along the rain-swollen gutters and disappear down the drain. To me they were beautiful and able vessels off on voyages to romantic and exotic lands just as the poem in one of my schoolbooks said:

The Ships of Yule

When I was just a little boy,
Before I went to school,
I had a fleet of forty sail,
I called the Ships of Yule.
Of every rig from rakish brig,
To gallant barquentine,
To little Fundy fishing boats,
With gunwales painted green.
They sailed around the world for me,
To Zanzibar and Rome,
And brought me back the lovely things,
We never had at home.

In the depth of the Great Depression, my mother sent me off on my bicycle to the little corner store to buy some oatmeal for porridge with the pennies she had scraped together. My eye was immediately taken by boxes of corn flakes, each with a model ship, the *Queen Mary*, *Normandie*, and the *Ile de France*, drawn on the sides that could be cut out and put together! I bought three boxes instead of the oatmeal. Surviving my mother's tirade, I ate corn flakes three times a day for the rest of the week. But I had my ships!

My father always had an old car and took us for drives on Sundays along the Halifax waterfront to see the vessels, yachts, ocean liners, and naval ships berthed there. A few retired wooden ships, barques, and tern schooners particularly took my eye. For a while the brigantine *Bear* was berthed in Dartmouth after she returned from her voyages taking Admiral Byrd to Antarctica, and I imagined what it must have been like in the ice as I looked up at her tall masts and rigging.

Summers were spent at St. Margaret's Bay in one of the summer cottages we had there. In a pond behind Meisner's Beach in Black Point I began to plan and build my first real boats. They were rafts made from old trees, which my young friends and I put together. I devised seats with rowing positions and homemade oars. Mine of course, was the flagship so had to have a mast and a flag. It was 1940, and World War Two had begun.

Halifax was a busy place in 1940 with her population tripled and her harbour a bustle of activity. As I walked Water Street and Hollis Street with my school chums, I was acutely conscious of the sights, sounds and smells of the waterfront. Vessels were lying in the stream waiting for a berth and cargoes. Hundreds of merchant ships of all sizes and descriptions were anchored so close together in Bedford Basin that it seemed one could walk from one side of the bay to the other from deck-to-deck. Troops with rifles and full packs, embarking for Europe and the war, tramped along the cobblestone streets to waiting troop-ships.

I can still smell the delicious odours of steam-tar, drying fish, oil, damp salt sea air, fresh-cut lumber, coal, hops, exhaust fumes and horse dung. I remember watching crews sloshing down the decks of wooden fishing and coastal vessels and thinking, "Isn't it great, those seamen are keeping their boats so nice and clean!" What they were really doing was keeping wooden deck planking swollen tight against shrinking by a hot overhead sun.

It was a heady mix, and one that made a lasting impression on a teenager attuned to the vibrant life and romance of it all.

During this period, I began to draw yachts and vessels in plan form. My marine heritage had gotten the better of me. I was determined to have my own boat.

My mother had bought a small house in need of repair on Edward Street in Halifax. She somehow had found a carpenter, Fred Dunsworth, who was wonderfully capable in all areas of house construction, and I became his helper as we re-built the old house.

In any spare time, I had Fred help me build an eight-foot punt rowboat in the basement from plans provided in *Mechanics Illustrated*'s "How to Build 20 Boats." This was a wonderful publication that came out annually and featured row, power, and sailboats from 6 to 50 feet. Luther H. Tarbox, Sam Rabl, L. Francis Herreshoff and others were my designer heroes as I avidly studied every detail described. I well remember such designs as *Poco Dinero* (little money), *Teal*, *Brenda* the 9-foot tender, a 27-foot Tancook whaler and Herreshoff's *H-28* and 50-foot three mast double-ender *Marco Polo*.

It was now 1945 and I was in grade eleven in high school. My determination in having my own boat had resulted in finding a derelict 30-foot schooner owned by a man named Ducky Farmer. Somehow, I found the $50 he wanted for her, which included masts, sails, and rigging. This was an open boat with no cabin and very slack bilges. I set to re-furbishing her with a will. Every day after school found me bicycling my way out to the shore of the North West Arm with a basket load of scrapers, nails, hammer, caulking, putty and paint. In the best naval tradition, I painted her pine plank deck red after the manner of Nelson's ship *Victory*. Of course, he had used red so that blood running around the deck during battle wouldn't upset the seamen, but to me it was all very romantic.

I inveigled the help of my school chums whenever I could as launching day neared. Someone had told me "she would need ballast," so I fastened a length of railroad rail to her keel. We launched her but she still would only float on one side or the other due to her slack bilges. The taciturn local ferry operator, Mr. Mont, watched the scene. I asked him what I could do. A man of few words, he replied, "ballast." I asked what could I use for ballast, and he replied, "rocks." So we rowed back and forth to the schooner all afternoon loading her full of rocks from the nearby beach. Having accomplished the labour of launching and ballasting, we stood back and admired my schooner jauntily tethered to her mooring.

Arriving the next day at the North West Arm, I was chagrined not to see my beautiful schooner anywhere! I asked Mr. Mont if he had seen her. His reply was, "Who tied her up?" I said that I had and he replied disdainfully, "Oh well, that explains it."

We rowed all around the nearby coves but could not see her anywhere! I figured that someone must have stolen her. Dejectedly rowing over the spot where she had been moored. I remarked to my chum, "This is right where she was." As I looked down into the water, there she was, sitting on the bottom with her bright red deck clearly visible! Not being swollen, she had leaked in every seam overnight and sank!

Fortunately, two of my mother's roomers were scuba divers in the Canadian Navy, and they volunteered to swim out to the vessel, dive down, and lift the ballast rocks out one at a time. It took them two full days! Then we attempted to pull her ashore but she would not budge. Mr. Mont mentioned a Mr. Purcell across the way who operated a very large and powerful diesel boat for Monstadt and Co. He sailed the boat home every evening and perhaps would hook on and tow my schooner ashore. The next day Mr. Purcell showed up for the salvage tow. I was positioned in the stern with rope and grapnel in hand. My instructions were to hook the schooner's deck, fast the line, and signal to Mr. Purcell to give it to her. I hooked the deck on the second pass, gave my signal, and watched as the deck broke water and we headed for shore. We arrived with the complete deck, and nothing more! We had succeeded in tearing the entire deck completely off, like ripping the top off a boot from its sole. There sat my red deck with the nails hanging down all around the edge like a beached shark.

The next day, my volunteer divers fastened a rope around the hull and I hired the biggest tow truck I could find to pull my schooner ashore. The balance of that summer was spent in rebuilding and re-caulking. The following spring, we re-launched with the benefit of hard lessons learned. We got the masts in, rigging and sails on. A cockpit floor was built out of an old picket fence discarded by a neighbour, and we were off sailing!

Our area of operation was confined to the North West Arm and Halifax inner harbour as a wartime submarine net extended from Maugher's Beach to Ferguson's Cove. There was a small opening near the shore and we sneaked out through it on a few occasions. These voyages were always curtailed by the howl of a siren and lather of wake as a Customs patrol boat came after us and towed us back inside the safety of the net. That was the fastest my schooner ever went! The skipper of the patrol boat would then appear and give us a thorough dressing down for violating orders. He was an old sea dog, used to being obeyed, as he warned us never to do that again.

Jack Grey, a friend whom I had grown up with, later a noted Halifax marine artist, sometimes crewed with me. He dubbed the schooner *Mud Turtle*, as she was always either stuck in the mud or moving slower than a turtle. Her response to steering was so bad that someone always had to go forward when we wanted to come about and back the jib to windward to force her bow around. This manoeuvre usually resulted in stopping her forward motion altogether and sometimes even sailing in reverse, which got us into all kinds of trouble.

After a few years, I sold *Mud Turtle* for $135 to an unsuspecting adventurer. The next day, I helped him get ready and he set sail, never to be heard from again, although many sea stories kept coming back about him and *Mud Turtle*.

During the time I sailed *Mud Turtle*, Halifax experienced its second explosion, this time at the Naval Armament Depot in Bedford. That day my father and I had been at Glen Haven near my grandmother's farm, building another cottage on family land. We heard what appeared to be thunder, although the sky was clear. As we motored back that evening, we met with heavy traffic streaming out of the city with all manner of household articles, mattresses and baby carriages on their roofs. They looked like a stream of refugees in Europe we had seen on the news. Occasionally, one would stop and tell us not to go into the city as a terrible explosion had occurred and that the whole city had been blown down—there was nothing left. This caused us great concern as my mother, friends and family were all there. Of course, the alarmed population of Halifax, especially its older members, still vividly remembered the great Halifax explosion of December 6, 1917 and the horror stories that ensued from it. On that fateful day, the French munitions ship *Mont Blanc* had collided with the Belgian relief ship *Imo* in the narrows of Halifax Harbour at 9:05 A.M. Much of the north end of Halifax was destroyed or damaged. Hardly a family in the city did not have relatives either killed or wounded, with much loss of property. It was then the world's largest man-made explosion. Over 1,600 persons had been killed and many more than that injured. It is no wonder that the population of Halifax feared the worst from the present explosion.

As we came into the city, the only apparent difference was the outgoing traffic. The radio was giving running accounts of a fire and explosions at the Bedford Magazine with predictions of possible larger explosions to come.

We made it home amid great confusion; neighbours had dragged mattresses onto their lawns, as they feared to remain indoors. One of my mother's roomers was a veteran soldier. A burly sergeant, he had seen many battles overseas, and advised us to remain calm, to open all doors and windows against concussion, and to cover them with whatever we had, and then go to bed. Following his advice, which seemed sensible to me, I dragged out my canvas sails from *Mud Turtle*, hung them over the windows of my bedroom, lay down and went to sleep. At 3:00 A.M. the big one came with a tremendous bang. The concussion blew the heavy sails over my bed and I awoke in great confusion thinking that perhaps the house had caved in on me.

The next day, as I was carrying glass bottles of water to friends who had abandoned their north-end homes and had pitched tents in the open Central Commons, there was a deep "carr—rump" and someone called, "Get down!" I dove for the ground and hung onto a bush. I felt the concussion, heard glass breaking, and felt something land across my legs. Fortunately, I was not cut, but my glass water bottles had bumped together and broken. That was enough for me. That day we left for Glen Haven and our partly built cottage where we stayed until the all clear was sounded.

With my newfound wealth from the sale of *Mud Turtle*, I bought another boat, which had been hauled out next to me at the North West Arm. This one was like a huge over-grown dory, but v-bottomed and fitted with a 6 h.p. Acadia 1 cylinder jump-spark engine as well as masts and sails, ketch rigged. She also had a centre cabin as well as a forward and after cockpit.

She was in better condition than *Mud Turtle*, so she did not sink. I named her *Frost Fish* after the cove at our cottage in Glen Haven.

I began to learn about engines. In order to start a one-lunger, one has to spin the flywheel by hand until she fires the first time, then quickly get out of the way of flywheel and handle. If the engine is stubborn, and your arm gets tired, you use your foot to roll the engine over. If the engine fires when not expected, you can end up with a broken arm or leg.

I was undertaking this leg start one day when she caught, kicked violently backwards and shot me up through the hatch, into the air and down into the ocean. My crew fished me out and I draped my wet jeans over the hot engine block to dry. I was grounded in my wet socks when my jeans made contact with the sparkplug. The voltage was ample enough to blast me backwards into the cabin on my behind. Another lesson learned!

Eventually we "mastered" the engine; learned how to shut it off, wait for the last revolution of the flywheel, then quickly switch it on again so that the next time the engine fired it would be in reverse, effectively stopping the boat.

With our new-found confidence, we approached the crowded and prestigious Royal Nova Scotia Yacht Squadron. We could see blue blazered, white-trousered members on the observation deck enjoying cocktails as we approached the dock. Unfortunately, it was low tide and the dock's large, tarred, pilings were wet, and slime-covered. Confidently poised on the bow with deck line in hand, I signalled my crew to cut the engine. However, when the crew clicked her back on for reverse, she caught in forward again. With the increased speed, the spoon bow hit, then climbed up the slippery piles. I lost my balance, dropped my rope, and wrapped my arms around the slimy pilings. The craft slipped back down the piles and shot stern first out while I slithered down the piling into the water.

After two years I sold *Frost Fish*, and later learned she was involved in the local fishery.

I was without a boat but busily engaged in my engineering degree at Dalhousie University. There were large classes of serious students at that time, as many returned World War Two veterans were intent on re-building their lives. I excelled at engineering drawing, leading the class of 138. I also enjoyed surveying and geology, but found that science was more than I could deal with. I did all the collegiate things: smoked a pipe, played a Hawaiian guitar, attended the football games and drove a Baby Austin, one of a kind in those days. Everywhere I went, people would stop and look. An Austin Seven was an oddity. One day, driving down the steep incline of Sackville Street, my cable brakes let go and I careened at breakneck speed down the hill. Halifax had no traffic lights yet, and a policeman was stationed at the intersection of Sackville and Barrington Streets, Halifax's main thoroughfare. As I came madly along, he held up his hand for me to stop, then, thinking better of it, dove for safety. I had no idea how I would stop, but when I saw the Irving Oil arch ahead of me I thought I could shoot through and find something soft to stop me, or run off the end of the pier into the harbour.

Just then, a huge fish-plant gurry truck lumbered along Water Street right in front of my path. The driver applied his brakes at the same moment I smashed headlong into his large rear rubber tire. Great piles of fish heads, guts and tails showered down from the truck and covered my little car. The truck driver hopped down from his seat, surveyed the ridiculous scene of my little car buried in gurry and the look of fear and relief on my face, and doubled over in gales of laughter.

I slunk home as unobtrusively as possible, postponing any plans I had that day for obtaining a driving licence.

Still boatless, I was working for the telephone company. I found a 48-foot fishing schooner advertised for sale in the newspaper and thought this would be just the thing. Enquiring further, I discovered a man named Bruce R. P. Parsons had her for sale in North Sydney, Nova Scotia. So my girlfriend and I boarded the train for a long and boring trip to North Sydney to inspect her. At this time, there was no causeway to Cape Breton Island, so the train had to be taken apart and loaded on three sets of rails on the ferry at Canso. This operation invariably took place in the middle of the night. The railway always loaded cars on an outside track first and it seemed the whole car would tip over as the passengers got dumped, half asleep, from their seats. I experienced the crossing several times and always the same thing. I never could understand why they did not load the centre rail first but deduced it must have had more to do with railways than boats.

Arriving at North Sydney, we were met by Bruce Parsons and taken to his residence. This was located in the rear of a second-hand goods and pawnshop, where he lived with his French-Canadian wife Colette, some babies and a huge black dog. Niceties were exchanged and he took me off to the harbour to see the schooner. She lay off at a small U-shaped rock island. This was locally called either Newfoundland Island or the ballast heap. Apparently, small Newfoundland schooners came over to North Sydney in rock ballast to load salt or coal for home. They would anchor near shore and dump their ballast until over the years the rocks got to form the island. In any case, there was *Agnes R!*, a 48-foot Newfoundland jack schooner. These vessels were termed jacks because they were shorter than a schooner, which had an overhanging stern and enclosed rudder-port. The jack's configuration was beneficial as the rudder could be hung outdoors on the transom stern. The south coast of Newfoundland was a winter fishery, where the more conventional enclosed rudder-port would freeze up overnight.

Now retired from fishing, she appeared a perfect jewel to my romantic, if inexperienced, sea-captured soul. A deal was struck and I bought her

THE 48-FOOT *AGNES R!*, "A PERFECT JEWEL."

from Bruce for $500. She had a defunct two cylinder Atlantic 20 h.p. marine engine installed, but very little other equipment in evidence. I asked Bruce if he knew where I might find such needed equipment as a windlass, anchors, deck pump, gas barrel, ropes, sails, and rigging. He replied that he just might happen to have such items in his shed. As I bought them one-by-one from him and carried them off to the vessel, I noted that they all fitted exactly into the holes and over the bolts of my ship. I accused him of selling me back the entire vessel's equipment, and insisted that this was less than honourable. He replied that selling boats was a very lucrative venture. Sensing that I might have a few more dollars somewhere, he further suggested we should go into the business as partners. I did not act on that suggestion at the time although it was to come up later with great force and effect.

In the weeks that followed, I made many drawings of converting the *Agnes R!* into my coveted dream-ship, with grand cabins, accommodations, and sail plans. I made several more 300-mile train trips to see and work on my schooner. Bruce had located a man to watch her, mostly to keep her pumped, which she needed continuously. Bruce said he had a payment policy for vessels he sold called, "Pay as you pump!"

I had the seized-up engine removed and taken to a small shore-side machine and engine shop run by a Mr. Clarke, for re-building. I hired a carpenter Bruce found by the name of Francis MacDonald. He came complete with glowing accounts of all the boats he had built and repaired. Over that winter I sent money from my pay at the phone company to Francis as he was, at my instruction, to cut all the deck beams out between the two masts and construct a long low trunk cabin for my accommodations.

The next spring, I discovered that Francis had spent most of the winter drinking my money away. But he finally got a roof on the cabin and I paid him off. Mr Clarke had installed the re-built engine and things were looking better.

I brought the equipment I had gathered over the winter—lights, buoys, charts, navigation, sea-keeping and camping supplies. Finally, I rounded up a crew in Halifax for the sail home. A Mr. Tanner came highly recommended, as he was part of that famous clan which had manned seagoing vessels out of Lunenburg to the Grand Banks for years. Two other friends were enlisted and off we went by bus for the grand adventure.

Supplies, as well as more ropes and a rowboat were purchased in North Sydney. We were ready for sea, but I didn't have the money to pay Mr. Clarke for the engine work. I promised to send him the $1,200 later. The next day my crew informed me that Mr. Clarke had come to the vessel and removed her two carburettors. When I went to see him he "explained" that he had to check them to make sure they were alright, but that by the time I had the money he was sure they would be okay. Upset at his unorthodox collection procedures, I went to the local police chief, who told me there wasn't anything he could do, especially for a foreigner from the mainland who hadn't paid his bill. It turned out that his name was Clarke too, and a brother to my engine re-builder.

I was caught! Out of funds, I was already a week overdue for return to my telephone company job. I called home and begged assistance. No one had any money except Aunt Lou, who had carefully saved a few dollars from her old-age pension, over the years. She reluctantly parted with the requested $1,700, in spite of her bitter experience with my father's business failure. She once remarked, "Rosborough men are lovely people, but don't ever give them any of your money!"

Finally, the bills were paid, the carburettors reinstalled, the dock lines cast off, and we were off to sea. In a few hours, a thick Nova Scotia fog set in and we were completely engulfed. Mr. Tanner had set our course and the engine pounded faithfully onward. Something bothered me, however, as I studied the chart spread out on the cabin roof. It seemed to me we were heading inshore rather than offshore. Hesitantly, I asked Tanner if he really knew where we were. He drew himself up indignantly and replied that he had been to sea all his life, and didn't need his expertise questioned by a young green-nosed neophyte.

Hardly were the words out of his mouth when there was a tremendous crash! Bang! Bang!

FRANCIS MACDONALD, WORKING ON *AGNES R!*

Looking over the side, there were rocks everywhere! We struck twice more as we turned the vessel and tried to find deeper water. Water in the bilge was rising alarmingly as we had to make a quick decision. I knew we had passed Glace Bay harbour an hour previously, and we made the decision to try to return there. Two of us were manning the large deck pump continuously while two more were furiously bailing with five-gallon cans. Still the water rose—we couldn't keep ahead of it. Finally, Glace Bay harbour buoy appeared as we crept out of the fog. The engine flywheel was now running almost completely under water, sending great geysers 25 feet into the air. We steered for the new government wharf dead ahead. The tide was high and we hit the side of the wharf at the exact moment the engine drowned and the schooner drove herself up the beach. We hastily got out dock lines, and assessed our plight.

We were indescribably grateful for our deliverance from a watery grave, but our situation looked hopeless. Time and money gone, we were all scared to death and simply wanted to be out of our predicament. After a hurried discussion, my crew stoutly refused to ever return to sea. Tanner was abashedly silent. As the tide went out, the water drained out of the schooner and it was apparent that her bottom planks had sprung off when she struck; some were broken and many fastenings had pulled. In my exuberance I had neglected to have the vessel hauled on a slip, have her bottom planking examined, re-fastened, re-caulked, and painted. Moreover, I had cut out all her main deckbeams, so there was nothing left to hold her together.

I instructed my volunteer crew to double the dock lines so she wouldn't fall over when the tide receded and I went uptown to see if there was anyone who wanted to buy a schooner. No one wanted to buy her.

It was swordfishing season in Glace Bay, and the whole harbour was crowded with hundreds of schooners and snapper boats. It was a sight to see. In desperation, I approached Mr. Liptkus, the owner of the local fish plant and threw myself at his mercy. He said he didn't need and didn't want such a vessel, but he would give me fifty dollars for her to get me out of my dilemma. This was quite a shock financially as I had spent thousands of dollars on her over two years not to mention the $1,700 I owed to Aunt Lou! He agreed to let me remove my personal things and he provided several very large wooden fish boxes for me to pack them in. Arriving back at the schooner, I told my crew I had sold her, but to remove everything they could and pack it in the boxes. Lights, buoys, ropes, sails, and everything loose was packed and a half-ton truck hired to take it to the railway station. We hastily went to the bus station for the long journey home. Broke, scared, exhausted, dejected, wet, and tired, we purchased bus tickets and two large bottles of rum for the trip.

Heyday of swordfishing, Glace Bay, 1950

As we pulled out of the station, I sat down in the crowded bus next to a pretty young lady and uncorked my bottle of rum. To console myself I invited her to have a drink with me. It was a very interesting 300-mile drive as the trauma of my horrendous experience faded and I began to embrace the future.

I often wished I could have seen the expression on Mr. Liptkus' face when he went to look at his fine new vessel and found her submerged at the wharf. I heard later that she was engaged as a gurry boat, hauling fish guts off shore to dump. A most ignominious ending for my beautiful dream ship!

Arriving home, I gathered up every snapshot and drawing I had of *Agnes R!*, and burned them, vowing never to have anything to do with boats and the sea again ever! The experience had been so painful I didn't want to remember any part of it. Later, as the pain diminished I regretted burning everything and longed for the memory of *Agnes R!*

More Boats—More Hard Knocks

ARMDALE YACHT CLUB, CIRCA 1960.

CHAPTER TWO

I WENT BACK TO MY JOB AT the phone company, but before long my attraction to boats and sailing prompted me to join the Armdale Yacht Club, then in its infancy, and buy a $50 12-foot sailing dingy. At the Club, which had just obtained a 99-year lease on the old military prison on Melville Island in the North West Arm, we built a marine railway out of old tram-car rails and wheels being removed from the streets of Halifax, and repaired the former warden's residence as our club house, and secured the stone cell blocks as member's lockers.

Money for the various projects was raised by organizing swish parties. Oak rum barrels were obtained from the liquor board, two gallons of boiling water were poured into each and they were rolled up and down the Yacht Club hill until the contents had soaked all the remaining rum out of the wood. The results were poured out, filtered through an old T-shirt and into empty rum bottles brought by volunteers. The powerful mix sold for two dollars a bottle. It was great fun and camaraderie with all the colourful characters of the day involved, and our building projects benefited immensely.

There was Frank Slaunwhite with his booming, friendly voice who told stories of running rum during prohibition days; Johnnie Snow, the undertaker, who drove his car off the yacht club causeway one night and drowned himself; Earnie Cameron and his pet monkey who sailed into the window of Earnie's motorboat; Ralph Woodward and his *Red Wing* sailing yacht out in all weather; Percy Hubley and his large motor-cruiser *Sea Mate*, and many others who made the world so interesting and fun-filled.

Through my work, I had met Courtney Jones, then Chief of Telecommunications at Halifax's Naval Dockyard, who had an old 32-foot motor-sailer, *Comeramie*, and dreams of setting out to sea in her, which matched my own.

Jonesy was older than I, married with a grown family, and was a tinkerer, fascinated by machinery and electronics. He drove an old Buick and re-built it periodically. His motor-sailer had a large Graymarine gasoline auxiliary motor that he had re-built and knew intimately. As our dreams merged, we talked of a great adventure in a cruise to distant places. We began preparations; he overhauled things mechanical and electrical, while I built on a stern cabin, added another mast, sail and rigging to make the vessel handle better.

Just before the day of departure, his elderly mother became ill and we altered our plans from a deep-sea cruise to a coastal one along the rocky Eastern Shore of Nova Scotia.

Supplies, spares, and cruising equipment were loaded while the news on the radio reported that a war had just begun in Korea. "Here we go again!" I thought, "Why won't people ever learn?" We completed preparations for departure. The crew, consisting of myself, my girlfriend Marian, Jonesy, his son, daughter, and brother-in-law were all aboard. Even though it was late in the day and the weather report called for light winds and coastal fog, we set

COMERAMIE READY FOR HER CRUISE, 1948.

off. The girls were jauntily dressed in white sailor suits, and the rest of us in our best sea-going attire. Spirits were high as we headed east, and as it was to be a long run, I offered to take first trick at the wheel. The engine was off, of course, to save fuel as we began a slow track through the quartering swells. First, one of the girls became seasick, then the other. Leaning over the rail, their white sailor suits soon became an interesting hue of yellow, red and green, while their faces turned as white as the suits used to be. Conditions were worsening, so Jonesy suggested all except the helmsman have a rest so they could be on deck later for a long night. Alone at the wheel, I stared intently through the thickening fog for any sight of land, buoys, or other boats. After hours of sailing, staring at the compass and peering through fog, I began to hear and see things.

I saw a shoreline with a road and people on horses and carriages riding along. There was a church with a bell tolling. The scene was one hundred years out of time. I had to be hallucinating. The fog does strange things when coupled with fatigue and anxiety. Suddenly there was a huge hotel right in front of the boat! Many storeys high, its top disappeared into the dense fog. I cut the wheel hard over, as crashing white water broke under the bow! As we turned, I saw that it was really an enormous sheer rock cliff! That made no sense, as we should have been many miles at sea. Jonesy sprang to the deck at the sudden shift of the vessel. I described what I had seen, although it was now lost in the fog. We realized we had forgotten to allow for a five degree set on the shore caused by the Labrador current! Once a new course had been set, Jonesy recommended I go below for a rest, while he took the wheel. When the vessel swerved and heeled, I had heard a muffled yell from below. Descending the ladder, I saw Marian holding her bloodied head. To ease her seasickness, she had gone to sleep on the cabin floor. On the sudden swerve, the ship's hammer had slid off the upper bunk and hurtled down on her head. She didn't even complain—the seasickness was still worse than the hammer blow.

Some hours later, a different motion woke me up. Going on deck, I saw we were sailing with the waves instead of across them. Jonesy explained that he thought he had seen a harbour entrance and had turned toward it. Hardly had he spoken the words when white water broke in front and on both sides of us. He quickly brought the vessel around, but now there were breakers everywhere! We couldn't find the way we had come in. Jonesy ran forward and threw over the anchor, while I volunteered to take the ship's little 8-foot rowboat to see if I could find a way out. The waves were steep and the fog allowed less than fifty feet visibility. I donned a life jacket, took the small mouth foghorn, and set out. Within a few oar strokes I could no longer see the yacht. I blew my little horn and they answered with the loud manual Klaxton horn I had installed on the deck of the new aftercabin. In this way, I could keep a bearing on where the yacht was, although it was still difficult to tell the direction of their horn in the thick fog. After rowing all around for a long time, I returned to the yacht without finding any break in the reefs. Jonesy decided to shut off the engine and stay anchored until daylight. Perhaps by then, the fog would lift and we could see. We all bunked in for an uneasy, broken rest amid the rolling sea and breaking surf.

Towards morning, someone who had gone up on deck yelled, "We're dragging!" Jonesy rushed to the fore deck, pulled in the anchor line and discovered it had chafed off! We were drifting towards the breaking rocks: Jonesy pressed the engine starter button–nothing! He tore up the engine box and tried to short the solenoid—nothing! By now, spray was landing on our deck from waves breaking on the rock cliffs behind us. Eight-foot oak emergency oars were brought out. The brother-in-law and I positioned ourselves on each side of the afterdeck and began to paddle madly. I looked at my sturdy oak oar and saw it bending like a bow under the strength of my stroke. "That's very odd," I thought, "I can't bend that oar like that." One's mind focuses on the strangest details when disaster is imminent. Jonesy yelled that he would put out another anchor, which was strange, since we didn't have one. He went below, threw aside the ladder, and tore up a floorboard where we had stowed huge blocks of lead for ballast. It had taken three strong men to get each of them aboard. Somehow he grabbed one, cradled it in his arms, and leaped up the three feet to the deck. He ran quickly forward and threw the block of lead overboard for an anchor, before realizing he hadn't tied a rope to it.

We kept paddling like crazy but the keel of the yacht bumped on the rocks with each wave. The girls who had forgotten all about their seasickness, were on deck screaming, "Help! Help! Save us! Save us!" This struck me as rather odd since there was no one to hear us. Marian was furiously cranking the handle of the new Klaxton horn with a superhuman strength, and tore it right off the roof! With the seas breaking, the Klaxton horn blowing, the yacht crashing on the rocks, Jonesy rushing about madly on the deck and everyone screaming, we must have looked like characters in Dante's Inferno.

For me, watching my oar bend and the waves crashing over us, everything seemed to be happening in slow motion and in complete silence. It was as if I was hovering over the scene as a casual observer from above. I could see myself, everyone else, the yacht, the ocean, and the action. It was all okay, calm and peaceful. I was having an out of body experience.

Then I heard it. Very faintly at first, then a bit louder. Putt-putt. Putt-putt. The sound of the small engine of a fisherman's boat. I snapped back into my body, and yelled, "Quiet everybody!" Then they all heard it. Putt-putt. Putt-putt. The screaming and yelling resumed with increased vigour as we saw the bow of a tiny fishing schooner poke out of the surrounding fog. Salvation! Two figures emerged clad in black oil clothes and Sou'westers in an open schooner-rigged boat. The one in the bow was preparing a rope as they headed towards us. It took forever for them to get close enough to throw the line, which fell short and landed in the water. They retrieved it, coiled it, and threw again. This time it hit our deck but Jonesy missed grabbing it. I dropped my oar and dashed forward. On their next throw, I caught the end and quickly wrapped it around our bitt. With a call of, "We got it! We got it!" the fishermen put their engine in reverse and began to tow us off. The yacht stopped pounding on the rocks, but then the towline broke! We drifted back, they recoiled the rope, I caught it and took another panic turn on the bitt. As I yelled, "Pull! Pull!" Jonesy looked down at me and cried, "My God, look at your hand!" I had caught my fingers under the rope and blood was running down the bitt, across the deck and into the sea. "I'll tell them to stop," Jonesy said. "No. No," I exclaimed, "Tell them to pull." I didn't feel a thing.

Gradually they pulled us out through the rock reefs to open water where we re-rigged the lines and they took us in tow. Quite a while later, we saw the end of a wharf appear through the fog. We had gone through reefs, passed close to islands and up the harbour and hadn't seen a thing. The fishermen knew exactly where they were going. Throughout the whole experience they hadn't said a word.

Once at the wharf, the fisherman-skipper's Sou'wester came off, and her long black hair tumbled to her shoulders. It was a startling revelation because in those days women were never fishermen. Midge Murphy and her son, who had fished these waters for years, introduced herself. She told us she didn't know why she was way down there, miles from her nets, where she found us. She never fished near the reefs, but this day, fog and all, she was close enough to hear our Klaxton horn and cries for help in the distance. Ignoring her own danger, she felt compelled to attempt the rescue.

We thanked her profusely, and as a small gesture of our gratitude we tried to give her money, but she wouldn't accept it. That was the law of the sea.

During the next two years, Marian and I got married and began to raise a family. I rented a small decrepit house on Windsor Street in Halifax with three bedrooms, a living room, and kitchen. The rent was $50 a month and to help financially, Marian rented one room to a friend and her husband and baby. Fortunately, he was in the navy and away part of the time. When he was in port, the house became a drop-in centre for many of his friends as well. Marian had a job so there was usually a baby-sitter/ housekeeper in the house, along with Marian's relatives and friends from the country. To say the place was like a zoo would not be too far off the mark.

I bought an old Fairbanks 5 h.p. two-cycle marine engine to power my next boat and kept it in the middle of the kitchen/dining room floor over the winter where I overhauled and painted it for the next boating season.

One day, an old 1,500 weight Army truck pulled up in front of our little house and out came Bruce Parsons with his wife Colette, two babies, and their large black dog. In the back was a huge 45 gallon drum of gas. Bruce explained he needed it because he had to vacate North Sydney hurriedly and didn't dare stop to re-fuel, or the people chasing him would catch up to him. He had rigged a hose from the barrel to his gas tank so he could keep on going as fast as he could. Apparently, his business dealings had so angered some of the local populace that they were out to tar and feather him. He asked if we could put them up for a few days before going to Montreal to live with his brother. Colette had a fiery temper and Bruce a huge ego, so it was an interesting, if volatile, visit.

Atlantic Marine: A Business Disaster

POD, A LOBSTER BOAT CONVERTED TO A SCHOONER.

CHAPTER THREE

I WAS NOW 25, WORKING for the phone company for $27 per week with a wife, and two babies. I drove my bicycle to work with my lunch pail on the handlebars.

Our little family was still poor and struggling when one day a huge surplus army truck jerked to a stop at our front door. Its cargo was strings of paper owls and barn lanterns. Bruce Parsons had returned! He was back in Nova Scotia, having made a tremendous deal on the paper owls and barn lanterns to start a new career. He asked if he could stay with us for a few days until he got situated. Over the next few weeks he began to buy and sell used boats and marine equipment. He said he could cut me in on some of the "deals" and I agreed as the money seemed opportune.

Bruce and I took a trip along Nova Scotia's southwest shore buying scrap rope and metals. On one trip, our old truck was piled high, it was 2:30 A.M., and I was anxiously anticipating arriving at Yarmouth, getting a motel room, and some sleep. My partner was slumped in the passenger seat, sleeping. It was dark and there were wisps of fog all along the highway. As I rounded a turn at Darling's Lake, my headlights showed a gaunt lady with long white hair and a long white gown standing in the middle of the road! I jammed on the brakes but couldn't get the old truck stopped. I drove right through her! My partner snapped awake at the sudden swerving stop and cried, "What happened, what's the matter?" I told him I had just hit a woman standing in the middle of the road! With hearts pounding, we jumped from the truck, our flashlights stabbing the foggy darkness. We searched everywhere, but could find no trace of her. Not knowing what else to do in this remote place, we carried on. Three years later at the same spot and time, I experienced the same apparition. Years later, I was visiting the area again and told a long-time resident my story. He smiled and said, "Oh, you saw her. That was the lady from the lake. She has been seen many times by travellers, always late at night when it's foggy and misty." Apparently the young woman had flung herself into the lake in a fit of unrequited love, and periodically comes out to look for her lost lover. Some unwary travellers have plunged their cars into the lake or gone off the road in an attempt to avoid hitting her. It was my first contact with the psychic realm, and gave me a lot to ponder about over the years.

Bruce suggested we open an office on the Halifax waterfront, so we obtained space on Pickford and Black's Wharf where we had a small warehouse and brokerage office. Atlantic Marine Brokerage and Sales was founded. Bruce explained that he was in bankruptcy from his business deal-ings in Montreal, so it would be necessary to temporarily put the business in my name until he could clear his affairs. Coincidentally, we had rented space at Privateer's Wharf where my ancestor James Heaton Tidmarsh had berthed his vessels so many years before.

Bruce had enough gall to match his huge ego. He would think nothing of helping himself to a drink from a stranger's refrigerator while he talked a deal to the owner. Nothing was sacred to him and no place out of his reach. He became one of Halifax's well-known waterfront characters as he roamed in and out of the many establishments there. He was liked in spite of him-self as his boundless energy and outgoing personality brought a spark of life to our otherwise dull existence.

As our little business became more diverse, more of my time and energy was required, and his personal financial needs became greater and greater. Soon new sales were being used to cover debts three con-tracts back. We were on a downhill slide.

My life was becoming busier and busier. I was on night shift at work from 12:00 to 8:00 A.M., then home for a few hours sleep and off to Atlantic Marine office until 11:00 P.M. As business debts piled higher, my disposable income became non-existent.

Bruce had rented a house in Halifax and brought Colette and the children down from Montreal. Both of our wives were becoming in-creasingly irate at the lack of money, lack of our attention to our growing families and lack of time spent with them. Additional staff was hired, but they required time and supervision, defeating their purpose. However, many interesting characters drifted into the wharf office making a cul-tural and intellectual hodgepodge.

There was Old Captain Giddeon Bower from Jordan Falls in Shelburne County. He must have been 80 years old then and still going strong. He had been in the old square-rigged ships earlier, and anything that floated after that. Cap would deliver any kind of a boat anywhere and do all kinds of odd jobs in the meantime. When asked what provisions he needed for a current delivery, he would reply, "Just a jug of water, a loaf of bread, and a chart." One hot August day he was painting along the cabin-side of a large motorboat tied to the dock. The day was hot and he had stripped to his old grey long johns and trousers. Lost in his work, he stepped right off the deck and landed with a great splash in the harbour waters. He came up still clutching the paintbrush in his right hand and the pail of paint in his left. A cry went up, "Caps overboard!" and the boys fished him out. Standing on the wharf, Cap quietly removed his trousers, picked up his brush and pail and, without a word, went back to work, his sodden grey long johns swaying back and forth with each brush-stroke.

Then there was Mexican Joe, a swarthy, stocky little individual with a brilliant flashing smile. Joe always carried at least two long knives thrust in his belt. He was the kind of person you wouldn't want to meet on a dark, foggy Halifax street if you didn't know him. No weight was too great for him to lift, nor any situation too fearful.

Newfie George (60 per cent of all Newfoundland males are called "Jarge") was a soft-spoken young man who knew engines and machinery intuitively. He could fix anything or make any engine run. He and Joe made a great team as we tried to coax the old boats we were buying back to life.

Another character that drifted by one day was Mad Jim Munster. Mad Jim had a wife and numerous children somewhere in Spryfield, then a suburb of Halifax, who were supported, I was told, by Mad Jim's affluent mother. But Mad Jim was in love with engines and things mechanical. He had made somewhat of a reputation for himself by driving a bren-gun carrier through the streets of Halifax with engines roaring, tracks clattering, and blue exhaust smoke bellowing. On one occasion, he brought an enormous V-8 Cadillac gas engine, unloaded it onto the wharf and announced that it would be just the thing to power one of our boats. He claimed he could make it run on diesel oil instead of gas, to make it more efficient. Batteries were bought, Mad Jim started it on gas, and then switched over to diesel oil. He had wound numerous coils of copper tubing around the red-hot manifolds to vaporize the diesel, while the exhaust was a vertical pipe without a muffler. The engine roared to life and began to leap and charge all over the wharf as Mad Jim, Mexican Joe and Newfie George tried to hold it down. Alarmed businessmen ran from their offices to witness what could only be the end of the world. Mad Jim managed to get it shut off just before the fire engines wheeled around the corner, sirens screaming.

Possibly the most colourful character of all was Lt. Commander Gordon Guthrie Keith Holder. Preferring to be called Don, he had been retired out of the Canadian Navy over some scam involving a shortage of stores. Don came from a long line of well-known yachtsmen, sailmakers and boat-yard operators in Millidgeville, New Brunswick. He was well educated and traced his ancestors back to the Loyalists. While still a bright, young naval officer he was married in Ontario. The ceremony was resplendent with gowned ladies, an archway of Navy officers' crossed swords, and all the appropriate regalia.

Waiting at the curb was a brand new Ford convertible, a present from his father-in-law, president of Ford Canada. A large polished desk in an office tower awaited him. But it was all too much for Don. By nature, he was a vagabond with a wry, keen sense of humour, who found the happenings of society too much to bear. Out of the Navy and out of the marriage, he came to us as office manager and sometimes boat deliverer. He dearly loved his drink of rum; in fact, it was the staple in his diet most of the time. I sometimes had to go looking for him when a job was at hand. He had befriended a small black and white female spaniel, which he called Sam. Locating his room in the dim recesses of a fourth rate hotel, I would pound on his door until finally answered by a staggering, bloodshot Holder. He would point to Sam, lying stiff on her back with four paws up in the air and say, "Its all Sam's fault you know, she drinks too much!" I would attempt to sober them both up and get Holder off on the boat to be delivered.

Eventually, he began to keep company with a pleasant, motherly woman called Rebecca Jane Macauber-Weaver-Holder. Becky had five or six children around her from time to time, like a mother hen with her chicks. She was a good partner for Holder. One summer we leased a waterfront property in Eastern Passage to use for a boat haul-out and storage yard. It was located behind Naugle and Pitts service station and Whip Naugle's pig-pen. Fortunately, the wind was generally southwest which kept most of the aromas away. As we began to gather boats and equipment on the site, we were increasingly concerned about theft, which was common in the area. Holder and Becky volunteered to camp on the beach and guard our goods. Two surplus army bell tents were purchased and set up. One accommodated a queen-sized bed and an old car radio hung on the centre-pole. This was Don and Becky's quarters while all her kids piled into the other tent.

One day I couldn't find a pile of lead ingots and rope that should have been there. I questioned Holder. He looked seriously and carefully about and remarked "Gosh, golly, gee!" (a favourite saying of his), "They were right here yesterday." There was a small scrap-yard nearby and Holder suggested we go there. There sat our goods! Holder accosted the owner, accusing him of theft and worse. The owner explained that some kids had brought it all in the day before. He gave it back to us to prevent further fuss. After this happened three or four times, I began to see the pattern;

Holder was recruiting the kids to carry off material to the scrap-yard for a few dollars for rum and other needed supplies.

Other characters come to mind: Ken Bacon of Seven Islands, Quebec, who came at just the opportune moment to finance part of our operation. He bought Courtney Jones' 32-foot motor-sailer *Comeramie*. Holder delivered her to him at Seven Islands where she later sank on moorings in a tremendous fall gale. Or the Partridge brothers, who ran their bum-boat service at the next dock. David Eaton, a young salesman from Canning, NS, who stayed with us as office staff for a while and was fated to be part of my life later on.

Nathan Hardy, a stout, rugged, red-faced fisherman from Burnt Island, Newfoundland, whom Bruce befriended. It was a trait of Bruce's personality to support anyone less well off than himself, while at the same time swindling anyone with more. He was the Robin Hood of the marine wharf scene. In any case, he bought a large dory and hand-line gear for Hardy so he could go outside the Harbour fishing. Hardy was full of grand plans to organize a huge fishery, or alternatively, to rob various banks. Friendly and helpful, he would offer various wisdoms in his booming voice, such as, "Yer got to eat lots of hungions, yer needs them to keep healthy." The only thing he loved better than fishing was wine. The cheaper and more abundant the better. His accommodations were at the Salvation Army hostel or any dry corner he could find. He was well known to Halifax Police, and they would compassionately gather him up on cold nights for overnight room and board.

During the stressful years of Atlantic Marine, my wife Marian was supportive and accommodating while she struggled with the responsibility of maintaining our home and children in lean and far less than ideal circumstances. She developed a strong dislike for Bruce Parsons, not without justification.

Eventually our business got into such bad shape that our creditors began to call in their markers. The Bank of Nova Scotia told me that since the

business was solely in my name, I would have to assume responsibility. They would continue to extend credit on the condition that I fire Bruce Parsons. He was both our spark plug and our problem; without his nerve and drive, the business sank into a sea of debt. I was faced with a $17,000 debt, which might as well have been 17 million!

Desperate, I did boat repair for some of the creditors with my own few tools. Others I paid a little each month out of my telephone company pay, under Court Order in Judgements. One day, Art Sibley, the deputy sheriff, came with his two huge dogs and seized everything I had, including some old engines and rope from the Eastern Passage yard, a small trailer (with only one wheel), and my bicycle. Now, I plodded my way back and forth to the telephone company on foot, often exiting via the back door to avoid angry creditors. These were the worst days of my young life.

Several months later, Art Sibley re-appeared at my front door with a huge city dump truck full of my junk. He announced that they had re-considered, and since I was such a nice young fellow and struggling along, they were returning all my seized equipment. The big truck backed into my driveway and unceremoniously dumped all my stuff, including engines, rope, my one-wheeled trailer, and my bicycle. As I retrieved my bicycle from the mess I thought, "Now, that Art Sibley is not such a bad guy after all!" It was weeks later before I found out they discovered it would cost them more to sell my stuff than they could get for it, so they were on their way to the city dump. My house was closer, so they decided it was easier to dump it there! "Life can be cruel, but does it have to rub it in?" I wondered.

Eventually, our landlord sold our rented house and it was slated for demolishment to allow construction of a new apartment building. We ignored the eviction notices until the wreckers were breaking down the back porch as we moved our furniture out the front door.

Fortunately, Marian had located a shabby house on Purcell's Cove Road near the Armdale Yacht Club, with water rights to a shoreline on Melville Cove. I realized it would be just the location I needed, so we bought the property and I began the long and arduous task of repair and renovation, including grounds, walls, and walkways. I constructed a wharf alongside the road, which is still berthing our boats to this day.

In the months that followed, the longing for a boat to sail began to return. I located a derelict 20-foot sloop, which appeared to be sound, but had been hauled out ashore for many years. I bought her for $50, hauled her back to my yard, and began rebuilding her. Planking, though sound, had opened from years of sun, and much of the white oak transom had rotted out. During her rebuilding, I noticed a pencilled note giving her original builder's name and date as 1947. My neighbours considered it a great waste of time and effort to make her sea-worthy again, and dubbed her "Rosborough's Folly." Eventually she was afloat with a new used suit of sails, mast, and rigging. My young sons and I sailed *Folly* for three years before I sold her to a yachtsman from Digby where she operated for many more years.

Next I located another derelict, this time a 27-foot lobster boat built during that change-over time when small fishing vessels were powered by a combination of sail and

Rosborough's *Folly*, a 20 ft. sloop.

small one cylinder putt-putt marine engines. I bought her for $100 and had the hull rebuilt in Ship Harbour. I then trucked her back to my yard, added a deck, cockpit, cabin, and furnishings. I re-designed her rig to a schooner and installed a 5 h.p. outboard in a well for auxiliary power. Painted a jaunty green, I called her *POD* as I pictured my sons and myself as three peas in a pod. She was a great training ground for my young family and we had much pleasure in her over the next few years. Anxious moments were experienced from time to time as they sailed off into the fog or stayed out over night alone.

I eventually sold *POD* and bought a Bill Roué designed 23-foot Bluenose class sailboat, which I re-conditioned, re-rigged, and re-named *MayBee*. Maybe she would float, maybe she would sail, and maybe we would have some fun with her. She did all three, as she sailed rings around the newer fibreglass boats of the same class.

LOOKING FOR BOATS IN NEWFOUNDLAND

JACK SCHOONERS IN PORT AUX BASQUES

CHAPTER FOUR

UNEXPECTEDLY, DAVID EATON re-appeared at my door one day. He had made a bit of money from his current business, and wanted to satisfy his longing for a boat. He thought there might still be a schooner or two left in Newfoundland, and since I knew about boats and had the time, he thought I might go there, search out a vessel for him and perhaps one for myself and one or two to sell. He would finance my search.

One of my telephone company co-workers, John Morse, also expressed an interest in having a boat, and since he had a car, trailer, and outboard boat, we made plans to "explore" Newfoundland. Expenses were to be shared fifty-fifty. We decided that the southern coast around Placentia Bay and Fortune Bay would be the best place to look first, and when our vacations arrived we were off.

We loaded our car through a side door in the ferry *William Carson* from North Sydney to Port aux Basques, where we off-loaded and began our

A VIEW OF A NEWFOUNDLAND OUTPORT.

CONFESSIONS OF A BOATBUILDER

arduous drive up the Codroy Valley. It was going to be a 600-mile trip over mud, gravel and partly built roads. Every car carried extra wheels and head-lights, as flying stones often broke out the glass, and it was not unusual to see a white-shirted businessman kneeling beside his car changing a tire. Service stations, motels, and large trucks were non-existent, while public transportation was by taxi from one outport to another. Gas was supplied from a single pump outside a small store every hundred miles or so. The only paved road in Newfoundland in those days was from St. John's up the road a few miles to Premier Joey Smallwood's farm.

As we proceeded up the Codroy Valley, the small wheels of our boat trailer hooked in every pothole until finally we had to abandon our boat and trailer at a farmer's barn, along with our plan to use John's outboard to scour the various bays looking for schooners. We had no idea of the vast distances involved or the roughness of the waters, so it was probably providential that we couldn't do it. At Port-aux-Basques, we had noticed local Newfoundland fisherman boarding the narrow-gauge Newfie Bullet for the train trip to the east coast. Each boarded the train with a large bag of oranges and a larger bottle of rum. The slow and tedious two-day trip did not appeal to us, even if the roads were terrible.

We went up past Cornerbrook, over the Halls-Bay line under con-struction, past the northern towns of Deer Lake, Grand Falls, and Bishop's Falls before we arrived exhausted at Gander, and found accommoda-tions. After resting, we struck out for Goobies, then down the Burin peninsula to Mrs. Murphy's boarding house in Marystown from which we fanned our search out in every direction. We found schooners in various stages of deterioration and I kept them in mind for our return trip.

Next door to Mrs. Murphy's was Grandy's boatyard, a relatively large shop, still building a few sawn-frame 40-foot vessels for the Labrador fishery—a distinctive blend of power and sail, having a spoon bow and schooner stern. Mr. Grandy was tired of the struggle in boatbuilding, but I learned later that the Newfoundland government began supporting his shipyard and it became a thriving business, bolstering the local economy.

In my visits north to Twillingate and Fogo, I found a similar fishing boat, usually 40 to 45 feet, with a straight but raking stem, larger engine power and one or two masts fitted. They appeared to be more of a motor-sailer and I was told they were called "Bully-boats" appropriate to the harsh northern fishery. In winter when the boats were hauled ashore, it was not unusual to see floe ice piled as high as a two-storey house on the shores of

Notre Dame Bay. The ominous sound of grinding and booming could be heard continuously from the groaners during an on-shore wind.

To get around Placentia Bay, we boarded the coastal boat *Petit Forte,* then just in her second season of commission. She was absolute luxury after what we had experienced. Unfortunately, John and

TYPICAL SCHOONER FOUND IN NEWFOUNDLAND OUTPORTS.

most of the other passengers were seasick much of the time as the wind blew and the vessel rolled and rolled. Sea air and the motion have the opposite effect on me, as I become ravenously hungry and ate for everyone.

As we roamed, we had a chance to study the land, the lifestyle, and the people; a simple folk, steeped in honesty by the unrelenting austerity of their life. They were uncomplaining, unquestioning, and uncompromising, like the cold hardness of the rock upon which they clung. I was struck by the neatness and order of their villages with small houses, held aloft by poles wedged in any available cracks in the rocks often surrounded by a rough white picket fence. I thought the fences were to separate and protect each owner's kingdom until I discovered they were meant to keep out the free-roaming sheep. Any plot of ground between the rocks was used for a graveyard as Newfoundlanders have great respect for their ancestors. There were no gardens or forests along the south coast since there was very little ground over the towering bedrock. There was no fresh produce or fresh milk for cereal—tinned milk, half-and-half with water was the fare.

Land transportation was almost an impossibility with commerce from port-to-port carried on by sea in small boats. Any little cleft or crevice between the rocky headlands was a small harbour running in from the sea.

In the late 50s and early 60s while I was there, most of the outports were being closed out as the inshore fishery had almost ended. Younger people had left for work in Canada's larger cities, while the older people and those remaining were moved to larger centres, where they could more easily be supported and cared for by the current welfare system, leaving their ancestors, their homes, and their whole way of life behind. It was a very traumatic change for them and many simply went into that twilight zone of their minds for escape.

The outports that remained were a perfect and startling example of the last days of the feudal system. The merchant-baron who owned the general store and kept each family's account book was king in each community. He would inspect the catch brought to the dock and decide what would be bought and what would be rejected, and what pittance he would pay for it. The value was then marked on the credit side of each book while foodstuffs, clothing, and household goods purchased by the fishermen were marked on the debit side. Most often the fisherman never caught up to the merchant, who set the prices, kept the records, and often did any personal paperwork for his chattel who couldn't read or write. Outside authority was

"WE THOUGHT THERE MIGHT BE A SCHOONER OR TWO LEFT IN NEWFOUNDLAND."

represented by the Catholic priest who swept up the bay driving his own motorboat with his cassock billowing out behind him, or by the local RCMP officer who might visit once a month.

I visited one small village to see the local merchant about buying an old schooner he owned, previously used as a boat-to-door supply. There was a one-mile gravel road in front of his store on which stood a brand new shiny automobile. I praised his new car and asked him how many cylinders it was. "I don't know, b'y," he replied, "I never lifted the hood." Such an attitude of casual affluence was his right.

One time I visited a small outport aboard the *Petit Forte*, squeezing into the tiny rock harbour. The skipper was astoundingly competent as he reversed engines, turned the vessel in her own length with bow and stern almost touching both shores, and brought her handily alongside the wharf. The harbour water was crystal clear and looked no more than three or four feet deep. A large crowd, probably the entire population of the village, had gathered on the dock to witness *Petit Forte*'s arrival, which was the highlight of the week. I asked the Mate how he was going to get the dock line affixed. "Just watch this!" he replied. "Hey Jarge, catch the line!" he called out to the crowd. Six men stepped forward as one; they were all named George! It seemed a risky way to depend on berthing a new multi-million dollar ship!

At one remote outport, *Petit Forte* discharged the new Catholic priest complete with all his baggage, and a large wooden crate marked Bathtub. The priest approached the men on the dock to carry his goods. "I understand you're a handy man George," he said to one man, "Would you take this bathtub to my house and install it?" The man doffed his cap and replied, "Yes, Father." When the priest left, the man's friend asked, "Jarge, what's a bathtub?" "I don't know, my son," was the reply, "I'm not a Catholic!"

John Morse and I visited many quaint fishing villages, some boatbuilding shops, the Friday night dances at Burin, attended mostly by local widows, and general stores to glean any information about schooners that might be for sale. It was a great educational experience in people, fisher-folk, and the sea. Once I asked a local what the cultural origin of Newfoundlanders was, and was told, "Well, we're one-half Irish, one-half French and one-half Portuguese." At Beau Bois, I remarked that there must have been a beautiful forest there once because Beau Bois meant beautiful woods in French. "No Frenchman ever lived here, b'y," was the reply. Our vacation time was drawing to a close, so John and I re-traced our journey, picking up our abandoned boat and trailer in the Codroy Valley and returned to Nova Scotia without incident.

We totalled up our expenses for the trip and divided them exactly in half. John even took a tire tread gauge from his pocket and measured the amount of wear we had put on his tires. It was a grand trip, and one that left me determined to return to Newfoundland as soon as possible on a boat-buying mission.

LAST OF THE NEWFOUNDLAND SCHOONERS

Susie Lockyer, towed from Isle Valen,
in Halifax for bottom cleaning.

CHAPTER FIVE

ON MY NEXT TRIP TO NEWFOUNDLAND, I stayed with Jack Ralph, who ran a small boarding house with his wife in Port aux Basques across from the ferry docks. He also drove the mail to Rose Blanche and Harbour Le Cou eastward along the south coast as far as the road went. Jack was a wealth of information in my search for schooners. His wife kept an immaculately fresh house, filled with warm aromas of baking, wax, and shaving soap. Supper was sometimes bottled moose-meat and bay-berry pie.

Jack sent me to Mr. Gus Buckland who owned a pretty 55-foot schooner named *Carolyn Marie* at Rose Blanche, and I bought her for $1,400. Built at La Poile Bay, she had operated the past two seasons transporting and accommodating big-game sportsmen along the south coast. In those days, it was said that you could shoot a moose or caribou on a cliff and it would

MARY J. HARDY AND *CAROLYN MARIE* AT BADDECK.

tumble right down onto the deck of the schooner. *Carolyn Marie* was powered with a newly re-built Acadia 87 marine gas engine, and was completely equipped with sails, rigging, anchors, lines, two dories, and other necessary equipment.

While I was in Rose Blanche I noticed a 40-foot powerboat with an outhouse built against the wheelhouse and overhanging the sea, "A tylet, for the Sports, ya know." Other equipment aboard also included three ATCs, for the hunters to chase after moose and caribou over the rugged barrens. Sport fishing was quite an industry for those with boats and camps since the fishery had ended.

I made plans to sail *Carolyn Marie* back to Halifax. Don Holder was pressed into service and sent up to be captain. In Rose Blanche, I had met Stan Rose and Alex Knee, two stoic, honest fishermen adept at maintaining boats and things marine. I hired Stan for engineer and Alex for crew for the trip. It was a successful voyage, and opened the way for Stan and Alex to join me in future adventures.

While I was in Port aux Basques, I had seen a handsome 47-foot jack schooner, *Lillian and Lizzie*, berthed near the ferry dock, and approached the owners, Jacob and Theo Hatcher, about buying her. She was no longer fishing of course, but the Hatcher brothers lived aboard, as she was the only home they had. They had already refused to sell her to numerous enquiring buyers. I asked them if they had ever considered living somewhere else and they replied they didn't know of any place. "What if I was to bring you up a house on wheels?" I asked, "You could live in it, and if there was any work anywhere, you could take it there too." They had never heard of a house on wheels. Roads were being built in Newfoundland then and a whole new way of life was opening up. I told them I could trade them a house-trailer and give them some money too, for the schooner. I said I would return to Nova Scotia, find a suitable house on wheels, and contact them. I asked them what they would want in it, and they replied, "Just two bunks, a table, and an iron stove." The deal was struck, and I continued with my schooner search in Newfoundland.

I motored back to Marystown on the Burin Peninsula and once again boarded the coastal boat *Petit Forte*. The skipper was Capt. Peter Drake of the small island of Oderin in Placentia Bay. He always blew the ship's horn when he passed by his mother's house there. Once he heard about my mission, he became very helpful in suggesting any schooners he knew of. The first was *Willis E.*, owned by Ron Manning also of Oderin. Enquiring had to be done quickly as *Petit Forte* only stayed at any particular port of call less than one hour, discharging freight and exchanging passengers. Manning affirmed he would be willing to sell his 39-foot jack schooner but time had run out; I told him I would be back to agree on details on *Petit Forte's* return run. Ron was a small weather-beaten sailor who sported a battered cap hauled down over one eye, and a seaman's eye focused on the distance as one looking for landfall or a buoy.

At Isle Valen, Capt. Drake told me there was a pretty little schooner just over the headland in a sheltered cove. I could probably see it if I hurried. I had found in my dealings with Newfoundland fishermen that a handshake and a drink of rum sealed a bargain with much more effect than a written contract. By nature, they were suspicious of paperwork, so I carried a satchel containing my camera, several pint bottles of rum, a contract pad and some money. In any case, Capt. Drake said he would blow the horn when they were ready to leave and when I heard it, I better come running or I would miss the boat. With this stern warning, I ran up over the headland and down the other side with coat tails and satchel flapping. Cresting the hill, I saw a handsome little green schooner named *Susie Lockyer* moored to her collar (mooring) in a picturesque little cove. A tall fisherman was on her deck with a double-bitted axe raised to chop up the cabin house. I ran down the hill shouting at the top of my voice, "Stop! Stop! Don't chop that schooner!" A young boy had a dory at the shore and without stopping I ordered, "Take me off to the schooner."

Boarding the vessel, I explained to William Lockyer, the owner, that I wanted to buy his schooner. He said it would cost me a lot of money since she would yield enough firewood for the winter. When he realized that I didn't want to fish with her, but simply "to sail around," he stepped backward as though I had something contagious. In his view, anyone who would go to sea for pleasure would go to hell for pastime.

He wanted $150 for her, $200 with gear—pulley blocks, ironwork, shaft, propeller, lines, ropes, and anchors. Not bad for an 18 year old, 39-foot schooner, tight and afloat! I agreed to his terms, opened my satchel, handed him a bottle of rum and ten dollars, and struck the bargain with a handshake as *Petit Forte's* whistle began to Toot! Toot! Toot! I left him staring after me as I beat a hasty retreat at full speed up over the hill! I expect he considered me a demon from hell. Life in Newfoundland had always been calm, slow, and deliberate.

Returning to Oderin, I stayed again with Ron Manning. In honour of my visit, his oldest son had been sent out with the family's old muzzle-loading shotgun to bag a black duck or coot, and the delicacy was carefully prepared and served by Ron's wife while their five children waited silently until we had finished our meal.

Ron showed me a little 31-foot schooner ashore on the beach, in rough condition with no masts or equipment, but he said he might be able to repair and refloat her. Her owner, William Mellay, agreed to sell her for $150 and help Ron do the necessary work on her. I shipped paint and tools from Halifax while they found other materials locally. She was aptly called *Hagdown* after the small sea bird that skims over the waves far at sea, never seeming to rest. Her deck was in bad condition so I told them not to bother with it, as I would probably have to replace it in Nova Scotia.

Ron was particularly concerned about the fate of his *Willis E;* it was almost a member of his family. I got the impression she had been named after an ancestor, whose spirit still inhabited the vessel. I assured him she would receive the best of care.

Willis E. was a 39-foot jack schooner with spars and rigging, windlass, pump, lights, anchors and lines, afloat and in good condition, available for $375. Ron agreed to replace some planking, caulk, fill and paint topsides and bottom. We were both satisfied with the deal.

HAGDOWN AS I FOUND HER, ODERIN, PLACENTIA BAY, NEWFOUNDLAND, 1964.

After I returned to Halifax, we experienced a disastrous and violent hurricane. Shipping had been lost and much coastal damage reported. In great concern for my schooners lying at anchor in Oderin, I finally contacted Ron by phone. Word had to be sent out to him, as the only phone on the island was in the general store. Eventually I heard his voice, faint, and scratchy at the other end. "Ron! How are the schooners?" I anxiously enquired. After much scratching and crackle, I heard his faint reply, "Ah my son, they's as safe as if they was in God's pocket." A perfect reassurance.

With boats scattered all along the south coast of Newfoundland, I began to plan some way to get them to Nova Scotia. It was impossible to insure them since so many small wooden vessels had sunk or burned after the fishery ended that the insurance companies insisted on a conditional survey, which was impossible.

A few vessels could make it under their own power, but the majority would have to be towed. Don Holder had located a 48-foot jack schooner built by Farrell's of North Bay, La Poile, named *Mary J. Hardy*. This schooner had undergone a complete repair and rebuild at the Halifax Shipyards on an insurance claim in 1961. He thought she would be just what we needed for

Willis E. AT OUR FIRST BOATYARD.

CONFESSIONS OF A BOATBUILDER

a towboat. However, her power was light for the job so we bought one of a pair of used 60 h.p. heavy duty Fairbanks-Morse diesel engines from Capt. Jack Cruickshank, late of marine interests but now operating a horse-racing track near Halifax, and had it installed in *Mary J.*

Holder installed a tall fore-topmast and rigged a variety of used jibs as staysails, not conventional, but effective. He also purchased a brand-new full-sized white enamel kitchen range to run on diesel oil, which he installed below, and then constructed his new cabin over it. Holder was not noted for paying his bills. Eventually the furniture store and finance company arrived with the sheriff to exact payment for the stove or re-possess it. Holder replied in his most innocent manner, "Well, I guess you'll just have to take it then." "How will we get it out? The companion-way hatch is too small!" they exclaimed. "Oh gosh, golly, gee, that's right, isn't it," replied Holder. When they decided to cut the cabin roof open, Holder remarked, "Oh, I couldn't let you damage my boat!" Stymied, they backed up off the wharf. Holder's methods were not always honour-able, but they were effective.

In due course, the *Mary J.* was ready and Holder began towing some of the smaller schooners over from Newfoundland and through the Bras d'Or Lakes to Halifax. Sometimes he would berth two or three at the govern-ment wharf in Baddeck in a shuttle-tow system. He always hired the most non-descript crew he could find, usually from the harbour front drinking establishments he frequented.

Staples of the ship's larder were peanut butter and rum. When I asked him how much a particular tow would cost me, he would reply, "Well, I don't know, the tanks are full of diesel, Becky's rent is paid and she has food, probably $400." Another time, when the larder was empty the tow from the same place could cost $1,500!

One day I received an urgent call from Holder from Ingonish in Cape Breton, Nova Scotia. The engine had seized up and thrown a piston right out through the block! *Mary J.* and her tow were alongside the government wharf as we discussed a rescue operation. I contacted Capt. Jack Cruikshank, and he still had the mate to the defunct engine. So I decided to buy it, as it should fit in place of its mate. I loaded the monstrous engine on a borrowed boat trailer and attached it behind my old 1958 Pontiac car for the trip to Ingonish, up over the famous mountainous Cabot Trail. My trepidation grew as I approached the 900-foot high Cape Smokey. My old car strug-gled up one side of the mountain, teetered at the top as I paused to let her cool off, then began the dangerous plunge down the other side. I knew there was a hairpin turn at the bottom, but I was preoccupied with trying to hold the whole thing on the road as we sped down faster. My brakes had been sending out great rolling clouds of blue smoke all the way down, but somehow I got to the bottom and around the turn safely.

Failing to find a crane or lift-boom in Ingonish, we waited until high tide and pulled the old engine with chains up to the wharf. The new engine was then rigged and slid down the planks. Unfortunately, the planks separated and our engine plunged into the water beside the boat! Sometimes if you don't have bad luck, you don't have any luck at all! Re-chain the engine, lift it up, take it apart, clean it up, re-oil, etc., and do it all again. This time we got it on its beds, hooked up and running with the usual expenditure of time, money, worry, and rum. Finally, Holder was under way again, towing schooners.

"Stop! Stop! Don't chop that schooner!" The *Susie Lockyer.*

LILLIAN AND LIZZIE:
TRADED FOR A TRAILER

THE *LILLIAN AND LIZZIE*.

CHAPTER SIX

MEANWHILE, BACK IN HALIFAX, I was busily engaged in finding a house-trailer that I could take to Port aux Basques to exchange for *Lillian and Lizzie.* Everything was too expensive, too large, or too small. I eventually located a homemade 15-foot round ended camper trailer being lived in by a young blind man who was going to move in with his mother and would sell it for $150. I tore out the old interior, scrubbed it up, re-painted, and installed two bunks, a kitchen table, and two chairs along with a Lunenburg Foundry Fisherman iron stove with pipe and smoke head. The finishing touch was a closet with an old toilet seat affixed to a five-gallon Irving Oil grease bucket. Now confident I had a complete house on wheels, I was ready to tow it to Port aux Basques.

When asked at the ferry dock in North Sydney, how long my rig was, I decided in the interest of cash flow to say it was 33 feet rather then the 35 feet it probably was. I expected someone to come out and measure, but they didn't. I pulled the front bumper of my old Pontiac right up to the ferry door when suddenly there was a tremendous crash behind me. I leaped from my car and looked at the trailer. A huge steel loading door had descended only a half-inch from the back of the trailer! So that was how they told if you were over length!

At Port aux Basques, I drove off the ferry and into the long freight shed as instructed where stevedores and forklift trucks were milling around. I waited and waited but nothing happened. Finally, I rolled down my window and asked a nearby stevedore, "How do I get through the shed?" "Yer blows yer harn, b'y!" he answered disdainfully. When I did so the wall of men and machines parted, and I drove sheepishly out onto the highway.

I stopped on the road in front of Jacob and Theo who were with *Lillian and Lizzie* when I arrived, and were all excited to inspect their new house. "Lard Jaesus, b'ys, she's even got a tylet!"

"Where do you want her boys, I can put her anywhere you want," I offered, feeling pretty cocky at having navigated the highway and ferry trip. In their sister's backyard over in the town was agreed. "No problem," I said and we set out. Their sister's backyard turned out to be an almost vertical rock face 50 feet high! Not to be defeated by this minor setback, I picked up three cases of beer and hastened to the local pub around the corner, quickly enlisting fifteen stalwart locals. They all arrived at the sister's house where I pointed to the rock mountain and said,

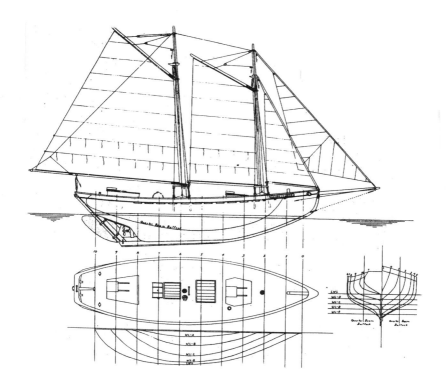

"We have to get this up there." Without a word they took hold of the trailer and nonchalantly carried it up the rock to its new home!

Stan Rose took the vessel to Rose Blanche where he could work on her, and I had a re-built 20 h.p. two cylinder, marine engine crated and shipped to him to install. He pronounced her ready for sea in September of 1963, and Don Holder and Tom McMartin were dispatched for captain and crew. Stan was to be engineer and Alex Knee also crew. I cautioned Holder to watch the fall weather and take every precaution about the vessel's seaworthiness.

After an uneventful nine hours steaming, the vessel encountered a freak sea caused by unpredictable rip tides. Just then, Stanley Rose and Alex Knee were busily engaged in transferring gasoline from drums lashed to the starboard main shrouds and bulwark rail. Solid water swept aboard, and Alex watched helplessly as Stanley was carried clear of the vessel. Holder immediately put the helm hard to port and brought the vessel around in an attempt to locate Rose, but there was no sign of him.

After a four hour search, and with weather continuing to deteriorate, the search for Rose was abandoned. Holder finally made port on Sunday afternoon at Dingwall on Cape Breton Island near Ingonish, after riding out a heavy gale. He went directly to the RCMP detachment there to report the loss of Stanley Ross at sea.

The first indication I had of any trouble was a phone call from Holder on Sunday. The seriousness of his tone prepared me for the worst. I dropped everything and drove immediately to Dingwall to bring the crew home. Holder had located a local man, Hugh Grover, who agreed to keep the boat pumped and tended until we could make arrangements to remove her from the small government wharf.

On the way back, I decided to drop into the RCMP detachment at Ingonish in case any other details were needed. The officer said the report was complete, as the engineer, Mr. Holder, had come in and reported their captain drowned! Clever, I thought, Holder is covering his tracks so as not to be responsible for the wreck and Stan's death!

I could not get over the loss of Stan and what it would mean to his wife and young family; I had instigated the voyage and felt responsible for it. After exchanging telegrams and letters with Stan's widow, I gathered up all the money I could find and went to Rose Blanche to see her. I hardly knew what to expect, but was deeply touched by Mrs. Rose's deportment. She said that accidents were the way of the sea and that every fisherman's wife expected her husband might not return every time he put out to sea. I gave her my pitiful funds and deepest sympathy.

Shortly after my return home, I had a call from Hugh Grover who reported that the *Lillian and Lizzie* had sunk at the wharf although he had been pumping her faithfully. She would have to be removed as a menace to navigation, without delay. So I filled my little camper trailer with air bags, two large pumps, chain hoists, a compressor, lines, chains, canvas, and all manner of salvage equipment, and set off again to Dingwall with Tom McMartin and a scuba diver. As we were driving along a remote section of highway along Nova Scotia's Eastern Shore at 2:00 A.M. there was a crash, swerving, and ripping sounds from the over-loaded trailer. We stopped and found an axle had broken and a tire had torn its way up through the trailer. There was nothing to be done at that hour, so we spent an uncomfortable night trying to get a sleep on top of the salvage equipment. The next morning we got the tire replaced at a nearby service station, rigged temporary blocking under the trailer and proceeded cautiously to Sherbrooke, the next village. We had the trailer axle welded and repaired there before continuing on our way and over Cape Smokey to Dingwall, where we found the schooner submerged beyond the capabilities of our floats and pumps.

The only thing to do was to somehow get the vessel pulled around the corner of the wharf and into shallower water so we could get our pumps to work on her but there were no bulldozers or heavy equipment in that end of Cape Breton. I finally arranged for the driver of the Department of Highways road grader to come from Ingonish on his own time the next evening, and drag the *Lillian and Lizzie* around the wharf and up the beach. There we coffer-damned the hatches and got our pumps at work. We gained on the water at low tide and when the six foot tide came in, she floated! Then we had a massive clean up and repair and before Holder arrived with his *Mary J.*, to tow her to our boatyard at Ship Harbour, near Halifax. It was all a costly, heartbreaking, and tragic exercise in futility.

I remembered asking Stan Rose one evening while he was staying aboard *Carolyn Marie* and working on the boats for me in Halifax, what he would do if he was ever faced with an imminent sinking in a storm. He replied in his own quiet and sober way, "I would go forward, grab up the anchor, and go overboard. It would be better to get it over with quick."

I often wondered what his last thoughts were that dark, fateful night in the storm in the Gulf of St. Lawrence.

When my Newfoundland vessels had begun to arrive in

ALL THAT ARRIVED AT DEBAIES COVE.

Nova Scotia, I had advertised for boatbuilders willing to come to Halifax and work repairing them. Cyril Russell of Ship Harbour had agreed to undertake the work, later joined by his younger brother, Donnie. At first they lived in my camper trailer at Melville Cove, and travelled home on weekends, but soon suggested moving the vessels to Ship Harbour to be closer to their families.

Cyril knew of a suitable property at DeBaies Cove near Ship Harbour, which I eventually bought and set up a boatshop there.

When I told my Ship Harbour boat-builders I intended to repair the *Lillian and Lizzie* and sell her they refused. In their opinion it would be more work than building a new boat. I insisted and they flatly refused. Arriving at the shop one day, I saw that *Lillian and Lizzie* had been rolled over on her deck; there she was, a door had been chain-sawed in her side and chickens were running in and out. They had won the argument.

Jack schooners had been built in North Bay by the Farrells who developed a strong yacht-like hull with a gracefully curved undercut bow, well-shaped sections and a smooth run to the stern. The inside sternpost in the Farrell boats is stepped on the keel in the conventional manner, and it carries the rabbet up to the horn timber, which is fastened to the top of the inner sternpost, where it runs out to join the outer sternpost. The outer sternpost is an integral part of the transom assembly, but it extends downward and joins the keel at its after end. The rudder outboard is hung on the outer sternpost.

This type of construction allows efficient positioning of the propeller as well as permitting a stout, nearly triangular system of timbering at this traditionally weak spot in a vessel's frame.

Witch hazel (similar to yellow birch) was used extensively as planking below the water line and very often in the frames, keelsons, keels, etc., while spruce is used in topside plank and decks which withstands the ravages of fresh water much better.

Construction was with frames of about 4 x 4 inches, practically double flitched. A heavy keelson was employed over the natural grown hooks and floors. Seams were caulked with oakum and payed with Portland cement, which stayed surprisingly tight.

All in all, we learned a great deal about construction and design of North Atlantic schooners from our experience in rebuilding Newfoundland jacks. It was a great apprenticeship for us as we progressed from rebuilding the old vessels to designing and building new yachts.

BACK AGAIN TO NEWFOUNDLAND

CLARY DeBAIE WITH *MARY GEORGE* OF RUSHOON IN THE NEW SHOP AT DeBAIES COVE, SHIP HARBOUR, NOVA SCOTIA.

CHAPTER SEVEN

BY 1965, I STILL HAD VESSELS in Newfoundland waiting to be towed to Nova Scotia. This was the height of the McCarthy era in the USA and the North American defence systems were a priority since the Russians were expected to arrive at any moment. This was ridiculous, of course, since the Russians had their hands full just trying to grow enough food and police their own countrymen. Nevertheless, a close watch was kept throughout the North and many of my customers were young American men stationed along the DEW (Distant Early Warning) line from Cape Dyer and its satellite outposts. In isolation, all they could think of was romantic tropical isles, dark-skinned maidens, and voyages to exotic lands. They were ready-made buyers for my schooners. I found that the best way to make a sale was to anchor a freshly painted old schooner in a picturesque setting, and have the prospective buyer "discover" it for himself while being driven around the area.

I would arrange to re-build the schooner at our Ship Harbour boatyard, which we had named "Bluewater Boats" and equip it from my stock of used engines, marine equipment, and fittings.

So I travelled back and forth to Newfoundland, while Holder continued his tows. He had taken a position as Mate on the Canadian Coast Guard ship *Narwhal*, so he had to tow between times.

I had once visited the small village of Fox Cove near Burin, and had seen a little 32-foot relatively new schooner built and owned by two brothers, George and Jacob Antle. They obtained their building materials by climbing up nearby cliffs, cutting out roots for knees and timbers, and tumbling them down to the beach, where they would chop them into the desired shapes. She was crude but sturdy and named *Bridgeth Josephine*. A long name

BLUEWATER BOATS LETTERHEAD.

for a little boat. They were fishing with her but agreed to sell. So Holder towed her to Baddeck and thence to DeBaies Cove.

Willis E., *Susie Lockyer* and *Hagdown* eventually made it under tow as well but we lost three of the older vessels while being towed due to their leaky condition and bad weather. These little craft were a unique breed of tough boats used to harvest fish from cod traps set by hand. They were usually 18 to 22 feet, carvel plank, and sawn frames. They were fitted with a single cylinder make-and-break engine, shaft, and propeller, and the rudder was hung outdoors on the transom. As in the larger jack-boats, they were ceiled-up part way from the keel to make a fish well; the ledge where the ceiling stopped was handy to stand upon while nets were hauled. They had nice lines and were great little sea boats. I have not seen them anywhere outside of Newfoundland, but together with the dory and jack schooner they were the backbone of the inshore fishery.

Another eastern-built jack named *Mary George* made it under tow from her homeport in Rushoon, Placentia Bay. Newfoundland vessels were often named after two family members of mixed gender. She was 46 feet with a 14-foot 6-inch beam without the graceful hull lines of the Farrell build boats, from North Bay, La Poile. I bought her from the four Wiffen brothers for $450. The Wiffens unstepped her masts and secured them on deck, with sails, rigging and other equipment put below for the tow to Halifax.

As I travelled around, I sometimes had to stay overnight with the fisherman I had gone to see, as

INSIDE THE SHOP AT BLUEWATER BOATS.

there were no motels or bed and breakfasts. One such time I was given a bed in a large upper bedroom. The family had a number of children, so sleeping arrangements sometimes had to be doubled up. I was made very welcome but told I would be sharing my bed with one of the younger boys. Bed time arrived and I crawled in. Small footsteps came down the hall and turned into my room. The nine-year-old went to his side of the bed and knelt down. Surmising he was saying his prayers, I thought I should follow his example, so I slid out of bed and knelt down too. My bedmate looked across at me and said, "What are you doing, mister?" To which I replied, "The same thing you are." Without batting an eye, he said, "Mum's going to be awful mad, the pot's on my side!"

The next morning it was quite a sight to see the older girls from each house emerge with their enamel pails, and engage in pleasant conversation while they walked to the wharf where they would throw their burden overside. Such was the efficient and accepted sewage system in the outport villages. On Monday mornings, putt-putt-putts could be heard everywhere around the harbour, and I assumed it was the small boats going out. I soon discovered that each house had a gas-motor powered washing machine on the veranda and Monday was laundry day. It made sense of course, as there was no domestic electricity.

During one of my trips to Rushoon, I had flown to Gander with a prospective buyer, Henry Crockett of Saint John, New Brunswick. He was an acquaintance of Don Holder as they were in the Coast Guard together. It was April 1965 with snow and slush still on the highway and we had rented a car in Gander for the drive to Rushoon. On our return trip, Henry was driving when slush built up under the wheels, froze, and sent the car into a spin and off the road. It rolled several times, coming to rest on its roof in the woods. Luckily, this was the only bit of level ground for miles, the rest being deep rocky gorges. We were shaken and disoriented—my glasses and hat had flown off and Henry was hanging upside down in his seat belt. He could not locate his release button so I crawled under him and pushed it; he came crashing down, knocking the wind out of me. He crawled out a broken window and I located my glasses and hat, put them on and followed him out. By this time, a curious group of Newfoundland fishermen had gathered. As I crawled through the broken window, I came eye-to-eye with a large black rubber boot, whose owner exclaimed, "Look, 'ees still got 'is 'at upon 'is 'ead just like the cowboys in the movies!" Boat buying was not without its hazards, but occasional humour helped to ease the pain.

Holder was quite busy now, so I enlisted other help in towing my purchases home. An acquaintance, Mike Crowley, who had an able vessel agreed to go to Harbour Breton taking my crew from Halifax to prepare the vessel *Bessie F. Appleby* for the sea voyage to Nova Scotia. I had bought the 55-foot schooner from Felix Johnson at St. Bernards, Fortune Bay for $2,500. When I first visited Felix to buy the schooner, I was invited to supper with his large family. The long table was piled high with steaming platters of lobsters and everyone hoed in. I took only two to be polite. Felix peered around the mound of lobsters at me and said, "Dig right in now, the season opens tomorrow!"

Since she was rigged and ready, we decided to bring the *Appleby* under her own power, but in company with Mike Crowley's *A. Halkett* for safety's sake. One of my riggers, Snook Caines, was to be skipper on the *Appleby*, with his crew. While waiting for delivery, I had sold the vessel to Lewis Glorsky of New Jersey who was waiting for her arrival at Nova Scotia. With so many interests involved, I had a conditional survey done by a local

DONNIE RUSSELL BUILDS ON A NEW CABIN.

surveyor, Sandy Hynes, and insurance placed on the vessel with Lloyds of London.

We outfitted Mike for the voyage with supplies and equipment for both vessels and they arrived at Harbour Breton without incident. There the crew completed preparing the *Appleby* for sea and both vessels journeyed in company along the South-West Coast to Rose Blanche, where Mike decided to rig towing bridles to keep both vessels together in case of fog and stormy seas. They set out, but sea conditions became so bad that Mike took *Appleby*'s crew onto his own vessel, and the *Appleby* was lost.

Unfortunately, the terms of the insurance on the vessel called for her to be under her own power and not under tow, so the insurance would not honour the claim. Once the owner had been paid, the crew had to be paid, the new owner had to be refunded and Mike Crowley sued me for the total delivery fee, although he had not delivered. I was facing a financial disaster in addition to my lost work, time, and salesmanship. Sometimes the boat business was one step forward and two steps back.

GEARING UP IN NOVA SCOTIA

THE *RED JACK* AT OUR DOCK IN MELVILLE COVE, READY FOR SEA.

CHAPTER EIGHT

THE NEWFOUNDLAND SCHOONERS that had made it were now at our boat shop, Bluewater Boats, at Ship Harbour, where they were repaired for their new owners. *Susie Lockyer* had been bought by Pete Tibbetts of Beverly, Massachusetts, *Willis E.* by Tom and Lee Janec of Chicago, *Mary George* by Larry Daugherty of Gloucester, *Bridgeth Josephine* by Glenn Plat of Toronto, and *Hagdown* by Kelvin Jarvis of Hamilton, Ontario.

Hagdown and *Bridgeth Josephine* were almost the same size at 32 feet. *Hagdown's* deck needed to be replaced, and Glenn Plat had decided he wanted a whole new deck and cabin arrangement for *Bridgeth Josephine*, so I told the boatbuilders to cut the deck off each boat and replace *Hagdown's* with *Bridgeth Josephine's*. My builders objected strenuously—such a thing had never been done before, and it wouldn't work anyway they said. I was adamant. *Bridgeth Josephine's* entire deck, complete with beams and cabins, was swung over and lowered onto *Hagdown*. A few well-placed spikes and bolts, and it looked like it had always been there. It wasn't really a working unit but looked great. The little schooner presented a pretty and perky picture once we painted her bright green and white. Kelvin Jarvis arrived in snow and ice to inspect *Hagdown*. She was more than slightly rotted, but frozen solid. He asked about her condition and I replied that, "She might have a few soft spots," but that I wouldn't like to make an opinion. I passed him my knife and invited him to test her for himself. Of course, the knife blade didn't penetrate the frozen wood, and he bought the boat. My boatbuilders who had been watching through the frosted shop windows informed me that my sales technique was less than ethical.

Glenn Plat took delivery of the rebuilt *Bridgeth Josephine*, now re-named *Red Jack,* and sailed her to my moorings at Halifax where he spent part of that summer before sailing off to cruise the Atlantic seaboard and Bermuda. While he was living aboard in Halifax, a prospective customer and his wife arrived. *Red Jack* was the only boat at hand so I called out to Glenn Plat and asked if I could row my customers out for an inspection. "Come right along," he replied. It was a hot August day and as I came alongside I discovered he was sitting in his cockpit full of water completely naked. He didn't bat an eye as he invited us aboard. I thanked him, but declined, and rowed my customer and his wife back to shore. Plat was a casual and easygoing character who had been an international roving reporter and photographer for the *Toronto Sun*; he went wherever fighting or political unrest was the greatest. Perhaps these experiences prepared him for his life at sea, single-handing his little schooner.

Larry Daugherty had bought the larger *Mary George*, re-named her *Constancy* and ordered a large aft-cabin built on her with large oval quarter windows. This was the first vessel we re-built with a raised aft deck and added considerably to her accommodation space, providing a higher deck from which to sail her. This was the prototype for the raised aft-cabins we were to later build on most of our new designs. Larry also acquired a red SL-300 convertible, a large local estate house, and a girl friend when he came to Nova Scotia to wait for his *Constancy* to be ready to sail away. He had found his own way to get de-bushed before his adventures at sea began.

One of the first Newfoundland schooners we had repaired, converted and sold was Ron Manning's *Willis E.* She was bought by another DEW Line boy, Tom Janec of Chicago, who was later joined by his brother Lee, and they prepared to make her ready for sea. They were both cold and reserved young men who seemed to have a chip on their shoulder, and a lack of experience with boats and the sea. They enquired what the iron and lead I was bringing aboard was for. I explained it was ballast to counteract the weight and pressure of masts, sails and wind. Without it, the boat could roll over. "You are not going to put any of that in my boat; if it filled up with water, it would sink," Tom exclaimed. No amount of reasoning could convince him of the necessity of the ballast.

One day, Tom and Lee decided it was time to take *Willie E.* out for a test run. Tom had his large volume of Chapman's *Seamanship, Navigation, and Small Boat Handling* spread out before him at the wheel, opened to the page for starting the engine and piloting. Lee had positioned himself up on the wheelhouse roof as lookout. Shortly after casting off, the steering cable jumped a pulley and jammed the wheel! In great panic, Tom called out to Lee, "I can't steer, what will I do?" "Well, turn the page, Tom!" was Lee's exasperated reply. Neither had thought of putting the engine in reverse before she hit the rocks with a loud "Carr—rump"!

The cost of the conversion work became much more than Tom and Lee expected, and postponed departure time until well into the fall of 1964. Departure day finally arrived and the Janec brothers came up my office stairs to say goodbye. Obviously exasperated from the extra time and money expended, Lee looked me in the eye and exclaimed, "Well, we're leaving; but if that boat sinks and drowns up, we're going to come back and kill you!"

Pete Tibbets of Beverly, Massachusetts was as pleasant as the Janecs were difficult. Pete bought *Susie Lockyer* and we did her conversion work at our Ship Harbour shop. He re-named her *Palaedes*, painted her black, kept her schooner rig and two cabin houses. We re-powered her with a Hercules-Kermath 27 h.p. diesel from a navy 27-foot motor cutter. Pete and my older sons had fun running around in the motor cutter while we were waiting to switch engines. Pete stayed with us and became like a member of the family. He sailed his schooner for many years and always sent us good reports of her throughout his days of cruising.

I had sold the 55-foot *Carolyn Marie* sight unseen, to Sid Rice, a bombastic little Jewish man from New York City. He was a most unlikely sailor and owner, but he had been bitten by the bug. Sid claimed to have been a nightclub singer for Al Capone when he was a young man, so we could guess his age and background. He kept calling me from New York wanting to know if his schooner was getting close to Halifax yet. Holder and his crew were sailing her over from Newfoundland, but had run afoul of bad weather and heavy fogs and had holed up in every harbour along Nova Scotia's Eastern Shore. He always managed to dock within easy reach of a liquor store, which also delayed his progress. Once, as he was trying to explain the current delay to me he protested, "Well, I got this

PALAEDES, CONVERTED FOR PETE TIBBETTS.

J.D.R., DONNIE AND CYRIL BUILDING AT BLUEWATER BOATS.

far didn't I, and I never hit one rock." "Yeah! Which one?" I replied, in frustration.

Sid could contain himself no longer and turned up at my door in his big yellow Cadillac convertible, with brightly flowered shirt and cigar. He had his two pet Schnauzers in the back seat. He passed out shining silver dollars to all the children who had come to see the unusual apparition, and told me he wanted to see his boat. I explained that it hadn't arrived yet but that we could drive along the shore and find her. He passed the keys to me and demanded, "Here, Doug, you drive, you know where we're going." As we drove along the fog-bound wooded road, Sid began squirming in his seat. I thought he might be having a heart attack until he exclaimed, "My God, Doug! You've got to get me out of here, there's nothing but trees!" We arrived with a jolt on the shaky wharf at Marie Joseph, where the *Carolyn Marie* was docked. I tooted the horn and three bedraggled hung-over heads appeared out of the schooners three hatches. One was Holder with stubble beard, a battered hat, and no teeth, while another was One-Eye Eddie from Eastern Passage who had lost an eye in a tavern brawl years ago and only the sunken socket remained. The third was Capt. Tom McMartin with long hair, a huge gold earring, and a two-foot long sheath knife on his belt. Tom's claim to fame had been as a sailor on the Lunenburg built *H.M.S. Bounty* and throughout the filming of *Mutiny on the Bounty* with Marlon Brando. Sid's mouth dropped open when he saw them. "On my God, look at them; Captain Blood and his Calcutta cut-throats," Sid exclaimed. They sobered up a bit, the fog lifted, and *Carolyn Marie* met us in Halifax a few days later.

Sid was pleased with the schooner but was convinced that nobody in Canada knew anything about engines or sailing so he would send a diesel engine up from New York, and look after the delivery himself. In due course, a crated G.M. 6-71 arrived and was taken with the boat to Construction Equipment, one of our best machine shops. The engine was uncrated and installed only to discover it was seized up and needed a complete re-build. I advised Sid by phone, who was furious at his supplier, but said to fix it anyway. We removed the engine, re-built it, and re-installed it, and she was ready to sail. Sid sent up his experienced U.S. crew. The captain, dressed in a neatly pressed khaki uniform, and his one-man crew soon disappeared into one of our harbour-front drinking establishments. Sid flew up, paid all the bills and boarded his vessel to sail away with his "highly qualified crew" after a whole year of grief and misery. As he offered me his outstretched hand he said cheerfully, "I just want you to know it is so good to say goodbye!"

Sid had the good sense to leave the vessel at Yarmouth after a rough sea voyage down the coast. Days later I was contacted by the U.S. Coast Guard who were looking for the seriously overdue vessel. They eventually found her drifting in the Gulf of Maine and boarded her only to discover the engine run out of fuel, the crew were passed out, and empty rum bottles were rolling around the cabin floor. They took her in tow to Portland, Maine where Sid sold her within six months to Dr. Albert Hickey of the Woods Hole Oceanographic. He re-named her *Tamarack*, re-furbished her including a suit of tanbark sails, and sailed her extensively for years around the New England coast. *Carolyn Marie* had found her new home and the life she struggled for, at last.

NEW BOATS—NEW WAYS—NEW DAYS

NEW BOATS BEING RIGGED AT MELVILLE COVE, HALIFAX.

CHAPTER NINE

MY BOATBUILDERS HAD become increasingly frustrated at the extent of necessary repairs. In some cases, we had to replace decks, some topsides planking, stems, sterns, and keels; there wasn't much left of the original vessel.

Cyril Russell insisted it would be easier to build new boats than to repair the old ones. "You must know about boat design since you've drawn all the plans for converting these old fishing boats," he said. "Why don't you design a new boat for us to build? We can correct all the mistakes made on the old ones, and build whatever the customers want." With this unusual and lengthy speech from Cyril, a new concept was born.

The closest course available in naval architecture was at the Massachusetts Institute of Technology in the USA. My job and family commitments precluded my going there, so I bought all the instructional books I could find dealing with wooden auxiliary yachts. Predominant were H.I. Chapelle's books on design and boatbuilding, L. Francis Herreshoff's *Common Sense of Yacht Design*, and others including Skene and Kinney. I studied these authoritative works without compromising their principles, concepts, specifications, or recommendations as I developed my new designs. My experience with the old vessels was invaluable as I married their sea-going qualities to more modern yacht design. The results were a series of able, handsome, sea-going cruisers capable of being built in Nova Scotia with local materials by our own expert builders. Designs such as the 32-foot Destiny, 46-foot Privateer ketch, the 55-foot Aquarius and the 65-foot Vagabond headed the list as we began to build our new fleet. Construction was very much in the manner of the seagoing Atlantic schooner, with sawn frames, white pine or mahogany planking, outside ballast keels cast of iron or lead, double plywood and fibreglassed decks. We started with basic designs and customized to suit individual owner's requirements.

By now, we had moved our repair operation to DeBaies Cove at the entrance to Ship Harbour, some 40 miles from Halifax along Nova Scotia's eastern shore. Cyril was in charge, his wife Jean valiantly keeping shop records of time, materials, insurance and necessary paperwork. Cyril's brother Donnie was the mainstay of the operation. They knew of a capable boatbuilder named Sid Butler from the neighbouring village of Tangier.

Sid was knowledgeable about ships, boats and the sea as well as being a craftsman with a gift for shaping and fashioning wood to his will.

Sid agreed to come to Bluewater Boats, and work with Cyril and Donnie. Everyone pitched in and built a small camp near the shop for Sid to live in. Sid had gained a nefarious reputation as an alcoholic—his wife, and children had long since abandoned him. I discovered that he was not attracted to alcohol for its own sake—Sid was unstable, and alcohol was his self-prescribed medicine. When things became too stressful in his life, which was about every four to eight weeks, the otherwise quiet Sid would let out an oath, hurl his hammer against the shop wall and stomp off to Halifax for a dedicated two-week bender. He would invariably take a room over the old Atomic Cafe affectionately known as the "A-Bomb" on Hollis Street in the prostitute district.

As his debauchery continued, he would sell off anything he had acquired for a few dollars. Shotgun, outboard motor, TV, everything went, until his devils were appeased. Eventually a taxi would bring Sid the 45 miles back and unceremoniously dump him in front of his camp. Cyril and Donnie would drag him into his camp, Jean would clean him up, along with his house, and fortify him with homemade stew.

I had transported almost all the materials to build the first boat shed at DeBaies Cove on my old 1958 Pontiac car and home-made boat trailer. In the spring of the year, the mud road became almost impassable and I had to get a good run on to get through the soft places, with wheels spinning and mud flying in all directions. I did not dare slow down or car, trailer and overweight load would simply settle down into the road. Later in the fall, a sudden night snowstorm covered the waiting boats and it became clear the shop would have to be extended to provide rudimentary shelter. All hands turned to for the addition, as I hauled load after load of framing, panelling and roofing.

Cyril would arrive early at the shop to get a wood fire going in the oil-barrel stove. As Donnie came in ten minutes late, Cyril would complain about some people never being on time, but by 10:00 A.M., he would return to his house up the hill for a drink or two of rum. It would be Donnie's turn to complain, "It's not what time you get here that counts, but what you do after you get here." Donnie was always hard working and conscientious as the boats began to take shape from my plans and instructions.

I had carefully researched and designed a new 45-foot vessel combining some of the good points of the North Atlantic schooners with modern materials and design concepts to suit the demands of sea going, live-aboard cruising yachts. At first, I offered the hull, deck, and masts at only $5,000, thinking there would be buyers interested in finishing a boat themselves. It soon became apparent everyone wanted a complete sail-away version. It was a good thing no one took me up on just the hull offer since it cost more than $5,000 thousand dollars to build!

Dick Shaw, a businessman and entrepreneur from Providence, Rhode Island, saw an ad I had placed in a sailing magazine and contacted me. We already had the first hull well along in construction as I picked Dick up at the airport to see her. He was impressed with what he saw, our sincerity, and the builders' competence. He said he would buy the boat but wanted it completed the way an American yachtsman would want her.

Dick was an astute man with experience in yachting and business having owned the very best yachts built in Holland and the U.S.A. He was president of Stackbin Corporation, building steel shelving in Rhode Island for domestic and foreign customers. His family was well known and respected in government and industry in Rhode Island and his money gave him the opportunity to expand his interests in yacht building and sales. He guided us in the completion and equipping of our first boat, which we called Privateer #1. He supplied a Perkins 4-236, 85 h.p. diesel engine, toilets, sinks, water heaters and other equipment. Dick helped us to develop a list of typical equipment while he explained that American yachtsmen wanted U.S.A. manufactured items. He formed a small business called Simplex Corp., hired a friend, Joe Brown, to administer it, and another acquaintance, Dick Allen, to do the leg work. It soon became apparent that Dick was going to re-sell the boats we built for him. He said he could take all the boats we could build, so after filling outstanding orders all our production was committed to him.

I realized that the output of Bluewater Boats with Cyril and Donnie Russell was not going to be enough to keep up with the developing demand. Cyril was an excellent craftsman, and a perfectionist, who consequently became dissatisfied with most carpenters and apprentices that came to work at the shop. We tried young eager men just out of trade school. They would arrive at the shop with a huge box of tools that took three men to carry. Cyril would look on disdainfully and remark, "When I was young, I had a toolbox like that. Now I can do all my building with what I can carry in my pocket!" Others were tried, but few met Cyril's expectations. I could see that no expansion was possible at our shop, so I searched out and hired a few other builders for my expanding demand.

The first yard I hired was Breton Gray's in Sambro, near Halifax. Next was Gerald Stevens' in Chester and Allan Mitchell's shop also in Chester. With the new sub-contracting boatshops coming on-line, I devised a numbering scheme to identify their boats. Bluewater would be the 1 to 100 series, Brenton Gray's the 100s, Gerald Stevens' the 200s, and so on. Eventually Donald Russell became the 300s, A.F. Theriault & Son the 400s and Osmond Yorke at Parrsboro the 500s. This gave each boat its own hull number, which was useful in identification, contractual reference, insurance, etc, as we expanded. My position was "constructor," to use the old-time term. Traditionally a constructor was a man who designed the vessel, took his plans to the builder's yard, and often lived there to interpret his design and the owner's wishes. After launching, he would be off to another yard and another vessel. As such, he was responsible to see that the owner's wishes were fulfilled and the boatbuilder protected against abuse. Often the boatbuilders had little or no formal education, so someone had to be in charge. I negotiated a building contract using the vessel's hull number with both the owner and the builder. I also re-

IN BUSINESS, BUT STILL WORKING FULL TIME.

searched, purchased, and delivered equipment to each yard. Buying in quantity gave better prices and kept equipment design and installation more standard. On the average 45-foot yacht there were 175 separate items of standard equipment as well as an extensive list of extra items as ordered by individual owners. All this required comprehensive lists and files to keep it all straight. It was also owner's choice of colours, upholstery, and layout, so it got quite hectic when there were fifteen boats building at one time at five different yards. Midnight would often find me flying home in my large Pontiac station wagon, having completed an inspection and delivery trip to the widely separated shops as each boatshop had to be visited at least once each week. I was still working a 40-hour week with the Telephone Company and helping to raise a family of five.

Allan Mitchell had bought the former Chester Seacraft, owned jointly by Gerald Stevens, his brother Emery and aged father, Perry. Allan was not native to Chester, had an inventive mind and a very high I.Q., but lacked the patience to manage the local builders he had inherited with the shop. Some were Heislers with a long ancestry of boatbuilding who worked methodically and carefully in the manner of their Dutch–German forebears. They were experienced and competent but firm in their opinions about "how it should be done."

On one visit to Allan's shop in Chester, he was not in evidence. When I asked his master–builder, Reuben Heisler, where he was, Reuben shifted his chew of tobacco to the other cheek, and replied, "Oh, he's up on Haddon's Hill playing with his model airplane." Later, Allan arrived in a cloud of dust obviously upset. He leapt out of his car, scooped up a handful of rocks, and threw them at the glass windows of his shop all the while yelling, "Stupid Nova Scotia boatbuilders! They're no good for anything!" As broken glass and rocks landed on the shop floor between our feet, Reuben gave his little wry smile, and calmly said, "That's Allan."

On another occasion, I noticed one of the older men at Gerald Stevens' shop in Chester building a mahogany drop–leaf table for the main cabin of one of my boats. He was doing a great job. On my visit the following week, he was still sanding and polishing it. I figured I could buy a whole living room set for what that table would cost. I spoke to Gerald about how long it was taking, and what it was probably going to cost us. "Yes," Gerald replied, "but isn't he doing a beautiful job."

Another time, my American customer wanted square windows in the break of his aft deck in place of the traditional round ones. I explained the requirement to Gerald, strengthening my argument over Gerald's remark that, "Grandfather never did it that way," by explaining that the yacht owner was an American, and consequently rather odd. Gerald reluctantly agreed to the change. On my next visit, the windows were built, but round! I asked Gerald if he had forgotten, to which he replied, "Yes, but aren't the round ones lovely."

Gerald had developed a unique manner of protecting himself from any unwanted conversation. His non–committal response to a customer's comment was always, "Uh–hum." When the accent was on the hum, it usually meant, "I'm not really interested" or "Go to Hell." This allowed him to do what he was going to do anyway without being rude!

One of the first new boats completed at Bluewater Boats was Privateer #1, Hull #1 for Dick Shaw. She was the first of the new 45-foot ketches, with a full wheelhouse midships. She also boasted auxiliary tiller steering on her raised afterdeck as well as a wheel in the enclosed cabin. She was powered with a Perkins marine diesel provided by Dick, Model 4.236, 65 h.p. continuous, 85 h.p. intermittent, giving the boat a steady speed of 7.5 knots through a Warner Velvet Drive, 2:1 reduction. We used a 21 x 18 inch 3-blade Michigan propeller in a Dynaflow pattern. Dick's

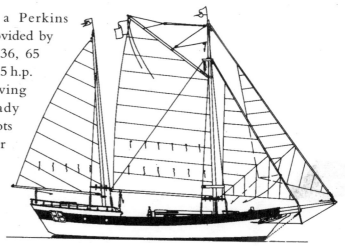

SKETCH OF THE KETCH "PRIVATEER."

experience and choice proved correct, and we employed the same power package in over 60 subsequent vessels. Dick named her *Esgrimidor*.

We enjoyed very good prices on the engines from Mack Boring and Parts in Union, New Jersey. The salesman was Joe Meehan, who told me early in the game, "Don't write us a letter, at the prices we're giving you, we can't afford to answer."

After launching and rigging at Ship Harbour, we held builder's sailing trials. It was a big occasion; the boat performed beyond expectations under sail and under power. Donnie Russell, his wife Annie and two young daughters, and Cyril and Jean Russell and their daughter were aboard. The day was sunny and the breeze gentle, so everyone enjoyed the maiden sail of the first of many similar vessels to come. Cyril took off his shoes and leaned back against the taffrail, commenting "If God made anything better than this, He kept it for Himself." Hearty praise from a man who was usually reserved and not often complimentary.

We kept her on moorings at Halifax for several weeks where she caused a stir in the local press as well as giving an opportunity to some of my other builders to look her over. It was the first time a local vessel had been built with a great aft cabin, stern and quarter windows and a taffrail for a long, long time in Nova Scotia.

Dick Shaw eventually sold *Esgrimidor* to Tony Gibbons who operated her for many years as a charter vessel in the Caribbean.

When I had first approached Cyril Russell about building aftercabins on the boats, he was adamant that it was a crazy idea, one that nobody ever

APOGEE, HULL #2, ON SAILING TRIALS WITH RENNIE LIVESEY AND CREW, WINTER, SHIP HARBOUR.

heard of, and one that nobody would want! He began the first construction reluctantly. The only reason he did it was that we were playing the game of boatbuilding by the golden rule—the man that had the gold, ruled.

Sometime later, I took a prospective buyer to see the boats being built, after several had already sailed away. He said he thought the hull shape and size was just right but that he didn't think he wanted an aftercabin. Cyril bristled and replied, "Well, we can't build her here then, because all the boats we build have to have aftercabins."

One of the next to be launched was *Apogee*, another 45-foot ketch, for 32-year-old Rennie Livesey. Rennie had arrived from the DEW Line to wait for her during the last weeks of building, launching and rigging. He was a really nice guy, quiet and unassuming, yet one of those worriers who doggedly continued towards his goal. Eventually by December 1966, she was ready. Rennie's brother Jerry, 28, and another DEW Line co-worker, big Al Janusson, also 28, arrived for final fitting out and departure for project Nassau. The news media quoted Rennie in an interview alongside the Royal Nova Scotia Yacht Squadron's dock, describing his *Apogee*: "She's suited to a T with all the room we wanted, rugged construction, and all the signs of Nova Scotian boatbuilding genius, something we'd only heard about before."

Their departure seemed to drag out as I visited the yacht after several days. It was a crisp, clear January morning as I stepped aboard the gently rolling vessel. I heard a clink-clink-clink from the forward cabin as I discovered an empty rum bottle idly rolling back and forth across the cabin floor. My attention was drawn to a twang-twang from the aftercabin where I saw Rennie sitting on the edge of his bunk, glasses slid to the end of his nose and a guitar in his lap. When I asked if he had gotten his compass swung yet, he replied, "No, but I got the guitar tuned." In a later postcard, Rennie said he and his crew were drinking their way down the Atlantic coast, and had only run aground three times!

Another 45-foot ketch was launched from the Bluewater yard the next spring for Dr. Barry B. White, a chiropractor from Dunk Rock Road in Guildford, Connecticut. Barry, with his wife, Betty, and three small children were to cruise around the world on a great voyage of adventure and discovery. I asked Barry what he would do about the children's schooling, to which he replied, "I never believed in letting their schooling interfere with their education."

Of course, they carried books and a full curriculum aboard, and Betty would be their teacher. They named the vessel *Whitewake* in honour of their family name. Their charted route was to encompass the Virgin

"SON, THEY HAD TO GET HERE!" *WHITEWAKE*, LANAI, HAWAII, AUGUST 1973.

New Boats—New Ways—New Days

Islands, Panama Canal, Ecuador, the Galapagos and sundry Polynesian Islands. Determination and patience got them through. I heard they had sold *Whitewake* to a dentist from Australia, when their cruising life ended in Bora-Bora.

Years later I was walking through the Ala-Wai Yacht Basin in Honolulu when I recognized *Whitewake* lying at a berth there. The owner emerged from the cabin and looked at me studying the vessel. "Do you ever have any trouble with her knightheads?" I asked. "Do I know you?" he replied. I was caught. I had to introduce myself as her designer/builder. A broad smile lit his face as he insisted I go aboard and meet his wife and young son. I learned my lesson that day. If you don't want to talk boats for three hours, keep your identity secret.

As I was leaving the marina, I noticed an old man with a white beard and battered yachting cap leaning back in his chair at the yacht-keeper's shack. "I see you have a lot of wooden yachts here, I expected to see many more of fibreglass," I said to him in passing. He lowered his chair, looked me directly in the eye and replied, "Son, they had to get here!"

DICK SHAW DELIVERS

BRIGANTINE *SEA QUEEN* ON TRIALS, HALIFAX HARBOUR.

CHAPTER TEN

THE AVERAGE 45-FOOT BOAT built in an established shop took almost 6,000 hours of experienced hand labour. That translates to 2,000 hours per man for a three man shop—a full year! We started building at Brenton Gray's yard in Sambro and the Stevens' and Mitchell yards in Chester, all charged to Dick Shaw's account. Everything went well for a couple of years until we realized that Dick had made some arrangements and promises to his customers that we had to honour. A friend of Dick's confided to me that Dick had had several mini strokes, which he did not want anyone to know about. Finally, he had to retire from the scene, and I was left with some mixed-up commitments to deal with. Most of the owners understood and we eventually got all the boats built and delivered, if late.

The first out of Brenton Gray's was *Sea Song*, the only 45-foot vessel of that hull design I ever built without an aftercabin. Her deck and sail arrangement was the style of a Maine coastal schooner with two low deckhouses on a gaff fore and main. This rig was not as handy on the deep displacement hull as that of a ketch, but she was a handsome and traditional schooner.

Designers and builders sometimes forget that a schooner sail rig should be installed on a hull with a pronounced cut-away forefoot, but deep aft! Her underbody profile should more nearly resemble a triangle. The hulls deeper forward are better balanced by a ketch rig. The forces on the hull must be understood: as the boat heels in the wind, her water line shape turns from a football to a banana — the leeward side gets fuller and the windward straighter, effectively forming a crescent that wants to turn to windward. As the leeward bow wave increases, the turning aspect heightens. The solution is to carry more sail forward and less aft to balance. In strong winds, the large mainsail aft on a schooner must be reduced by reefing or removal. In a ketch, the mizzen sail can simply be lowered and balance is restored. A greater variety of light-wind sails can be carried on a ketch, which is a further advantage.

However, *Sea Song* was built, launched and delivered by Dick Shaw and his handpicked crew. Murray Gray, one of her builders went along, which was his first real adventure at distance cruising at sea. He talked about his experience with a smile and sparkling eyes for a long time after his return to Nova Scotia.

Murray had diabetes, so Brenton always stocked soda pop and candy bars in the shop. One of the men would shout, "Murray's taking a fit!"

and there would be Murray ram-rod stiff, tipped back with his heels dug into the floor, his head against the wall and his hammer still gripped in his hand. The shop then sprang into action with men running in from everywhere. Some would lower Murray to the floor while others forced open his mouth and poured in soda pop and a candy bar. Slowly Murray would begin to chew and flutter his eyelids. Five minutes later, he was back hard at work and the shop returned to normal.

Dick sold *Sea Song* to Garfield Langworthy who did charter sailing out of Shelburne, Vermont. In the fall, he would unstep her masts and rig, motor her down the Hudson River, re-step spars in New York and sail off to the Caribbean for charter work there during the winter.

Years later, she was sold to another American, Bill Nagy, who sailed her across the Atlantic to Greece and at last account was chartering with her in the Greek Islands near Athens.

Another schooner-rigged Buccaneer out of Gray's yard was for Bob Row, M.D., of New Hamburg, Ontario, but this time the vessel had a conventional great aft cabin, raised deck with stern and quarter windows. After launching, Dr. Row sailed her in Ontario for several years before selling her there to Ian Hardcastle. Ian cruised the vessel extensively, and

DECK AND BOW FRAMING, *SEA SONG.*

years later brought her back to our boatyard in Parrsboro for re-build and re-fit. My eldest son, Bob, and our delivery captain at the time, Don Webster of Halifax, sailed her back to Ian, where, we understand, she still goes strong.

Ian enjoyed being a hard-nosed businessman and he and I spent hours hammering out details of the repair contract and payment in his great aft cabin while our riggers, and crew were enjoying the fruits of his generosity in the forward cabin. When an irresistible force meets an immovable object, both have to give a little.

Another customer of Dick's was Ken Gifford of Augusta, Maine who owned a fuel delivery service there and had a large family of teenaged boys. He wanted a training vessel for them and approached me about rigging the yacht as a brigantine. This was a new concept for me and a new challenge. I had always been impressed by square sail and now investigated how that rig could be adapted and modified to suit our smaller craft. At first glance, it appeared that those old timers of a hundred or more years ago used square rig simply for convenience. Their wisdom soon became apparent however.

A square sail is hung from a yard, which is attached at its centre-point to the mast. So no matter how hard the wind blows, it balances itself allowing the sail to be easily managed since the force of the wind does not have to be pulled against. With other more conventional fore and aft sails as well as genoas, spinnakers, staysails and the like, great force needs to be applied to haul them in, requiring winches, a larger crew, or both. The square sail is picturesque and draws attention to the vessel wherever she goes.

It seemed logical to me that with modern materials like stainless steel, Dacron, and nylon, the rig could be simplified, lightened and more easily constructed and handled. After studying the older designs and arrangements for square sail, I devised a method of attaching the sail to its yard using stainless steel sail track and slides. With a system of in-hauls and leech lines, the sail could be easily gathered in by the crew on deck, and furled vertically in front of the mast.

In the first boats we had converted and built, I had developed contacts with marine suppliers and chandlers in Lunenburg, Nova Scotia. Lunenburg is a wonderfully picturesque and productive port with its aura of marine life centering on the fishing industry and the vessels it required. The local populace are of Dutch-German descent, generally referred to as Dutchmen. With their own particular broad accent, ready smiles and eager co-operation, they were a joy to be around. As a boy, I remembered seeing Lunenburg harbour crowded with two and three mast tern schooners, in from the Grand Banks to discharge their catches and re-supply. These were hard but happy days with plenty of fish stocks for all. Later, fish harvesting vessels became ever larger and more efficient, and the fishing grounds were systematically decimated.

The large side-draggers dragged their huge, steel-bound doors back and forth across the ocean bottom, opening their trailing nets and scooping up everything in between, thus destroying the garden on the ocean floor that fed the smallest marine life. These smaller animals fed the larger, and with their demise so went the whole fish stock. It would be the equivalent of dragging old car bodies back and forth over a vegetable garden continu-ously and expecting anything to grow there. In addition, the Canadian government made trade agreements with numerous foreign nations, allow-ing them to harvest as well. The end result is that today there are virtually no fish left and the government is paying fishermen not to fish!

Lunenburg Foundry supplied me with a variety of cast and manufac-tured equipment from their exotic catalogue and well-stocked shelves. Their pattern makers could develop white pine moulds to my design for hawse pipes, deck plates, rudder fittings and the like. Their foundry, machine shop foremen and stockmen were always pleasant, and capable.

WORKERS POURING MOLTEN STEEL AT LUNENBURG FOUNDRY.

Vernon Walters, of Thomas Walters and Son, had inherited his father's small blacksmith shop and was a one-man whirlwind producing anchors, mast and hull fittings. The old system of wrought iron was good since it resisted rusting, but our more complicated fittings required steel and welding fabrication. The large ones were sent away for hot-dip galvanizing if Vernon's pot was too small. It was always a joy to visit his shop and take in the glow of the forge, the ring of his hammer on the anvil and the odorous black dust that covered everything.

Later, when we began to work in stainless steel, the individual boatshops could weld their own mast and hull fittings, requiring less legwork from me. My drawings were still referred to as "Ironwork" for each vessel, and still carried the simple flavour of the older days.

Dauphinee & Sons blockshop on Montague Street was a holdover from the old days of fishing schooners. One was greeted at the door by the rumble and slap of overhead pulleys and belts that powered the whole operation. The dust of ages was in every corner, shelf and bin, piles of oars, pulley blocks, handles, and galvanized fittings waited expectantly as old Mr. Dauphinee appeared from the back to take orders. He was a small man, but powerful even then as he managed the sprawling business of several adjoining buildings and scores of employees. Although elderly he still had a full head of unruly grey hair, and was usually covered from head to toe in hardwood sanding dust. On one occasion, attempting to get his attention, I remarked, "Gee, Mr. Dauphinee, you seem to be awfully busy." His reply, which I found strange for the owner of a going concern, was, "Yes, but we try to discourage this kind of thing as much as possible!"

His son Arthur worked in the shop too, and had the same dusty appearance as his father, was a bit taller, and just as cooperative. Years later when I had six yachts on the slip, late for delivery with lawsuits threatening from irate owners, I received a letter in reply to my current orders for pulley blocks from Arthur. It began, "There is no good news in this letter." He continued to list his problems with wood suppliers, and his backlog of orders. "If I was to supply your orders, I would have to increase the cost of each block by sixty cents," he continued. "Knowing that no sane man would want such an increase and late delivery, I have cancelled all your orders." Recovering from this shocking announcement, I hurriedly phoned him, explaining I was imminently in danger of being thrown into prison, and imploring him to get me some blocks as rapidly as possible, regardless of what they would cost. I could just imagine him shaking his head in disbelief as he went back to work to save my hide.

The pulley blocks that we chose for our vessels were three-and-a-half-inch and four-inch, which was the measurement of the length of the varnished ash shell, bronze sheaves, bronze roller-brushed, with stainless steel pins and copper cover plates, galvanized banded and available in single sheave or doubles, barefoot or becket. They were fitted with chain links or shackles, upset, plain or twisted. Careful planning was needed. Each had to suit its position on the vessel and use intended. We invariably rove them with half-inch laid nylon or Dacron rope, hand spliced. Other items we got from Dauphinees were one-inch wooden belaying pins, spruce or ash oars and lignum vitae (tree of life) deadeyes and yacht blocks. As rigs became more complicated and our customers more demanding, I spent much time in Lunenburg with our suppliers supervising design and supply. Ken Gifford took delivery of *Sea Queen* in the summer of 1967 in Halifax. After sailing trials and provisioning, he, his wife, and five sons set out on a cruise of northeastern Nova Scotia.

A BEVY OF NEW SCHOONERS AT MELVILLE COVE.

Cape Breton boasts an inland sea that has been described as the third best cruising grounds in the world, next to the Mediterranean and the Caribbean. Baddeck is the friendly and picturesque seaport town in the centre of the Bras d'Or Lakes with a good government wharf and yacht facilities. It was the summer home of Alexander Graham Bell and was described by him as the prettiest place in the world. He carried out much of his invention of aeroplanes, hydrofoils, and electronic devices in his laboratories there. Baddeck provided a sheltered resting place for Don Holder as he towed our schooners from Newfoundland to Nova Scotia many years ago where he re-grouped and re-organized his tows to continue.

Ken then cruised through the Strait of Canso and on to Prince Edward Island before returning to Halifax and leaving *Sea Queen* on our moorings in the North West Arm over the winter of 1967–68. The following year he returned to complete the rest of his voyage home to the United States.

In these days, our wharves and moorings were crowded with masted vessels awaiting pick-up by their owners. My residence and adjoining design and sales office was situated on the shore of Melville Cove, with moorings directly in front of the office windows. It was a picturesque and much photographed setting as we went about the final stages of rigging and commissioning each new vessel as they arrived from their builder's yards.

As his business grew, the highway was modernized and re-routed around the small village of Meteghan River. One-by-one Gus bought the store, blacksmith shop, and other buildings, establishing them as riggers loft, welding shop, machine shops, and slips. When I arrived on the scene in 1968, his yard was an active and thriving boatbuilding village.

Gus and Elizabeth had four sons who inherited their parents' industry, honesty, and drive. Ernest, the oldest, was in charge of general slip repairs, and spent time with Gus in the woods, harvesting and milling stocks of white oak and black spruce. Their trailers brought load after load to the yard for air-drying and milling as needed.

Arthur, next eldest, was in charge of the office—accounting, and purchasing equipment and supplies. He also supervised a staff of draughtsmen and clerks.

The third son, Russell, who had just graduated from trade school was introduced to me by Gus. "This is Russell, he'll work with you, so tell him what you want." With this introduction, Russell and I began building the first of 30 yachts. Russell had a quick and keen grasp of what was needed and how it could be accomplished. This combined with an unwavering sense of honesty made working with him over the years a real pleasure.

The fourth son, Larry, came into the business later to take over much of the accounting and office procedures.

Some time after my trip, Osmond Yorke from Parrsboro showed up at my Halifax office and announced that he would like to build boats. He had heard of me and had seen some of my yachts.

Osmond was a descendant of the established Parrsboro Yorke family and acquainted with local suppliers of boat-building materials and boat builders there. He had owned and operated a grocery store and a shoe store and now wanted to satisfy his maritime blood by boatbuilding. I decided to give him a try. The larger, old yard of Wagstaff and Hatfield

GUS THERIAULT. HIS ACADIAN HERITAGE MADE HIM A METICULOUS CRAFTSMAN.

had just closed down at Port Gilville, so Osmond and I went there to see what could be salvaged for our purpose. The old shop had supplied fishing vessels for the Bay of Fundy for many generations, as well as building barges and floats for World War Two. It now lay virtually abandoned in a dilapidated state. Eventually Osmond purchased the old tilting-wheel bandsaw, planer, and other necessary equipment from part-owner and master boatbuilder Charlie Murphy, and we located a temporarily unused boatshop and began to set up the keel for *Scaramouche*, the first 45-foot vessel out of Parrsboro. Charlie Murphy, then 65, and Freeman, 75, joined the shop. Later Lamont Anderson also came to work there as well as a few others Osmond located. Lamont had been a mechanical and electrical technician in the Canadian Air Force, and so provided welcome expertise in those departments. He was sincere, neat, and exact, if sometimes exasperatingly slow, in his work. After a few more boats, Osmond purchased land near the Parrsboro government wharf and built a new Quonset style shop there, which he named Windjammer Yachts.

So now, with the extra shops, I was able to settle into boatbuilding in earnest.

Building schooners at A.F. Theriault & Son.

I. Chapelle; *Dictionary of Sea Terms* by A. Ansted; *Young Sea Officers Sheet Anchor* by Darcy Lever; *Masting and Rigging the Clipper Ship and Ocean Carrier*, and *Sailing Ship Rigs and Rigging*, both by Harold A. Underhill.

These works gave me a look at traditional square sail and its management which I could adapt to my smaller and more modern vessels. My requirements were different, and anticipated crews would be much smaller, less experienced and not as hardened to the sea, wind and weather. There were many things to remember, weigh, and decide as my designs were developed.

As I travelled to my far-flung boatshops I discovered that Nova Scotia had a shoreline of six distinct districts and personalities. Halifax and area had a more cosmopolitan outlook and acceptance of new ideas; the South-Western Shore had a rich German heritage with their own methods and opinions on boat building; Yarmouth through to the Annapolis Valley maintained their skilled Acadian heritage; the Eastern Shore was suspicious of city mentality and had developed a self-sufficient attitude; the North Shore was of solid Scottish and English descent surviving by hard work and patience; and Cape Breton was an independent society, fun-loving and hard-living.

It made an interesting mix of personalities, and I began to appreciate their differences.

I also found resources in myself that I didn't know I had. Once, while designing and working out engineering problems for my yachts I stumbled upon a perplexing problem to which there seemed to be no solution. I pondered and fretted about it all day long, and it totally consumed my mind as I went to sleep. I am not a morning person but the next morning I awoke with a start at 5:30 or 6:00 a.m., sat bolt up-

"I FOUND RESOURCES I DIDN'T KNOW I HAD."

right in bed and before my conscious mind could even form a thought, I exclaimed, "I know! I know what the answer to the problem is!" I leapt from bed and hurried down to my drawing board where I began to mark down furiously the solutions as they tumbled into my head. It was most uncanny and completely different from anything I had ever experienced before. There was my requested answer, and it was perfect.

I experienced this process many times thereafter, always with the same amazing results.

This contact with a higher level of mind coupled with my ability to see a design complete on my board before it was drawn enabled me to go on to new heights in my chosen field.

However, it was still a lot of hard work, and I discovered that every success was 10 per cent inspiration and 90 per cent perspiration.

New Yards—New Boats

Gemjig under full sail.

CHAPTER TWELVE

THE FIRST NEW VESSEL—a 46-foot gaff-headed Buccaneer schooner named *Eileen*—came off the ways of A. F. Theriault's shipyard in June 1969. Her owner was Scott Blanchard of Brookville, Long Island, New York, who wanted to cruise with his son, with whom he had a difficult relationship. Unfortunately, the son died before delivery, so launching day was a somewhat sad occasion. However, she lived up to our expectations during sailing trials in St. Mary's Bay, justifying the 6,000 hours of hard work put in by the boatbuilders, Russell and myself during one whole year of construction. Her final sail-away cost was $37,343. Today she would cost eight times as much—$300,000!

In 1969, owners were willing to spend $40,000 to $50,000 for a yacht to sail during their vacation and spare time, but when the cost of the boats rose to $250,000, not including insurance and maintenance costs, it was a different story. A charter yacht could be hired for a fraction of the cost without any of the attendant worries. Interest on investments also rose, so prospective owners were unwilling to commit funds for a yacht. However, in the early 70s, demand was still high and we were building to capacity at all five yards.

I had devised a method to control construction of the vessels by making a building contract with each of the owners and the builders, setting out details of the boat design, and payment schedule. Attached were plans, specifications, equipment lists and any extras ordered by the owner. In addition to the 175 standard items of equipment on an average 45-foot yacht, there were many ordered extras. Builder's insurance was also arranged to cover loss during construction.

In the owner contract I included colour choice, and upholstery specification.

In addition to my design work, I researched, located, and purchased most of the needed equipment; duty on imported items was paid and reclaimed as the vessel was exported from Canada.

I was using a large new Pontiac station wagon by this time, so I picked up the equipment and delivered it to the yards during my inspection and instruction trips.

I developed detailed general specification and hardware and equipment lists to accompany the building contract and further define the vessel. As each item was delivered for inclusion by the builder, it was marked off the list so some control could be maintained.

As each stage of construction was completed, I exchanged photographs for cheques from each owner. In all the years I built yachts, I never borrowed any funds, always keeping ahead of my expenditures with monies arriving from the owners. My profit was no greater than current bank interest, so loans could not be considered in any case.

Among the suppliers I located in those days were Manhattan Marine and Electric of New York City who had a fine catalogue and could supply most items from their comprehensive stock; Mack Boring and Parts from Union, New Jersey who supplied our Perkins marine diesel engines and Buck-Algonquin Iron in New Jersey, who supplied bronze cast stuffing boxes, bearings and fittings, marine windows and ports.

USA suppliers also included Raritan, Groco, Gem Products, Wilcox-Crittenden, Bliss and Co, Danforth, and Morse Controls, as well as many more.

EVERY EQUIPMENT ITEM, INTERIOR AS WELL AS EXTERIOR, HAD TO BE PURCHASED.

Simpson-Lawrence Ltd, Glasgow, Scotland supplied traditional yacht hardware and equipment in the British style—tile fireplaces, galvanized mast and deck hardware, and anchors were specialties. W.H. Den Ouden of Holland supplied stainless steel and brass items such as portholes, windows, exhaust systems, small fittings, rubber tanks and much more. They imported stainless items from Norway and Sweden as well as brass items from Italy, France, and Spain. They were the largest supply house in Europe at that time. Munster-Simms, Belfast, Northern Ireland provided Whale pumps, while Irish Preston, U.K., provided anchors.

As well, local suppliers of hardware and materials were able to provide a good deal of our equipment. All of our sails were made by R.B. Stevens and Sons, Lunenburg, Nova Scotia, with great attention to detail. Harold Stevens and his son Robert provided us with many suits of sails throughout our busy years.

Harold was one of the industrious and tenacious clan of Stevens who had developed family businesses at Second Peninsula, Lunenburg. His father, Randolph Sr., had taken up land there, and he had established a farm, and a boat-building and fishing life. Eventually his son, David, became the boatbuilder, Harold became the sailmaker and Randolph Jr. ran the farm. They had a knack for handling animals and a green thumb for gardening; their prize-winning formal flower gardens were a joy to behold.

The sail loft, accessed up a ladder-stair and trap door occupied the upper floor in one of the barns where Harold, Robert and several helpers sewed and stitched the snowy white sailcloth over an immaculately clean and polished planked loft floor. It was mandatory for a visitor to remove his shoes on the mat provided upon entering. The sailmakers all wore slippers, while their shoes waited in neat rows near the trap door. Later Harold devised a method of recessing each worker and his heavy sewing machine into the loft floor so that the table of the machine was level with the floor. In this way, the heavy sailcloth did not have to be dragged up and over the machine, making it easier for the sail to be worked. I was invited for dinner at Harold's table many times; his home was like an island of peace in my otherwise hectic boatbuilding life. The Stevenses were deeply religious, and supper was always preceded by a heartfelt grace.

I remember when we were dealing in scrap rope and marine artefacts, arriving with Bruce Parsons at Randolph's farm one evening. We were dirty and unkempt. Church missionaries were visiting from Boston and they were just about to start a service in his parlour. The room was crowded, but Randolph insisted we come in and join the group. Chairs were brought and we were seated in the very front row. We were uncomfortable in our dirty work clothes but Randolph would not discuss any business with us until the service was concluded and we had something to eat.

Harold's brother David had his boatshop in a large barn beside his house where he usually built boats to his own design from half-models he carved himself. He had been hired by the Province of Nova Scotia to go on site at Expo '67 in Montreal to build a schooner there as a living demonstration of the art representative of Nova Scotia craft. His son, Murray, later followed in his father's footsteps as an active boatbuilder.

Harold was very co-operative in my designs, particularly in square sail as we adapted new and lighter materials. He explained that Dacron was DuPont's trade name for terlene fibre, which had been developed in England on their narrower at 30-inch American looms instead of 36-inch looms. So, six ounces of British cloth was equal to eight ounces of American, the running yard being different. I worked out design problems with Harold's suggestions, such as the management of light leech lines on squaresails by attaching the line at the forward centre of the sail, then leading it through a series of grommets around the sail to a small band with bullet blocks and thence to the deck for handling. In this way, the sail could be furled without the crew having to go aloft.

Boltropes were seldom used, with all tabling and hemming being doubled, tripled, and then double stitched. Stitching always wore out long before the sailcloth itself, and sails were often re-stitched to prolong their useful lifetime. The enemy of Dacron was sunlight, so acrylic canvas sail covers were often provided in either dark blue or green to protect furled sails. We also used a variety of light striped sails, awnings, and dodgers on some boats, so the loft was kept busy with new inventions. Harold Stevens was one of those real craftsmen who contributed so much to the building of wooden boats in the last days of wooden ships and iron men.

Foundrymen were often helpful sub-contractors in the early days. Originally, ballast keels for the 45-foot models were cast iron, 8 x 10 inches x 24 feet. Hillis' Foundry in Halifax was first to cast iron keels for me, and later a foundry at Industrial Marine Products in Burnside took over. Freeman Cox, their foundry foreman, was always very helpful.

The original pine plank mould had been built at Bluewater Boats, and I transported it to Halifax late one evening on the roof of my old '58 Pontiac. It was an ungainly load and I was hoping not to run into local authorities. As I neared the black community of Preston on the eastern Shore along the only existing highway one of my back tires blew with a tremendous bang. As I surveyed the blown tire and sagging load, in the beam of my small flashlight two men came out of a nearby house to see if I was alright. They rolled up their sleeves, and together we got the old car jacked up and the tire changed. They waved goodbye good naturedly and I continued my journey with that feeling of gratitude that comes when the human heart crosses the boundaries that so often divide us.

The iron keels weighed 5,000 pounds but were relatively inexpensive. However, as foundry costs increased and transportation to more distant yards was more difficult, it became more expedient to deliver scrap lead to the shops and have the builders pour their own keels. This increased the total weight of the same size keel to 7,000 pounds, which provided a better righting movement with the increased weight on the bottom of the hull. Inside ballast could still be iron scrap ingots or cast lead, as an extra.

Standard planking was traditional one-and-a-half inches North Eastern white pine, but we offered Honduras mahogany as an extra. Pine cost 50 cents per board foot while mahogany was $4.00. Since there were 2,000 board feet used in an average 45-foot yacht, the extra cost for mahogany was $7,000. Invariably, when using mahogany we fastened with 3 inch Everdur ring-barbed nails in place of the 4 inch galvanized square-cut boat nails traditionally used in the pine planking. Either fastening was counter-sunk and glue-plugged.

As materials became more exotic, we offered stainless steel as an op-tional material for keelbolts, mast, deck and hull hardware, and standing rigging. Most of the custom hardware was weldments, often by the indi-vidual boatshop that had that particular capability.

Frames for the vessels over 40 feet were usually four x four inches double-fliched oak, butts staggered, and bolted. They had to be bevelled on a tilting-wheel bandsaw, with bevels determined on the loft floor from patterns.

Smaller yachts 40 feet and under usually were framed with steam-bent oak of perhaps 1-3/8 x 3-3/4 inch dimension. This was another of those operations requiring haste and experience as each timber was ex-tracted very hot from the steam-box, carried to the battened hull, and tramped into its place. The ribs or timbers were held in place by dogs or wires until the planking was attached. Larger vessels could have doubled frames, one on top of the other, if needed. Plank fastenings were invariably ring-barbed nails in place of galvanized formerly used.

An interesting event in the life of the smaller boat shops was keel-pouring day. A female plank mould would be set up on the blocks where the vessel was to be built, and a cast iron bathtub set up outdoors on a steel and brick frame, with two oil-fired furnace burners directed under-neath. Scrap lead would be placed in the tub as the operation began. Often more heat than could be provided by the burners was needed to melt the lead, so an extra fire of creosoted railway ties would be started under the tub as well. It was found that the melting could be aided by liberally dous-ing the ties with P.C.B. transformer oil, which we obtained from the scrap yard that had sold us the lead. Sometimes it was also thrown into the tub with the lead until the whole hellish cauldron was a roar of fire and smoke with the lead spitting and hissing as the dross was skimmed. A procession of boatbuilders, each with a long-handled homemade ladle, would dip from the tub, carry his load of molten lead to the mould inside the shop and carefully pour it in. The process was repeated over and over until the 7,000-pound keel was poured.

Sometimes it seemed like an endless procession of overall-clad legs and boots moved through the dense clouds of smoke and steam from tub to mould. Great care had to be taken to ensure the mould was built strong enough to carry its load of molten lead without rupturing. If the pour was lost, it all had to be repeated the next day, weather permitting.

In a small yard of four or six men, the pour began at 7:00 A.M., sometimes not finishing until 9:00 P.M. that evening. It was a long, hard day's work. Once the pour was started, it had to be continued until finished so that the lead would not congeal between pours. There always had to be one or two men feeding the fire, stirring the molten lead, adding P.C.B. oil and skimming the dross. P.C.B. oil is now considered a hazardous material and outlawed, but we were not aware that it was carcinogenic, even though there always seemed to be a new man at the scrap yard when I went for more oil, because the previous one had died. I did not relate the two occurrences until many years later.

Building at A. F. Theriault's yard in Meteghan River was gaining momentum with Hull #402, *Serendipity*, for Ed Beaupré of Newport, Rhode Island, and #403, *Gemjig* for George Hofstetter of Mississauga, Ontario set up on the ways.

Ed Beaupré told me that his name meant bowsprit in French, which reminded me of the shrine at Sainte Anne de Beaupré and the story of its founding. Apparently, sailors were shipwrecked there, but were able to crawl to safety ashore over their bowsprit. In gratitude for their deliverance from a watery grave, they erected a shrine to Sainte Anne.

Ed owned a company in Rhode Island manufacturing electronic components and wiring for telephone companies. He was a sharp businessman, as I would soon find out. His Buccaneer schooner was built to specifications and equipped with numerous extras he ordered. The total price for the vessel with extras was $41,896 in 1969. He paid the bulk of the cost throughout construction, and gave a final cheque for $1,925 upon delivery, after trials and acceptance. Shortly after, however, he put a stop payment on the cheque, claiming that electrical wiring and installation was not satisfactory. I have no doubt that the meticulous wiring necessary in telephone equipment was a far cry from that in general use by boatshops in Nova Scotia, and that Ed's ideal was different from ours. He said he would have his own electricians re-wire to suit him, and deduct the cost from the amount outstanding. I realized that he didn't intend to make the cheque good when he wrote it. It was an expensive lesson as the cheque represented half of our profit for the year it took to build the vessel. My contracts with local boatbuilders were often merely a handshake and a promise—I was used to dealing with men of integrity who believed that a promise made was a debt unpaid. In some cases, when I knew a yard was losing money on a particular item, and I offered to cover their shortfall, I was met with a firm, "No! We made the deal, and we'll honour it." They would rather loose money than cut back on the quality of their work or break their word. After Ed Beaupré, I introduced a no cash—no splash policy: final payment always in cash or certified cheque.

Hull #403, *Gemjig*, for George Hofstetter was a happier experience. George was a friendly and outgoing businessman from Mississauga, Ontario. Three years after he had taken delivery in 1970, and had cruised extensively he wrote me a letter in which he said he always recommended "the high calibre of the designer and construction engineer as well as the quality and workmanship that comes out of the yards under his supervision," to anyone who asked.

Gemjig was a 45-foot Privateer ketch with a full wheelhouse and many extras. She was launched from A.F. Theriault's yard in June 1970. After trials, acceptance and payment by George, he asked us to have her sailed around the southern tip of Nova Scotia to Halifax where he planned to begin cruising. We hired an old skipper from Maitland familiar with the waters and Russell Theriault and I joined the vessel for the two-day trip. As is often the case in early summer in Nova Scotia, we were in dense fog the entire trip. Fortunately, George had us install a good Plessy radar and a sophisticated echo sounder, both of which ran continuously for the whole voyage. Winds were very light so it was a power run. Going through the narrow and treacherous Schooner Passage near Pubnico, the audible alarm on the digital depth sounder suddenly shattered the air, inducing panic stations aboard. We knew we were in dangerous, rocky, and shallow waters. I made a dive for the wheelhouse door, flung it open, tearing a gash in my hand in the processes, and jumped out on deck to peer into the fog-shrouded, murky water. A huge black shape was directly beneath our hull and moving along with us! It was a large whale swimming in company, probably thinking our gracefully rounded bottom was another of his kind. Captain Gates who had remained calmly at the wheel, pipe in mouth, commented casually, "That kind of thing happens all the time, you often see whales in these waters." I glanced aloft up through the fog and saw the red round roof of the local lighthouse moving by right alongside of us! A good radar and an experienced skipper were worth the investment. George picked *Gemjig* up at our wharves in Halifax that summer to begin his cruising of Nova Scotia and homeward voyage to Toronto. He cruised Georgian Bay, the Thousand Islands, and the Great Lakes over the next number of years, ending up in Halifax in 1977, when he left the vessel with us for sale. We eventually sold her to David Howard, also of Mississauga, for $53,000. I did a calculation at that time of replacement cost which came to $109,103, over twice her original cost, a scant seven years before. Costs of building yachts were escalating rapidly while interest rates were dropping on owner's investments, all of which began to spell the death knell of our business.

Meanwhile, construction had begun at Parrsboro, with Osmond Yorke and his crew at Windjammer Yachts. The first keel laid was Hull #501, *Scaramouche* for Raymond LaRose of Montreal. She was a Privateer ketch, semi-wheelhouse, gaff main, and fidded topmast. Raymond was one of those wild, longhaired, secretive young men of the hippie generation of 1973. We did custom design of accommodations and equipment for him, and after one year of building, Raymond and his friends as crew completed sailing trials at Parrsboro. As he couldn't make final payment, we let him sail *Scaramouche* around to our wharves in Halifax, where she spent the summer. Raymond and his friends stayed aboard from time to time, altering fixtures and equipment. On one occasion Raymond left a pretty tan Husky dog aboard alone for many days without our knowing about it. By the time Raymond returned, the dog had chewed through much of the wood window trim in the aftercabin trying to escape his confinement. Eventually in October of 1974, Raymond resolved his financial difficulties and cleared for the USA.

Another very strange building contract was at Windjammer for a young man named John Skinner from Buxton, North Carolina. She was to be another Privateer ketch but with a varnished mahogany full deckhouse amidships. Her name was to be *Wooden Ship*, Hull #502. John was very clean-cut and pleasant on the few occasions I met him as we worked out his custom design and equipment. He said he planned to go treasure hunting in the Caribbean and ordered much exotic search and navigation equipment to be installed including a Wesmar undersea sonar, a Raytheon radar, a Decca LORAN, an OMEGA navigation receiver, a single sideband SSB radio, and a Kenyon digital sounder.

Her final cost was $87,000 of which $37,000 was for extras.

John ordered the vessel through his company, Independent Research and Investment Corp., Grand Cayman Island, B.W.I. Half way through the building period, John simply vanished, and although I no longer heard from him, funds and decisions came from his lawyer, in Florida. We completed building, launching and trials, and still no John, although all payments came promptly. We had found Michael Cassidy, a local mariner and yachtsman who with a crew of two delivered the vessel as requested, to Florida. It was all very mysterious. I don't know if *Wooden Ship* ever went treasure hunting, but heard she was sold shortly after her arrival in Florida. We were told she also had a tile fireplace and spinet piano installed in her deckhouse for casual, comfortable, and long range cruising. We did a replacement cost estimate for her in 1980, which came to $165,000.

By this time in my boatbuilding career, most of the heavy materials were being delivered to the various shops by truck, but I was still required to supervise and deliver much of the equipment and sometimes make an emergency delivery when time had run out. One such situation was a need by Bluewater Boats in Ship Harbour for three trees in the rough to be made into masts. The sticks were 50 feet long and some 18 on the butt. I took my old Pontiac car and boat trailer to Greenfield, Lunenburg County to get them, a delivery drive of 100 miles. I loaded them in the afternoon with their butts tight to the back seat in the trunk of my car, and the back bumper was almost on the road! I put my boat trailer out at the end of the logs and firmly lashed the whole load to car and trailer. The tail light for the trailer was a lantern flashlight with a red rag tied over it—a wild and highly illegal load! It was now after dark, and I hoped I could slide the whole thing through to Ship Harbour without being noticed. At the town of Mahone Bay the long load began to feel different, so I stopped and found that the logs had almost pulled out of the trunk. It was quite a dilemma. There was no one to help and the logs were far too heavy for me to push back into the trunk. Then I noticed the large stone monument to the casualties of World War One in the centre of the town crossroads.

Aiming my load carefully, I put the car in reverse, and forced the logs against the monument, driving them back into my trunk. After three or four of these attempts, I had them back in place. The monument shuddered a little each time but appeared to be withstanding my attack. As I was re-lashing, I saw the headlights of the town police car coming, so I silently thanked the monument's builders and hastily went on my way, discretion being the better part of valour. I delivered my load, and our boatbuilding continued without pause.

BLUEWATER BOATS BUSILY BUILDING
PEREGRINE, GOLDEN VANITY AND *TERN*
1966-70

PRIVATEER, *GOLDEN VANITY* ON SEA TRIALS.

CHAPTER THIRTEEN

BACK AT BLUEWATER BOATS at Ship Harbour, Hull #4, another Privateer ketch, *Peregrine*, was up in frame for Dick Shaw's Simplex Corporation. He very quickly sold her to Tony Carlucci and Tom Cutler of New York City. They ordered a comprehensive list of extras and delivery by June 1968 for $35,000. Later, we heard from several of her new owners as she was sold and re-sold. We had reports and photos from them over the years showing careful maintenance and custom items each owner added as she cruised the Atlantic and Caribbean. In August 1973, Elmer Smith of Fort Myers bought her for $45,000. In July 1975, John Larouche owned her and was living aboard with his wife, son and daughter in Tampa, Florida. By 1978, she was owned by William O'Donnell, West Palm Beach, who reported a very happy cruising life aboard. In August of 1982, we heard from George Marcus who regrettably had just sold the vessel after re-naming her *Fourth of July* and sailing her for three years with his family. He told us she was going to be used by her new owner for charter work in Jamaica. So *Peregrine* had a very active life with many owners as she brought a lot of pleasure into the yachting world. As I recall her story, I can't help but think of the yachtman's axiom, "The two happiest days of a yacht owner's life are the day he buys her and the day he sells her!"

The next vessel at Bluewater Boats was Hull #5, *Golden Vanity* for Reuben Trane of Scranton, Pennsylvania. I went to the Halifax Airport to pick up young Reuben and his new bride, Rosanne. Reuben, part of the well-known Trane manufacturing family (heating and air-conditioning equipment) was tall and husky, resembling an American football hero. Rosanne was petite and pleasant. They were very much in love and were, in fact, on their honeymoon. They were both dressed in leather clothes with decorations and fringes; Reuben with a large brimmed hat. "Uh-oh, hippies," I thought. When my teenage children met them, they soon corrected me, "They're not hippies, Dad, their clothes are very expensive, and very much in style where they come from."

Being in love, Reuben and Rosanne (whom he affectionately called Rosietoes) saw love in everything and thoroughly enjoyed our quaint boatshop, the builders, and the countryside of Nova Scotia. As *Golden Vanity* began to take shape, they returned several times to stay with us, roam the province and take in the sights of Canada's Ocean Playground. Towards completion of the vessel, they took up residence at a nearby lodge with cabins, visiting the boat almost daily. On one occasion, I overheard Reuben say, "Yes, Uncle Dick is certainly going to like this boat." It wasn't until later that I learned that Uncle Dick was Richard Nixon, then President of the United States. Reuben's mother was a Scranton, descended from the original founders of Scranton, Pennsylvania. Reuben's star was rising, and the world was a wonderful place for him in the days before Watergate.

Golden Vanity was delivered to Reuben at the builder's yard, in sail-away condition, with nine typewritten pages of extras for $42,000 in June 1969. When launching was at hand, Reuben flew his cousin, who was a priest, up to Nova Scotia with his full regalia, to bless the vessel as she was launched. It was a beautiful sunny day, the boat was bedecked with christening flags, the entire communities of Lower Ship Harbour and DeBaies Cove turned out for the occasion as *Golden Vanity* slid into the water for her exciting and colourful life. Reuben would not think of having it any other way.

Final shakedown and provisioning was done at Halifax. My oldest son, Bob, then 15, joined Reuben and his crew for the maiden voyage to the USA. It was his first long sea voyage as he was answering the call of the sea and his Maritime heritage.

Reuben wrote in March 1970 that they had a great winter aboard the *Golden Vanity*. "We are making a nursery out of the fo'cs'tle as Rosanne is expecting a baby in September." He wrote, "this should be a first for one of your boats!"

Also set up at the same time as *Golden Vanity* was a new schooner I had designed and called *Tern*. She was a smaller yacht, which I thought would appeal to buyers wanting a more compact and less expensive craft. We built, launched, and equipped her as planned. She had a few unique features such as a particularly adaptable cabin layout, large afterdeck with cockpit and schooner rig featuring a marconi main and overlapping foresail reminiscent of our famous Tancook whalers and older Pinky schooners. By roller reefing the mainsail, the rig quickly gained the balance of a ketch, a feature we later employed with some of our larger marconi main Buccaneer schooners. We showed her at schooner meets, boat shows and yachting displays, but found that most buyers still preferred our larger, great aft cabin models, so we didn't go into production.

The *Tern* was a good boat, but I was sorry I hadn't rigged her with a conventional boomed foresail for ease of handling. My third son, John Patrick, was six months old then and sometimes sailed with us on *Tern*. I rigged paddled pen boards on the navigation table for a combination crib/playpen, and slung a playpen under the main boom near the mast so

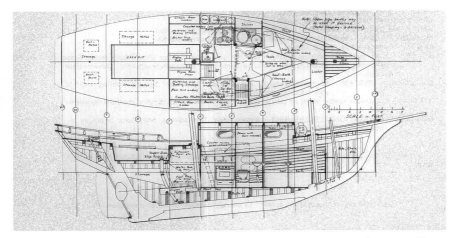

that it was always gimballed but stayed over the deck. The sight of the little schooner barrelling down the bay with a baby hanging from the boom always caused a double take from onlookers. In later years, John Patrick became an excellent sailor.

As my business expanded and became more demanding, I had to hire additional office staff. I had been running all aspects of the business myself with occasional help from my wife and teenaged children. Now my oldest daughter Kathy's husband, Jim Heffernan, joined the company as office manager. He was helpful and cooperative, quickly learning boating terms and requirements. Next, I hired Lloyd d'Entremont from Pubnico, near Yarmouth, as draftsman. Some of his Acadian cousins were boat builders at A. F. Theriault's yard, so he was already conversant with boatbuilding and easily fell into the designing mode. Lloyd worked on the drawing board under my supervision, and gradually picked up the style and nature of my designs. Having these two young men on board relieved the mounting pressure as we moved into "my golden year," 1973, with 15 boats being built at 5 yards.

Donnie Russell had decided he wanted to do more than his 40-hour week at Bluewater Boats, and built a small shop beside his house in Lower Ship Harbour. I told him if he were determined to expand his efforts, I would find customers for smaller yachts to suit his shop.

Consequently, in 1971 I modified L. Francis Herreshoff's H–28 design to what I called R–30 by slightly raising her freeboard and adding a higher high-crowned trunk cabin to provide standing headroom below and a more commodious cabin plan with enclosed head, galley, settee berths and drop-leaf table. Herreshoff's thinking was more in accord with the British notion that "If you were comfortable, you weren't doing it right!" I maintained her original hull lines and marconi ketch rig which made her a smart and comfortable sailor.

Dr. Fred Shaw of North Plainfield, New Jersey, visited us and bought the first R–30 out of Donnie Russell's shop. He named her *Sagittarius*, and we delivered her to him by truck and trailer in August 1973.

During this period of my life, another strange occurrence took place one day when I sat down at my drawing board to draw a particular design. I stared at the empty, white paper, and drifted off into an altered state where I could see the whole design complete on the paper in every detail, just as though it were all done. I then started with my pencil at the lower left-hand corner, drawing in the design, working my way across the page without looking back at what I had already done, nor ahead to what I had yet to do. It was like doing a pencil rubbing of a treasured artefact. After what seemed like a short time, I began to feel an ache in my back, realized that I needed to go to the bathroom, and that the room was getting dark. Looking up at the clock, I saw that five hours had elapsed! Stiff and incredulous, I unfolded from my drawing board and revived myself. Next day, I thought, "I'd better go look at the drawing, since it must be a mess and need fixing up." But everything was perfect, and the design was complete! It was almost as if someone else had done it.

This occurrence happened repeatedly, and to me is an indication of a connection deeper than our conscious mind is aware of.

My boat building life became busier and more hectic as a variety of new customers turned up monthly. Some of our customers were rank amateurs when it came to sailing and the sea. On one occasion a young owner from Hilton Head, South Carolina, was standing on the deck of his boat at our wharf in Ship Harbour ready to sail. The vastness of the ocean dawned on him as well as some of the dangers he might encounter. He looked at David DeBaie, one of our local builders, standing on the wharf, and asked timidly, "Can you tell me anything I should particularly watch out for?" "Wall yes, you should watch out for them nits," replied David. "Oh, you mean those little black flies."

"No, No," exclaimed David exasperatedly, "Nits, nits, fish nits!" The local Eastern Shore dialect had its differences. Later, the owner asked me, in all seriousness, "When I get out of the harbour into the ocean, which way do I turn?"

One cold winter day, the men at Bluewater Boats were gathered around the oil-barrel stove for morning coffee, when one remarked, "I haven't seen old Ned lately." In fact, no one had seen Ned in days. Ned was a wizened old bachelor who lived in a small shack across from the boathouse. He kept his cow pastured in the shop yard and used our wharf for his little fishing boat. He often showed up with a potato bag to gather shavings off the shop floor to take home for his pig. He was the butt of many good-natured jokes by the boatbuilders. "Well Ned! Have you found that woman yet," or, "I expect you had six barrel of fish this morning." Ned would always grumble a reply, but secretly enjoyed the attention.

It was decided that someone should go over and see if Ned was all right. He came back with the news that he had found Ned "head-first in the woodbox." Apparently, a day or two before Ned had suffered a massive heart attack as he was putting wood into the box, and died instantly.

The men got him unbent, cleaned him up, and after a respectful service, buried him. Later they all sat in a kitchen on straight-backed wooden chairs holding their ball-caps in their laps, and staring intently at the floor. After a long, thoughtful silence, one of the men cleared his throat and said solemnly, "Waal, leastways he got the wood in."

The Eastern Shore idioms were often colourful. Cyril Russell was once trying to remember the name of a local woman with piercing eyes and a head of wild hair. As his listener failed to grasp his description, he exclaimed, "You know who I mean, the one that reminds you of a rat looking through a ball of oakum!" The light went on and Cyril continued his conversation.

"THIS ONE IS FOR MY GIRLFRIEND." *ROAMER IV*, A CHESTER 50.

Chapter Fourteen

Dick shaw had met gerald stevens in Chester, Nova Scotia as we were building *Que Sera*, Hull #301, at Alan Mitchell's yard in the Back Harbour next to Gerald's shop. Gerald, although still a relatively young man, had built many yachts over the years together with his brother, Emery, father Perry, and others. They had gained a widespread reputation as yacht builders, mostly to Gerald's design.

Chester is a summer resort town picturesquely nestled in Mahone Bay with its 365 islands. The local populace, descended from hardy fishermen, were care-takers and retainers for wealthy American and Halifax landowners who had estates at Chester, invariably with older staid houses, grounds and yachts. The Stevenses, Heislers, Schnares, and others built and crewed the owners' yachts, each carefully maintaining his position in the social order. Chester's summer population was three times her winter one of local families, and each "caretaker" was intensely loyal to his employer, opening and closing the estate houses and readying the yachts according to the season.

Gerald was a likable, outgoing person, a product of a traditional society with definite opinions of how things should be done. This attitude carried over into his yacht building, design, and methods. It so happened that Dick saw and liked a 42-foot power cabin cruiser called *Buccaneer Lady* that Gerald had designed and built as a party boat for a local tourist lodge. He asked Gerald if the design could be extended to 50 feet and Gerald agreed to give it a try.

So Gerald drew the extension, and he and I designed a new cabin and equipment layout according to Dick's recommendations. Dick had considerable experience with a wide range of yachts, both power and sail, having had the best built worldwide. At that particular time, his own personal yacht was a 50-foot steel-hulled ocean cruising ketch built by Kok of Muiden, Holland. Superb in every detail, Dick maintained her meticulously and cruised widely. He sailed her to Nova Scotia and cruised our coasts, where I was invited to join him. He found our many sheltered harbours and their inhabitants quaint, relaxing and pleasant. He liked to tell the story of berthing at the small government wharf at Lower Ship Harbour and walking up the gravel road to old Lee Siteman's little country general store for a dozen eggs. Lee put each egg in its own little brown bag, and then the whole dozen little bags in a larger one.

We began building our first Chester 50, Hull #201, for Dick Shaw in a new shed Gerald erected for the purpose. She had two private double staterooms in an aftercabin, with galley, dinette and crew's quarters forward. Topside was a large saloon and windowed pilot deckhouse. Her power was a pair of Perkins T-6.354, 160 h.p. diesels, with large tankage for distance cruising. Dick sent the engines up from New Jersey along with much of her other equipment of U.S. manufacture. Planking was of 11/8 inch local pine, bronze fastened over steam-bent oak frames. Trim was Honduras mahogany, varnished. We delivered her to Dick in June 1970 for a total of $24,000, exclusive of the equipment he supplied.

CHESTER, HOME TO WEALTHY AMERICANS WHO HIRED LOCAL "CARETAKERS."

In Rhode Island, Dick showed her to another long-time yachtsman, Frank Prue, who owned Woonsocket Textiles, was in his seventies at the time and wanted one similar. We laid the keel for our second Chester 50, Hull #202, to be called *Roamer IV*, Providence, R.I. As construction continued, Frank visited the shop with Dick. In casual conversation with him I remarked that the yacht would provide some great cruising for Frank and his wife. "My wife hates boats. This one is for my girlfriend," he replied. I had to admire his optimism.

Frank's boat was the same hull design and construction as her predecessor, but cabin layout was altered to include an owner's day/night cabin aft with private toiletroom. Her power was a pair of G.M. 6-71 diesels, 2:1 reduction, shafted through quarter logs. As building neared completion, Frank, Dick, and two acquaintances visited for inspection. The yacht looked great with many extras of equipment and finish installed, including indirect fluorescent lighting all around the main living room saloon. As she was being admired, the saloon lighting was switched on but nothing happened. Several attempts failed to work. Frank's friends were electrical engineers, so out came their calculators and meters. Weighty theories were offered including volts, amps, microfarads, and resistances. Still no lights. One of Gerald's older builders walked through the cabin and overhearing the technical conversation, asked if we wanted the lights on. The answer being in the affirmative, he walked over to where the ship's power cord was plugged into the shop wall, removed it, turned it over, and re-inserted it. Miraculously, all the fluorescent lights came on. "Should be okay now," he said.

Soon after *Roamer IV* was completed, launched and was off for her homeport in Rhode Island. It was about this time that Dick Shaw began having a series of mini strokes, which resulted in a confusion and disagreements over equipment and payments. Dick's office manager, Joe Brown, attempted to fill the gap without really knowing Dick's wishes; as with most successful entrepreneurs, he kept his thoughts to himself.

Completing the building process was frustrating for us as we tried to work around the difficulties. Dick wanted to conceal his physical condition, which complicated matters even further. He and Frank finally came to loggerheads over extra-billings and guarantees. I never knew of the outcome as my relationship with Dick gradually terminated although I was left to conclude business arrangements begun by Dick with several owners. I was also faced with sales responsibility for future contracts, having to fill building berths at my five shops.

I began advertising nationally in the *American Yachting* magazine and several other periodicals. I designed my ads for the greatest impact, a generally expensive one-quarter page horizontal format. From one $900 monthly ad in *Yachting*, I received 400 replies, and could count on selling at least eight boats per year. I sent out brochures and information sheets to each enquiry. If the customer liked what he saw and could arrange the finances, he generally called to arrange an inspection visit of boat building. I was amazed at the number of prospective buyers who would make the trip to Nova Scotia, often at considerable time and expense, state emphatically that they were going to buy one of our boats and leave, never to be heard from again. After many such visits, I concluded they were just out for a joy ride with no serious intentions, regardless of what they said. Nevertheless, it took up a great deal of my time and attention as I listened to their pet ideas, time which could have been more profitably spent in serious pursuits.

I designed and produced a design brochure and a picture brochure, with inserts, which were used in our direct mail-out. They cost $5.00 each with postage. From 1,000 brochures sent, there were one to two contracts realized. I was selling a romantic dream, and dreamers are often notoriously poor.

Alan Mitchell's yard in Chester now being defunct, I contracted my next boat with Gerald Stevens. She was to be one of my designs, a 46-foot Distant Star brigantine, Hull #203, named *Morgan*, for Russell Morgan Tuttle, of California. I had been in correspondence with Russell for several years as he was trying to arrange finances. Finally he came through with enough money to enter into a contract and at least build the hull. I knew it would be an extended project, but believed I could at least get the hull built at Gerald's. Her design and specifications were foreign to Gerald's normal type of construction, and I had to spend considerable time with him in Chester.

By this time in his career, Gerald had seen a lot of boats and too many crazy customers. He was always pleasant and polite with a wry sense of humour, but he had become indifferent to the business. Uninteresting jobs had diminished his enthusiasm. I often arrived at his shop only to be told I could probably find Gerald at the Legion having a few drinks with a friend. It seemed that the arrival of anyone at the shop occasioned Gerald's invitation, "Let's go have a drink before we talk."

We set *Morgan*'s keel up as I began to take truckloads of lead to Chester for her ballast keel. It seemed never-ending and I wondered where Gerald

"JUST OUT FOR A JOY RIDE." RESPONSES TO ROSBOROUGH'S ADS RANGED FROM THE SERIOUS TO THE FRIVOLOUS.

was putting it all. She was finally set up in frame and planked. As decks went on, Gerald's building got slower and slower, with a large turnover in workmen. I could see years of prodding and coaxing stretching into the future, so after the first phase was completed for *Morgan*, I decided to remove the hull to Donnie Russell's boatshop at Lower Ship Harbour for completion. It was a sad day for me when she left Gerald's yard as it signified the end of the glory days of wooden boat building in Chester. With the spirit and the heart gone from the builders, the industry rapidly declined.

I heard later that Dick Shaw had retired from business in Rhode Island, left his wife and family, and gone to live in an apartment in Florida. Two years later, his wife called to say that Dick had died in Florida and that she thought I might like to know.

While I was building boats at Chester, I appreciated the interest and expertise of Frank Hawbolt, president and hard-working owner of Hawbolt Industries, a local foundry, and machine shop that manufactured propellers, pumps, hydraulic gear and shafting. Frank was an inventor at heart, so he appreciated the challenge of a new concept or piece of equipment. He was one of those people who saw a challenge in every problem, not a problem in every challenge.

SIMPLY GORGEOUS HAL
AND THE MAGIC BURNING BOAT

"UNUSUAL, ROMANTIC, AND ATTRACTIVE": THE *WANDRIAN II*.

Chapter Fifteen

THE MAJORITY OF MY CUSTOMERS were middle class New Englanders. They were enamoured of old pine furniture, older wooden houses in quaint and peaceful suburban towns, and things that were steeped in history, solid graciousness, and permanence. Our heavily built wooden yachts of a design harking back to another era particularly appealed to them. Occasionally, we found buyers in California, Florida, and west coast U.S.A., even Europe, but hardly ever in Canada.

There were many more yachtsmen in the U.S.A. than Canada due to the much larger population. They made bolder decisions and were more willing to take a chance. Canadians were more reserved and cautious. I noticed that if a Canadian had twenty dollars, he might spend ten, but carefully put the other ten in the bank. On the other hand, an American with twenty dollars would rush out and spend forty.

One day a local resident, Dr. Hal Tucker, came into my office, introduced himself, and began to talk about having a new boat built for himself. Hal had been born on the island of Grand Manan and as such claimed both Canadian and American citizenship. He had a quietly aggressive personality, purposeful and decisive. He had applied himself, completed medical school, and became a respected neurosurgeon. At the time I met him he lived in a handsome older estate in prestigious Boulderwood on the shores of Halifax's North West Arm, and was an avid yachtsman at the Royal Nova Scotia Yacht Squadron. After he explained his requirements and preferences, a 45-foot Privateer ketch was decided upon. He wanted his boat to be the best quality, including Honduras mahogany plank, bronze fastened and quality stainless steel used throughout in bolts, mast and deck hardware, and standing rigging. Although he appeared soft-spoken and easy-going, he knew exactly what he wanted. As each item was decided upon, he would signify his agreement by saying, "That would be simply gorgeous, that would be fine on my boat." I came to think of him affectionately as "simply gorgeous Hal."

As the various sets of design drawings and specifications were completed and building commenced for Hal's *Wandrian II*, Hull #404, at Meteghan River, a close friend and occasional sailing partner of Hal's, Dr. Ernest Guptill, came to my office. Dr. Guptill was a professor of physics and research at Dalhousie University. He introduced himself and said he wanted me to understand the man for whom I was building the boat. Hal had been a commando during the latter part of World War Two, in command of a group of young men storming an enemy beach from a submarine. Their mission was to steal quietly up the beach, dispatch the German sentries, wire explosives and blow up a radio tower. While he explained to his men they had precisely so many seconds for this, and so many seconds for that, one young man enquired, "Sir, if we are ten seconds late what happens?" Hal's reply was, "Son, you go up with it." Ernie told me that Hal could go up a beach, come quietly behind a German sentry, reach up, grab his helmet, jerk his head back and slit his throat, before going on to the next. His purpose was his goal and he would let nothing interfere with it. Of course, Ernie's purpose was to ensure that his friend got the best deal possible in his new yacht and that I did not take advantage of his seemingly easy-going and pleasant appearance. I hardly needed the advice.

Wandrian II was the fourth vessel of the same design being built at A.F. Theriault's so progress went well as equipment arrived for her. Russell Theriault was in charge, had met Dr. Tucker, and was intuitive enough to realize just who he was building for. The boat took shape, resplendent in her shining paint and gleaming varnish.

Launching day was a grand occasion. Hal had hired the dining room of the local motel, had a bar and food set up, and had a launching party for his friends and the young men who sailed with him. They called him "Chief." The boat was bedecked with flags, with sailing trials off Meteghan River in St. Mary's Bay. The next day they left for Halifax and *Wandrian II*'s grand entrance there. Local press covered the event on June 10, 1971 as the vessel was unusual, romantic and attractive, and her owner a man of prominence in the community.

Dr. Tucker sailed the vessel locally as he prepared her for a trip south to Florida and the Caribbean. He engaged Ron and Maureen Glendinning as captain and crew for the upcoming voyage. They took her south in October of 1971; Hal joined them periodically for cruising over the next year, then returning the vessel to Halifax.

Over the next months, Dr. Tucker showed boundless energy in his position as Chief of Neurosurgery at the Victoria General Hospital complex and on the management executive of the R.N.S.Y.S. He expected to gain a directorship at the V.G. and to be elected Commodore at the prestigious Yacht Squadron, but neither appointment was forthcoming and Hal, I expect, was bitterly disappointed. He sold his beautiful wooded estate including his private dock where he had berthed *Wandrian II*, and resigned from his positions at the V.G. and R.N.S.Y.S., removing his family inland to Moncton,

New Brunswick. At this time, he came to my office to say that he wanted to sell *Wandrian II* immediately, and asked if he could leave her on our moorings for us to help him sell her. We, of course, agreed and made room for her at our floating wharves in the centre of Melville Cove in April 1972. We began the sales process by sending off ads and talking about her to any prospective customers. Hal called several times over the next few weeks asking if we had any prospects. We had to report we did not but explained such a sale often took months, perhaps years.

In deciding a sale price for *Wandrian II*, Hal said he had paid $52,863 for her in June 1971. He later installed electronics and other equipment and fittings, bringing his total cost to $65,000. He felt he should get $52,000 for her, as she was only one year old. He retained her custom lap-strake dinghy, life raft, and some equipment for himself.

I returned from a two-day inspection trip to Meteghan River on the evening of Wednesday, June 27, 1972, and was met at our office by my son, Bob who said, "I have some bad news to tell you. Dr. Tucker's boat caught fire this morning and had a bad fire." Bob described the damage

WANDRIAN II IN THE LAUNCHING YARD.

as confined mostly to the engine room, and the scene with the firemen and onlookers. Early the next morning, I went off to the boat to inspect the damage. I was dismayed to see the mess that black smoke, oil soot and water had caused. Dr. Tucker had installed white styrofoam sound insulation throughout his engine room, and apparently it was this that had caught fire and burned with a thick acrid black smoke. The fire began on an otherwise calm Wednesday morning when there were normally few people around. Luckily, a yachtsman at the Armdale Yacht Club across the Cove, John Pauley, who knew us, spotted smoke coming from the vessel, and quickly alerted our office, the fire department and rescue boats. It was only by chance that John had dropped into the Yacht Club and was looking out the window at the time. It was only his quick action that saved the boat from total loss.

CONFESSIONS OF A BOATBUILDER

I looked the damage over carefully and determined the structural damage to be minimal. Three of the main spruce deckbeams in the engineroom were scorched, some hoses and wiring were burned, and pumps, fuse panels, and the like were melted by the quick, sudden heat. The greatest damage was from smoke, and fire department water. Upholstery, cabin paint, and varnish were a soupy mess. *Wandrian II* had beautiful Honduras mahogany cabin doors and skylights, which the fireman had chopped to pieces. The doors were held closed by a small padlock, easily popped off. I could not understand why the fireman had chopped them to pieces. I asked the deputy chief the next day when he came to complete his report, why he chopped up the doors and skylights. He replied that their first action is to gain entrance to a burning structure in case anyone is inside. I don't know why even the greenest rookie would assume there might be anyone aboard with the doors padlocked on the outside. Even if their first action were to gain access, "Why wouldn't they pop the hatch open?" "Policy," he replied. In spite of the damage, I really was appreciative of their putting out the fire so quickly.

As I was collecting myself and pondering about how to tell Dr. Tucker of the disaster, a young man who kept a rowboat at our wharf came in to tell me about the fire. He had been around the wharf that morning and said, "Dr. Tucker arrived in his station wagon and asked me to row him out to the boat as he wanted to get some of his personal belongings. He got his rifle, some books and clothing and other items." I told the young man that he must be mistaken because Dr. Tucker lived in Moncton now and wouldn't have been around. "No," he said, "It was Dr. Tucker all right or I wouldn't have let him go aboard." After the fire was out and the firemen had left, he said that, "Dr. Tucker showed up again and asked me to take him out to see the damage." "What did he say?" I asked apprehensively. "Not much, he was pretty quiet," he replied. "What did he do?" I asked. "He just looked around, and threw some burned things overboard, including the bottom of a red plastic jug."

Although Hal had obviously been in Halifax, he did not contact me then. In a few days, he called to say he had an appointment with his insurance underwriters, and would I accompany him to their office. In the meeting, condolences were expressed by all at his loss. After pleasantries, the conversation settled down to what payment they would make. Hal listened politely as they explained that they would replace upholstery, wiring, hoses, and equipment. They would clean the vessel and have her painted and varnished. They would replace damaged doors, skylights, and furniture. As they concluded, Hal withdrew a copy of his insurance policy and turned the pages to the fine print. "And what do you intend to do about the burnt deck beams?" he asked. "Why," they replied, "we will have the charred wood scraped off and repaint them." "Not on my boat, you won't. It says right here that any damage will be repaired like new. I insist on three new deck beams!" The room fell silent. All knew this would entail the removal of cabins, bulwark rails, decking, knees, fastenings, etc. It would almost be like building a new boat! The cold-blooded commando had re-surfaced and won the day. The underwriters and adjusters held a hurried consultation while Hal and I waited at the conference table. They returned and offered him a cash settlement in lieu of repairs. Their first two offers were unacceptable to Hal, but when their offer hit $30,000, Hal replied, "Well, alright, I will accept but, only because I am a reasonable man." The deal was struck and payment made. As we left their office, Hal pocketed his cheque and asked me, "Do you want to buy the boat? All I would require for her is the difference between the insurance and my ask-ing price of $52,000." I told him it was a generous offer and a wonderful bargain, but I simply didn't have the money. He replied, "You could take your time and pay me later." I agreed, and he suggested we go to my office and draw up a letter of credit in the amount of $22,000, cash or kind, at his option. We did so, and as he pocketed our agreement and headed for the door, he turned and said, "Now, I meant what I said, payment later will be fine, anytime within the next three weeks." Hal had done it again! It was a neat coup all the way around. He had his price and was relieved of further responsibility for the boat. A deft operation in two or three bold strokes.

As I scrambled to obtain funds to pay Hal, we began an extensive clean up and repair to the vessel. My teenaged children and I scrubbed and scraped, cleaned and painted. I had new upholstery, cabin doors and other equip-ment installed by my local men. Don Webster of Nauticus Marine was a great help in the new wiring, electronics and new radar. We re-furnished the forward cabin with two large swivel rockers to starboard and double settee berths to port. Many other refinements were added over time as we sailed the vessel and found what worked best for us. We showed her at local boat shows and regattas in Halifax and Mahone Bay. We cruised the coasts of Nova Scotia and into the Bras d'Or Lakes, centring our operation there in beautiful Baddeck. We explored the many hidden coves and harbours before returning to Halifax. We sailed her from our wharf from July 1972 to September 1978, during which time my young family and their friends enjoyed growing up with the boat as we sailed many pleasurable hours, living and cruising aboard, as well as time in displays and shows. We took prospective buyers sailing and demonstrated her as typical of our boats. She was instrumental in closing many contracts, some signed on board.

I remember one time showing *Wandrian II* to a new prospective customer and his wife. They were neophyte yachtsmen and would-be cruisers. As they stood on the docks admiring the yacht, he peered in through her aft-cabin windows, noticing her quarter-berths. My customer turned to his wife and said, "Oh, look dear, she had afterbirths." His wife, gazing at *Wandrian's* Blue Belle figurehead, replied, "Yes, and look she even has a maidenhead!" From this somewhat dubious nautical expertise, I had to begin to sort out what would work for them.

Another interesting phenomenon between our U.S.A. and Canadian customers was that if we had a serious problem during construction, a Canadian would invariably respond, "How can we fix it?" The same report to an American customer would result in the question, "Whose fault is it?" He wanted someone from whom recompense could be claimed.

The last time I saw Hal Tucker, he was aboard his new fibreglass boat, *Wandrian III*, docked at the Lido wharf in Chester one summer evening, lounging in his cockpit in his blue and white striped pyjamas. When I spoke to him, he replied briskly and quickly ushered his guest below. The next morning, there was a roaring southwester, and as I looked seaward, I saw Hal double reefed, beating out with determination directly into the teeth of the howling gale. He was bravely doing battle once again with forces that would intimidate ordinary men. A few years later, I learned he had died, and I assumed his foes, the forces of nature, had finally caught up with him.

In June 1978, we had *Wandrian* on display at an in-the-water boat show in Halifax when a

WANDRIAN II FINALLY CATCHES A LADY'S EYE.

lady came by, saw her, liked her, and wanted to buy her. She was Amanda Taylor, who ran a daycare centre, but wanted to leave for a cruise to Florida, the Caribbean, and perhaps to Australia. It was her husband, Brian's birthplace and perhaps they thought it would be good to sail there. Unfortunately, they had a very precocious and hyperactive five-year-old daughter. After sailing to Florida, it must have seemed like a very large ocean for a hyperactive little girl cooped up in a small boat. In any case, Amanda and Brian had bought *Wandrian* and had us install distance cruising equipment including an A/C generator and large freezer. With re-fit completed, they sailed for Florida in November of 1978. I learned later that the Taylors sold her to Don Colley, who sailed her back to Canada where he operated her out of Toronto. Unfortunately, for Don, he had a bad fall from her topmast, seriously injuring his back. Although he did survive the accident and valiantly sailed her again, in 1991 he sold her to Vernon Fairhead, a young, energetic man who re-furbished her and made her ready for the impressive gala bicentennial re-enactment of the historical landing of Governor Simcoe at Niagara-on-the-Lake in 1792. *Wandrian* was dressed and polished in all her period finery, and with all sails set and flags flying, joined the flotilla of other period and square-rigged vessels sailing dignitaries across the lake to Niagara.

A 20-foot longboat that I researched, designed, and built for the Nancy Island Historical Society, Wasaga Beach, Ontario, was also used in the same re-enactment. She was an authentic replica of a pulling boat for H.M. Schooner *Nancy* on duty on Lake Ontario in 1792. We built her for Eric Macklin, organizer of that historic project.

Wandrian II has had a varied and colourful life through a number of owners who have brought out the best in her. She maintains a special place in our hearts from the years we sailed and cruised aboard her, becoming a treasured memory.

A LITTLE HELP FROM PIERRE TRUDEAU? *ARCTIC WITCH* .

Chapter Sixteen

In october 1973, i had another Canadian enquiry, from E.L. Mac MacKay of Cobble Hill, British Columbia, Mac operated Tundra Technical Industries and Arctic Communications Ltd. out of Edmonton, Alberta, supplying and maintaining electronics throughout Canada's north and into the Arctic Circle. Consequently, he was very interested in how electronics would perform close to the magnetic pole with all its inherent electrical influences. It had long been his dream to traverse the North West Passage in a small vessel, testing as he went. He estimated the project as several years duration, during which the vessel would be frozen in over the winters, with research being carried out each summer. The season there was short, from mid–August to mid–September, so he needed a sturdy, seaworthy, and comfortable craft for the icy voyage. He had promise of financial support from the Pierre Trudeau government, then in power in Canada.

Mac was a pleasant, kind, well-mannered entrepreneur with a charming social personality who deftly balanced his businesses with the help of two ex-wives while awaiting the arrival of a child with his third. Slightly on the heavy side and balding, he said that all the energy that would have gone into growing hair went into virility. His life-style certainly bore out his theory.

After several letters and packets of plans and information were sent to him, he visited me in Halifax and eventually a Privateer ketch was selected with lists of special extras compiled to suit his proposed voyage. After his new baby was born in April 1974, he was prepared to launch the vessel. Our building contract #503 was drawn in April 1974 for delivery in 1975 out of our Parrsboro shop, Windjammer Yachts by Osmond Yorke. The contract was for $63,300, with a base price for a Privateer at that time of $51,000. Extras included Greenheart sheathing and steel bowplates for ice; an enclosed deckhouse, including electronics; plank bowsprit, extra anchors, chains, and rodes; an eight foot dinghy with davits and insulated backstays; stern sailing position, engine controls, and life lines; a radar, diesel furnace, an Onan 7.5 kw generator; Constavolt charger, extra batteries, engine pumps; extra 2,000 lbs ballast and water line 4 inches higher; and a host of other items to make operation, safety and life aboard easier in the Arctic.

By the time the vessel was completed, she cost $81,780 after other extras were added.

Mac visited us many times during construction. His visits were always pleasant and we enjoyed his dinner meetings and conversations. While in Parrsboro, he stayed with us at Mrs. MacWhinnie's White House guesthouse, one of the older, gracious houses in the town. Mrs. MacWhinnie was a sweet little lady who provided clean, comfortable rooms and good home-cooked meals. My workmen and I often stayed there in spite of local tales of the house being haunted by an older man who would clump along the halls at night, dragging chains and banging on tins. We sometimes heard strange night noises, which provided interesting jocularity at the breakfast table. One night David Whitehead, of Halifax, while working on *Arctic Witch* with us, claimed he saw the ghost; he packed his bags next day and refused to ever stay there again.

One time Mac brought his wife and new baby. They were leaving in Mac's big yellow Cadillac, and with the motor running Mac placed the baby in a car seat in the front seat. He and his wife hurried back into the house for something forgotten, when a loud crash was heard. The baby had pulled the gearshift into reverse, and the car shot backward over the

MAC MACKAY ABOARD *ARCTIC WITCH*.

lawn and through a picket fence, smashing to a stop against the brick wall of the local hospital across the street. Once Mac had determined that the baby was okay and damage to his car minimal he smiled and said, "I guess the child is starting to drive early." It seemed to me the child was exhibiting Mac's penchant for adventures, even then.

Later Mac came to Parrsboro and lived there until launching day arrived. He became part of the Parrsboro scene during that time, meeting a young lady, Sherry, who accompanied him on his seagoing adventures for the next three years. Sherry was petite, smiling, and redheaded and I am sure she helped make Mac's cruising experiences a whole lot more pleasant. This time Mac was driving a small convertible MG sports car, gadding around with beret, flowing scarf and petite Sherry in the passenger seat. He made quite a dashing sight as he explored the countryside while waiting for *Arctic Witch* to be finished.

Unfortunately at this time, Canada's government changed. Pierre Trudeau was gone, and with him, Mac's funding for his Arctic voyage. Undaunted, Mac decided to take the vessel south for a well-deserved vacation from his business life. *Arctic Witch* sailed around to Halifax with a young crew that Max engaged, and stayed at our wharves while he concluded his arrangements to leave Alberta for an extended time.

Arctic Witch left Halifax in August 1975, cruising southern waters and the Caribbean for over a year. She spent Christmas 1976 in Nassau and transited the Panama Canal in January 1977. Mac left the boat in San Diego, where she was later sold to Robert Fellmeth. He re-named her *Kailua* and sailed her in California and the Pacific for eleven years. In September 1998, I heard from Ron McElroy who was owner then, living on the boat and refurbishing her, that she had been neglected in recent years and sank twice, ruining most of her electronics, although her engine and other equipment were saved.

Mac eventually moved back to Cobble Hill, British Columbia, although he often visited his old haunts in Parrsboro. He bought part interest in Windjammer Yachts and a large farm property at Port Greville. Unfortunately, most of Windjammer's older builders had died by then and wooden boatbuilding had almost ended in Nova Scotia so nothing ever came of the boatshop. Lamont Anderson was the only builder left, but he was getting tired of the game also, and he too died a few years later. The shop, a quonset-shaped building next to the Parrsboro government wharf, lay derelict, the builders gone and Mac departed for his retreat in Cobble Hill.

The Russells: Flying on their Own

Cyril Russell waving to the world.

CHAPTER SEVENTEEN

BACK AT BLUEWATER BOATS in DeBaies Cove, Cyril and Donnie Russell had the idea they would like the freedom of owning and managing the boatshop themselves. Although we had founded the shop in partnership with me supplying most of the funds, I agreed to their proposal with the proviso that they build only for me until the agreed sale price for my share at $5,000 was paid off. Cyril made one payment of $500, but I never did see another cent. They struggled along, but became increasingly in conflict with each other. Cyril was drinking heavily and Donnie felt he was carrying the load. His solution was to bow out of the business, leaving his share to Cyril and build full time in his small shop beside his house in Lower Ship Harbour. Donnie enlarged his shop as I advertised for new customers for him.

Cyril continued his downhill slide at Bluewater, until the business failed and he was in serious financial and alcoholic difficulties. Cyril and his wife Jean had been living in a large house trailer at DeBaies Cove, heavily mortgaged, as was his shop. After the demise of Bluewater Boats, Cyril went back to work with Donnie. In his best moments he was a real craftsman who could fashion a piece of wood, feel its curve and make it fit in impossible places. But, like old Sid Butler before him, who also had the craft, alcohol got the best of him. It is ironic, but years earlier, he used to look up at Sid's shack and say, "Look at that crazy thing, up there drinking himself to death!"

One day, I arrived at Donnie's shop to find Donnie working up inside a boat and Cyril climbing up the rickety staging with a timber on his shoulder. I had cautioned the men repeatedly to build sturdier stagings with a handrail, but they dismissed my idea as too cautious for real men. They took pride in just how shaky a structure they could get away with. Suddenly there was a tremendous crash as the staging collapsed and Cyril went hurtling down in a tangle of timbers, and planks on top of the shop's large black dog, Sport, who had been asleep in the shavings below. Donnie peered over the side of the boat, took in the scene of devastation with Sport yipeing off towards the door, and asked quietly, "What's the matter Sport, is he getting in your way?"

Later, when I visited again, I greeted Cyril with an exuberant, "Well Cyril, so how are things today?" He grumbled a gruff reply and shuffled off. "*That* was not the question you should have asked him today!" Donnie

explained. Cyril's wife left him a few days ago, he just had a fight with his daughter, Ella, and she left; the mortgage company had seized his house trailer, and the sheriff has seized the boatshop. That morning a neighbour had called to complain that Cyril's German shepherd had broken its chain, gone over to her house, and killed some of her chickens, so Cyril had borrowed his shotgun and shot his dog! "Yes sir," repeated Donnie, "that was not a good question to ask him today!"

The last time I visited Cyril he had moved into a cabin that they built behind Donnie's boat shop at Lower Ship Harbor. Cyril was obviously well in his cups and had been attempting to bake a loaf of homemade bread. He had rolled out the dough, set it to rise, and then baked it in his woodstove oven. The loaf was cooling just as I arrived. We had just exchanged pleasantries when a couple of his drinking buddies arrived to scoop Cyril up to go to the local "time."

Cyril replied that he would have to change his clothes and then asked, "Where's my watch? I had it right here on the table when I was rolling out the bread dough." He looked all around and couldn't find it. "Ohmigod, I can't go without my watch." Then, as though he'd had a brainwave he went to the new loaf of bread and held it up to his ear. Then carefully broke apart the loaf and there was his Timex watch, complete with silver expansion bracelet. Holding it to his ear he announced, "It's still tickin'." He brushed off the crumbs, put it on his arm, reached for his cleanest dirty shirt and announced he was ready to go. I remembered the popular Timex slogan, "It takes a lickin' and keeps on tickin'" just like its owner, I silently observed.

Nevertheless, life at Donnie's boatshop went on as I turned up with a new customer. He was Capt. Tom Follett, a deep-sea captain on various tankers and ocean freighters. Capt. Tom loved the sea. When one might suppose he would want to get as far from it as possible during his months off duty, he in fact wanted his own small ocean-going yacht to single-hand around the oceans of the world. He selected R-30, my modified H-28, for his purposes and chose *Teredo Verde*, green worm, for her name. When I said I thought

TOM FOLLETT had sailed Three Cheers from the Virgin Islands alone to the start at Plymouth. Austere in his needs, he claimed to need five hours of sleep in 24, existed afloat on one hot meal every two days. Very popular with the British.

CAPTAIN TOM FOLLETT.

that was an odd and ominous name, Capt. Tom said, "It's to remind me that green worms are the boat's enemy, and for me to always keep her bottom well painted with copper." He also would not let me plan for lifelines around the boat, which struck me as a foolish decision for a single-handed ocean sailor until he explained, "No, if they were installed, I would come to depend on them, and one day I would go overboard. If they are not there, I will have to be very conscious of the danger constantly, and never forget to hang on." I could see that Capt. Tom was a determined and self-reliant man.

CONFESSIONS OF A BOATBUILDER

As *Teredo Verde*, Hull #302, took shape at Donnie's yard, Capt. Tom arrived to live in Ship Harbour and wait for delivery. He rented a picturesque little cabin in the woods next to a quietly flowing river, and he enjoyed sitting on the veranda strumming his guitar at evening sunset. His quiet, patient nature showed me how he could successfully spend so many months at sea alone. He was always pleasant and friendly with the builders, striking up a warm relationship with them during construction. Eventually, all was to his liking and he headed off for the Bras d'Or Lakes in Cape Breton where his wife, Priscilla, joined him for a shakedown cruise. I joined him there also for a few days of sailing. Priscilla was a legal secretary in Beverly Hills, California and maintained a home there for Tom whenever he wasn't off sailing around the world.

Tom struck off across the Atlantic, destination Spain. I had a letter from him from Horta, Fayal, Azores, in which he reported:

All has gone well so far. Departed Cape Breton July 27, arrived here August 19. Twenty-three days for about 1,500 miles. No speed record but not too bad single-handed. No problems. Only bad weather was three days of fog on the southern Grand Banks with lots of fishing boat traffic. But here I am and what a delightful spot it is! A beautiful town, a very pretty island, nice people and cheap (but good) wine. What more could I want? Perhaps if I had any brains I'd stay here from now on. But Spain calls and I'll be on my way again. Should arrive Malaga late September.

Cheers - Tom Follett

In the weeks that followed, Capt. Tom made small-boat nautical history by accomplishing a predicted-log rendez-vous with another small yacht, skippered by his friend, Bunty King. Tom arrived first and stayed on station at 40°N–29°W for a day and a half before he spotted Bunty's sails in the distance. They had a grand reunion and sailed in company 130 miles back to Horta. Priscilla joined him in Spain, where they spent that winter before Tom cruised the Mediterranean and England, returning to Florida via the southern route in 1978.

Tom sailed and cruised *Teredo Verde* over the years until February 1990, when we heard from Priscilla that he had suffered a sudden and fatal aneurysm of an artery to his heart. Priscilla had Tom cremated, then hired a small plane to take his ashes out over the Atlantic and scatter them over the ocean he loved so well.

Over the next few years, we built two other R-30 designs at Donnie Russell's. The first, Hull #303, was *Daisy* for Bob Barnstead, a young Halifax man who planned to sail south. On her maiden voyage to Boston, she inexplicably filled with water and sank. Bob was alone and barely had time to get off in his dinghy with his emergency transmitter. Fortunately, he was rescued within hours, but *Daisy* had found a watery grave. Bob told me that he was at a loss to explain the sinking, but thought perhaps that a sink drain hose had come loose.

Another R-30 was *Switchel*, Hull #306, for David Murphy of St. John's, Newfoundland, a schoolteacher with some experience. "*Switchel*," he said, "had two translations. One is a cup of wild tea that Newfoundland women used to brew. The other is a stick or switch cut to legal size for a husband to beat his wife, under the old law." The name caused many interesting comments as David cruised around Newfoundland.

The next boat out of Donnie's shop was a 32-foot Destiny that I had designed years before my active boatbuilding life. She was a pretty, compact little cruiser that I had thought I might be able to afford someday. So the design was resurrected and construction begun on Hull #304, *Dawn of Destiny*, for Rick and Muriel Harnett of Ontario. The Harnetts were not wealthy, working at ordinary jobs in Peterborough, Ontario, but they were romantically enthralled with the idea of living aboard a small vessel and cruising. Their dream was almost palpable as they telephoned each week to eagerly discuss it. They had no sailing experience, but were sure everything would be wonderful.

They visited our office in Halifax, and we spent considerable time with them, going over their requirements. After they left, we drew up a contract, including their specifications, and sent it to them for approval and signature. It was for $41,000 for the complete sail-away boat.

Although they were determined to sail off into the sunset, after carefully considering their income, they realized they could not finance the complete boat at that time. They offered an alternative proposal of sending us $15,000 to build as far as that would allow it, then to discontinue work and store the hull until they had accumulated more funds to continue her construction. No set price had been established. We agreed, and laid her keel in August 1975. In the months that followed they phoned us almost weekly and sometimes visited the boatshop, where relationships were cordial and friendly.

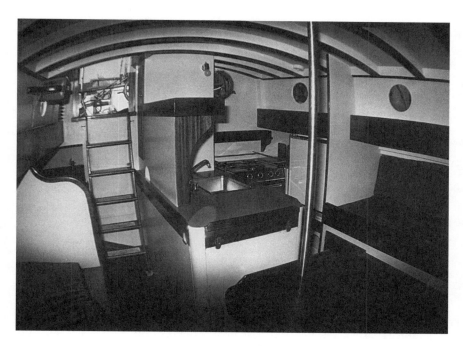

Among other custom specifications, the Harnetts wanted the 32-foot boat rigged as a cutter, against my recommendations. By September 1976, she was well along in construction with much custom equipment on hand.

When funds were exhausted, the Harnetts said they could get more money, and to keep on building. By March 1977, they had paid a total of $32,700, and were again out of funds so construction stopped and she was hauled out of the shop, and stored in a custom cradle. Regular maintenance was carried out as required. Costs of building were increasing, but finally in July 1979, Harnett arranged more funds, and she was moved back into the shop for completion. She was launched in September 1979 and motored to Halifax for rigging and final fitting out. The Harnetts moved aboard, but when they learned their final bill was a total cost of $53,340 they were shocked, handed us the keys, told us to sell the boat to recover our final payment and costs, and went back to Ontario.

It is common for first owners to be frustrated and unhappy. The dream they had carried for years does not necessarily turn out as planned; delivery is usually late, and final costs higher than estimated. The measure of an owner is determined by whether he survives the trauma and goes on to accomplish his cruising plan, or runs away with his tail between his legs. Our customers did both. Fortunately, the majority faced up to reality, overcame their disappointment, and went bravely on. Second or third owners are always more reliable.

With the Harnetts we were caught between the proverbial rock and a hard place. All through the years of construction, we had tried to keep costs as low as possible. Yet, here we were, holding the bag, with a custom designed yacht of limited buyer appeal.

In addition to not taking possession of their yacht, they sued us to recover all the money paid to us over the years, plus all the associated costs of the failure of their dream. This necessitated a lengthy and expensive court case while the boat remained at our wharf in limbo.

They contacted Howard Epstein to represent them. As the case unfolded and Epstein doggedly pursued dates, agreements, costs and correspondence between Harnetts and us over four years, it became clear to him that if there was any claim, it might well be between the Harnetts, and the builder, Donnie Russell. As Epstein and I happened to ride down in a court elevator on one of the trial days, I said to him, "You know, there really is no case against us." "That may be so," he replied, "but if Donnie Russell has no money and you have..."

The case concluded with each party maintaining part of the loss. The judge ruled that the yacht was built to the customers specifications, the workmanship was satisfactory, delivery was on time, and the bill was not unreasonable enough to entitle the Harnetts to repudiate the contract.

Although he ruled against their claim for damages, he also ruled that because there was no firm building contract with agreed to prices, some of our billings were in question. He agreed that we should sell the yacht to recover the balances owing. Each party had to pay their own legal costs, a further blow to us in an already losing situation.

For us, the anguish, time consumed and financial losses taught us that we should never build without a firm contract, or build ahead of the customer's ability to pay.

In July 1980, we sold *Dawn of Destiny* to Marcel DuPont of Quebec for $41,000. Marcel had her trucked from Nova Scotia where we loaded her for him.

The next boat out of Donnie Russell's shop was *Liberation*, Hull #305, for Milton Taylor, of Okemos, Michigan. Construction was carried out through 1977 and 1978 at a total cost of $71,000 for the 35-foot Pilgrim ketch. Pilgrim was a compact version of our 45-foot Privateer, complete

Rosborough Boats – Price List

Model	Dimensions length width draft	Tons*	Total Building Time	Kit #1 Plans	Kit#2 Frame Kit	Kit#3 Hull Kit	Kit#4 Bare Hull	Kit#5 Total Hull	Kit#6 Power-Away	#7 Complete Sail-Away
R-30	30'X24', 8'10", 3'8"	5	2,200 hrs	$400	$2,650	$3,600	$6,875	$11,500	$18,400	$27,500
DESTINY	32'X26', 11', 4'5"	7	3,300 hrs	$450	$3,250	$4,210	$8,950	$15,500	$23,900	$43,000
PILGRIM	35'4"x30', 11', 5'7"	14	4,000 hrs	$550	$4,510	$5,546	$11,000	$19,500	$27,950	$50,500
PRIVATEER	45'8"x35', 13', 5'11"	21	6,000 hrs	$650	$6,270	$7,660	$16,500	$29,000	$41,000	$74,500
LOYALIST	55'8"X46', 14'6", 6'6"	35	9,000 hrs	$700	$9,200	$11,680	$28,750	$52,000	$68,000	$140,000
AQUARIUS	55'6"X45', 15'9", 6'	38	10,500 hrs	$750	$11,930	$14,020	$42,600	$75,000	$91,500	$180,000
VAGABOND	64'6"X52", 17', 7'	55	11,000 hrs	$800	$14,500	$17,160	$48,200	$90,000	$110,000	$190,000

*Tons – approximate displacement in short tons (or deadweight).

CLIENTS COULD CHOOSE FROM A VARIETY OF MODELS, SIZES, AND PRICES.

with aftercabin, stern and quarter windows, a flush deck with mid–ship enclosed wheelhouse, and aft-deck sailing station. With ketch rig, she sailed well at over 7 knots, and maintained 6 knots under power with a Perkins 4-108, 50 h.p. diesel. Altogether, she was a competent little pocket cruiser. Milton was an economics professor at Michigan State University with a bent for sailing wooden boats, so with a few minor financial setbacks toward the end of building time, he sailed away to enjoy his cruising life.

Early in 1978 we had an enquiry for a custom Tancook style schooner from Dr. Erik Hansen, a professor of sciences at Acadia University in Wolfville, Nova Scotia. It was a bit ironic that Erik had been instrumental in the development of fibreglass resin, yet he wanted his own yacht to be of wood and in a traditional Nova Scotian style. Consequently, I designed a 36-foot schooner for him and we began construction as Hull #307, *Rayon d'Or* (golden ribbon), at Donnie Russell's shop. The whole building was a pleasure throughout for all of us. He sailed his yacht around Nova Scotia for many years, centring his sailing activity at his summer home in Mahone Bay, among its 365 islands. *Rayon d'Or* was named after Erik's grandfather's fishing trawler. Auxiliary power was a Perkins 4-108 diesel, a very reliable and satisfactory unit. Her cabin layout was conventional with long trunk cabin housing sleeping accommodation for five in two separate staterooms, full galley, enclosed head, swivel armchairs and Scottish tile fireplace.

Erik did his own maintenance and repairs over the years, and his very patient, accommodating manner allowed him to enjoy his yacht to the fullest.

As his family grew, his son Rick became involved with ongoing maintenance and sailing the vessel. In 1997, they completed a major overhaul, preparatory for a cruise to Caribbean waters, and in December Rick and two friends set off. Unfortunately, they were caught in a tremendous early winter gale off New York. *Rayon d'Or* sank under them but a nearby Dutch ore carrier was able to rescue them. It was a sad end for a gallant schooner, especially after all the loving, hard work everyone had put into her. The crew were safely ashore in London, England and returned home in time for Christmas. When Erik called me with the news, he understandably had mixed emotions about the loss of his lovely vessel, but he was thankful for the rescue of his son. Sometimes the sea can be cruel, and the sailor can never be too prepared.

Sea Chase - Trillium - Sea Trek II - Lesana

"I was caught in a whirlwind of my own making." Another Privateer
being rigged at Melville Cove.

Chapter Eighteen

At the same time as all the activity at Bluewater Boats and Donnie Russell's shop was going on, we were busily building a host of vessels at Breton Gray's in Sambro, Windjammer Yachts in Parrsboro, and A. F. Theriault's in Meteghan River. I had graduated to a large, new Pontiac station wagon and was flying low on my busy schedule of weekly visits to all the shops. I was concurrently working a forty-hour week for the telephone company and raising a family of five children. To say my life was a merry-go-round of mad work would be a grave understatement.

I had to have lists and reminders to keep track of my lists and reminders. Each owner had comprehensive lists of his own particular extras, colours, layout, equipment, wants, and schedules and I had to keep track of them all. In addition, the builders, their workmen and families need a good deal of psychology. Their personal difficulties had to be remembered and considered to maintain a productive flow of construction. I became an obsessive workaholic!

My addiction was all the more serious since people thought I was doing wonderful things for everyone involved and making it all happen. However, beneath it all, I knew I was living a lie. What had begun as a pleasant and satisfying life of yacht design and construction had become a cycle of sales, design, construction and delivery that I couldn't escape. I was caught up in a whirlwind of my own making.

Bob, Kevin, and sometimes Lynda joined me part-time in my design and sales office. We usually rigged the locally built boats in Halifax, so we all got involved in phases of masting, rigging, ballasting, trials, and delivery. My wife, Marian, was also doing part-time office work and when my third son, John Patrick, got old enough, he too assisted in rigging, sailing trials and deliveries. It was a very busy time, without much opportunity to see where we were all headed.

We had *Wandrian II* at our wharf in Melville Cove where we used her as our demonstration vessel to show prospective customers, sometimes taking them for a sail if their enquiry proved serious enough. My eldest daughter, Kathy, helped with the entertaining and sailing. It was a pleasant though hectic time, and I expect everyone has memories of all the activity, and family togetherness.

Sea Chase, Hull #7, for J. Fletcher Chase, was the next Privateer ketch out of Bluewater Boats. Her name, of course, was a play on her owner's name, who originally contacted us from Italy where he has business interests. His home base was Greenwich, Connecticut, but he travelled extensively. He was a member of the prestigious Explorer's Club in New York City where he entertained me at an exclusive dinner, discussing the construction and equipment of his yacht. Our white linen tablecloth was resplendent with an array of silver cutlery, china and cut-glass goblets, and each of us had a personal waiter standing behind our chairs who filled our water glasses whenever we took a sip of water. The dinner was many courses, taking several hours and giving us time to discuss all the details regarding the yacht. From a base price of $28,750 in 1969, she was delivered to Fletcher for a total of $35,000 with many extras.

After he sailed away, Fletcher sent long and detailed reports on his experiences

GEMJIG. OTHER COMPARABLE YACHTS COST THREE TIMES AS MUCH.

concerning maintenance of the boat, with accompanying critical comments from the experts who worked on her for him. He probably didn't tell them her price, and that other comparable yachts of her day cost three times as much.

Around this time, I noticed another phenomenon among owners. When the boat was working well, they would report, "We had a wonderful sail on *my* boat, with dinner aboard." If things weren't going so well, they would report, "Your boat is leaking again." It was odd how the ownership would change, according to how much sun was shining.

Even with all his problems, Fletcher, I believe, had a good time with *Sea Chase* over the years, eventually selling her to Jessie Knight in 1976 who lived aboard with his wife in Miami and cruised the Eastern seaboard. Edward Harrison, who bought her in April 1979, did custom modifications and sailed her after that.

In 1970, we delivered another Privateer, *Trillium*, to Syd Firminger, of Willowdale, Ontario, who sailed her out of Antigua, West Indies. She still cost only $42,000, and was named after the provincial flower of Ontario. Syd sold her to Henry Van L. Baay of Fort Lauderdale. Henry had successfully operated a boat yard for many years and selected *Trillium* for his own personal yacht for cruising in the Bahamas. He wrote a very informative book titled *Boats, Boat Yards and Yachtsmen* chronicling the problems of both the yard owner and the customer. It makes useful reading for prospective boat owners and boat yard owners. He cites serious legal considerations that the yacht owner seldom thinks of, and illustrates them with actual experiences. Henry had experienced various traumas in his lifetime, including repair, labour problems, and robbery.

Henry had an operation for cancer in 1971 and a serious heart attack in 1972. In spite of everything, he continued to enjoy cruising and sailing, and sent us many prospective customers over the years. In his final communication with us, he wrote, "The world around is getting gloomy, but not mine. I may be anchored somewhere in a sandy cove in the islands, or at the house in Lauderdale, but you can always contact me if you call. If you call my executor in the future, he will advise you of the time of the funeral at Park Street Church in Boston." Henry had his last cruise all planned and provisioned as all good sailors do.

Henry reached his final harbour in September 1975, age 72.

Hull #9, at Bluewater, was *Sea Trek II* for Paul D'Onofrio of Cohasset, Massachusetts. Another 46-foot Privateer Ketch, our costs in 1971 were:

6000 hours labour at $3.00	*$18,000*
Materials (all)	*$5,500*
Equipment (standard)	*$10,500*
Overhead	*$2,500*
Total	*$36,500*

Paul also ordered many extras, which were duly installed. After trials at Halifax, *Sea Trek* sailed away on June 7, 1971 at a total sale price of

$39,000. In June 1976, she again visited us as her new owner, Dan Ladrigan, his family and crew cruised back to Nova Scotia. He was pleased with the boat, and she was performing well.

In 1971/72, we built *Lesana*, Hull #10, a bald-headed gaff main Privateer for Edwin Ray Phillips of Miami Springs and Maine. When he first came to us, Ray was well over 70 and had been a vice-president and comptroller for Morton Salt for the greater part of his working life. Being in the salt mining business, he was well acquainted with Nova Scotia and our salt mines. Now retired, he travelled with his little Corgi dog, and entertained himself in painting and sculpting. We custom furnished his great aft cabin to accommodate a comfortable berth and large potter's wheel. His dream was to cruise the St. Lawrence River, Great Lakes, Mississippi, Florida and Caribbean. *Lesana* cost Ray $42,000 including extras such as Diesel generator, water maker, semi-enclosed wheelhouse, sounder, compasses, dinghy and special wiring.

After launching, rigging, trials and delivery, Ray stayed for a time at our wharves in Halifax. One day, I noticed him come ashore dressed in his best clothes and finery. I asked him where he was going. He replied that his grandniece was in town, and that she was taking him out to supper. It turned out that she was Miss Nude America, here on an official tour. He was very proud of her and her accomplishments. A large stretch limousine pulled up to the wharf and Ray was off! After that, little Ray's stature increased enormously in the eyes of our workmen and staff, and he was always greeted with a smile and a wink.

Eventually *Lesana* left Halifax with Ray, his little dog, and a paid crew of young men. Ray made it to his granddaughter's wedding in Chicago, and continued on down the Mississippi to the Gulf of Mexico.

In 1973, he became ill in Miami, his weight went down to 117 pounds and his strength diminished. With regret, he offered *Lesana* for sale, abandoning his plans for cruising South America and the Mediterranean. He was asking $44,000 then as he had added more extras of his choice. These obviously had value to him, if not to prospective buyers. Carl Palmer bought her in 1975 for $27,000 and sent to us for a topmast package for her mainmast. By October 1979 Frank Stone, who contacted us for replacement items due to a recent robbery, owned her. We lost track of Edwin Ray and *Lesana* after that, but perhaps both are still going strong.

During this period of my boatbuilding career, I was offering a standard design at a set price. Invariably when a new customer came to me, he would sit down in my 10 per cent chair (the mark-up I was trying to achieve), look over my offering, and begin to whittle the price down. Excuses were many and varied. "The market was poor," or "business reverses for two years," or "just waiting for rich Aunt Minnie to die," etc, etc. Having obtained their lowest-price deal, they then began to list their necessary extras, which every boat should have. Some were sensible, but many were quite ridiculous. They never argued the cost of their extras, and most times didn't question the final cost at all. Another interesting psychological phenomenon for my collection!

Customers kept arriving; more boats were planned and keels laid, leading up to my peak year of 1973, with 18 boats building at 5 yards!

THE ADMIRAL'S CANNONS:
GEMINI, *VALKYRIE*, AND *SNOW GOOSE*

BRIGANTINE *VALKYRIE* WITH HER OWNER, ADMIRAL RICHARD BLACKBURN BLACK.
"I DIDN'T GET SICK, DID I?"

CHAPTER NINETEEN

AT BRENTON GRAY'S YARD IN SAMBRO, two new keels were laid. The second was for Admiral Richard Blackburn Black of Woodbridge, Virginia, and the first was for Mimi Thygeson of Atlantic City, New Jersey.

They were both to be 46-foot Distant Star brigantines and contracts for them had come through Dick Shaw.

Brenton Gray was a very shrewd and intuitive man. He had little formal education, but had learned about life and people by observation and instinctively knew how to work things out. Being close to Halifax and having a good slip, he enjoyed much work on servicing and repair of federal boats. This experience taught him the value of proper estimates and calculations. He always expressed everything in terms of percentage. He would raise his ball cap, scratch his forehead, and announce a 20 per cent chance of rain that day, or an 85 per cent probability of completion next week. With his pleasant smile and outgoing personality he was liked by all as he organized his boatyard into action.

Admiral Black was a fine gentleman of the old school; his life was steeped in U.S. Naval tradition. At 21, he had been to the Antarctic aboard Admiral Byrd's brigantine *Bear* as a dog-sled driver and radio operator. Black's tales were spellbinding. He told of ice and cold as forages were made over the frozen wasteland. At one time, I asked him, "Why didn't you use ski-doos instead of dogs?" His quiet reply was, "You couldn't eat the ski-doos." He was no stranger to privation, cold, and hardship, even then.

Byrd's expedition sailed south to the Antarctic in 1933. As ship's crew, Admiral Black was assigned to the lower topslgang, and was frequently aloft in gales and cold. He went to Antarctica on four scientific expeditions at various times and was in command of the East Base there 1939-41, displaying the U.S. flag on that continent for the first time.

Black's adventures with Byrd on the *Bear* and his subsequent Naval service life left him determined to someday own and command his own brigantine. With the design, construction and delivery of *Valkyrie* his dream was finally realized.

Dick Black was of Norse ancestry and explained to me that the *Valkyrie* were mythical Norse maidens who swept down to earth and carried off valiant slain warriors from the battlefield to Valhalla, their eternal reward. Naturally, his brigantine had to have a carved Valkyrie figurehead, Norse raven on her squaresail, and appropriate mythical and nautical decoration throughout. His old-time friend, Capt. Jack Shickel, curator of the floating museum aboard the square-rigged ship *Balclutha* in California, made him decorative rope-work handles for his deck gearboxes and other ornamentation. The entire vessel was reminiscent of centuries of naval history as well as Admiral Black's own personality, and charm.

Dick had already enjoyed a long and colourful naval life when we first met him. In 1937, he had been stationed on Howland Island in the South Pacific and was part of that historic search for

MURRAY GRAY, TILTING-WHEEL BANDSAW.

Amelia Earhart after her plane went missing, never to be heard from again.

Later, he told me that he was also stationed at Pearl Harbour at the time of the infamous attack by the Japanese in World War Two. Expecting some grand and momentous tales of his experience during that fateful bombing, I asked him, "Where were you on that day?" "I was hiding under a deck," was his honest reply.

Dick lived in a columned old southern estate house originally owned by his grandfather, who at one time had seventy slaves on the 21,000-acre plantation. His wife, Eliza, was a direct descendent of Daniel Boone. I got the distinct impression she was a no-nonsense lady and ran their lives and home with firm decision, leaving Admiral Black to his pet nautical and historical interests. The estate house was named Rippon Lodge at Woodbridge, Virginia, steeped in colonial history.

At the time I met Dick and built *Valkyrie*, his 46-foot Distant Star brigantine, he was retired as custodian of various U.S. Naval museums in New England. He had acquired oak removed from *U.S.S. Constitution* during a recent re-build, and used the historic material to fashion gun carriages for small cannon to be used on *Valkyrie*. He had located an actual signal gun from a castle in Italy, using it as a foundry pattern for the one-inch bore bronze cannons. At his request, I also researched, designed, and had cast at Lunenburg Foundry, one-inch bronze swivel guns for mounting on her taff-rails aft. When I showed the pattern to one of the older workers there he said, "I haven't seen any of those for a long, long time. Just a minute," and disappeared into the blackness of dusty old shelves at the rear of the pattern shop. He returned with an ancient pine pattern for a similar swivel gun, saying, "At one time all the fishermen installed one of these on their bow rail to ward off poachers." His eyes sparkled with pleasure as he prepared to make the pine pattern for my swivel barrels, handle and yoke.

During the yearlong construction, Admiral Black visited several times and kept up a lengthy, interesting, and informative correspondence with me. He knew naval history well and wanted his brigantine to be as authentic as possible to that colonial period. He began his letters to me by quoting from Longfellow's poem, "The Building of the Ship":

"Build me straight, O worthy Master!
Staunch and strong, a goodly vessel,
That shall laugh at all disaster,
And with wave and whirlwind wrestle!"

Such was his admonition to me to build him the very best vessel we could for his nautical adventures.

Dick had been an armchair admiral during most of his naval career, and was now looking forward to the colourful life under sail that he was denied for so long. His dream began to unfold and his enthusiasm was contagious. The boatbuilders were fascinated when he arrived at the shop with his cannon. Nothing would do but a firing demonstration, which halted all work in the shop and brought the entire village to attention as the thunderous roars and bellows of black smoke drifted over the harbour waters.

Eventually, *Valkyrie* was completed, christened by Eliza, and launched. Sailing trials were held in a piping sou'wester in Halifax's outer harbour. The crew consisted of many of her builders, her riggers, myself, and Dick, who was jauntily attired in his best yachting togs. He clamped his peaked cap firmly down in traditional yachting style as he held firmly onto the main shrouds and taffrail cap. All sail was set, and as the vessels wild plunging and dipping increased, we all had our hands full just to hang on. It was one hand for yourself and one for the ship during the exciting and wild sailing trial. When we got into somewhat quieter waters under the lea of Chebucto Head, I turned to look at Dick. He was still clinging to his shrouds, but his trousers had descended to half-mast, his pipe had gone out, and the ashes had dribbled down over his blue blazer and old-school tie. "Well, how was that for a sail, Dick?" I asked. "Well, at least I didn't get sick, did I," he replied confidentially.

As we came in closer to land, Dick pointed up on the promontory to Fort York Redoubt and a crowd gathered there. We could make out brightly uniformed military officers with flashing swords and a host of colourfully dressed ladies. As we watched, a cannon boomed out from the fort and a large Union Jack was raised to the flagpole head. Dick said, "They seem to be having some kind of ceremony, I think we should fire them a salute." He had brought a huge U.S. revolutionary flag about half the length of *Valkyrie*, which, of course, we were flying from *Valkyrie*'s main gaff. Orders were given, gunports opened and the Admiral's cannons run out for the salute. A broadside salvo was fired out from the little U.S. brigantine. It was a great deal of fun and Dick was well satisfied with the performance.

The next day, our local paper screamed with the headline "U.S. Vessel Fires on Fort York Redoubt!" The article went on to explain that York Redoubt had originally been built to guard against American invasion during the War of 1812, and that this was the first time that an American warship had fired on the fort. What made the event even more dramatic was that it should happen exactly during the re-opening and re-commemoration of the fort, almost as a planned part of the event.

Dick and I were both contacted by CBC TV to go on-air for their evening

VALKYRIE "ATTACKING" YORK REDOUBT.

interview segment. As Admiral Black's colourful past and our boatbuilding heritage and activities came to light, the story mushroomed and filled the local spotlight for quite some time. The CBC interview was ably conducted by Don Tremaine, and the whole thing became great fun.

Eventually, Dick sailed *Valkyrie* away to her homeport at Pirate's Cove Marina, in Galesville, just south of Annapolis and Dick's home in Rippon Lodge.

From there, *Valkyrie* took part in many historical re-enactments and galas, such as the burning of the tea-brig *Peggy Stewart* at Annapolis in 1774, and the defence of St. Michaels, Virginia, 1973, by *Patricia Blues* under the US Command portrayed by Senator Barry Goldwater, and the repulsion of the British Naval ships attacking it.

The principals were costumed in full colonial military attire, with Admiral Black in command of the attacking British ship *Valkyrie*, circling the harbour with all cannons blazing. After the battle, cheers went up from the crowds as British commander Admiral Black surrendered his sword to the victorious US land forces, General Barry Goldwater, with Admiral Black, saying "We have met the enemy and we are theirs."

At the launching and commissioning of *Valkyrie* at Brenton Gray's in 1969, Admiral Black presented me with one of his historic ship's cannons, in appreciation for his staunch and sturdy vessel, a keepsake that I treasure to this day.

The other brigantine on the ways at Brenton Gray's at that time was for Mrs. Mimi Thygeson of Atlantic City, New Jersey. This proved to be an entirely different experience from the pleasant one with Admiral Black. I first met Mimi when her large custom camper van pulled to a stop in the front yard of my design office in Armdale. Mimi was buckled into a wrap-around aircraft pilot's seat while her girlfriend was the driver. Mimi stormed into my office, demanding to see her boat. She was an arresting vision. Her attire was a red mackinaw jacket and cap over close-cropped hair, khaki battle-dress army pants with patch and ammunition pockets, and army boots. Mimi didn't just appear, she exploded onto the scene. As she sat in my 10 per cent chair and we prepared to go to Brenton's to inspect her boat, I noticed her right hand made quick twisting movements. Later, when I had a chance for a private word with Mimi's girlfriend, I asked if Mimi had an epileptic condition. Her reply was, "No, she is a championship motorcycle driver, and she is re-living the memories."

Among her other achievements, Mimi owned a house construction business where her husband was chief finish carpenter. In addition, she had a flying school, which taught skydiving. As we grew to know Mimi, it became obvious why anyone in a small plane with Mimi would want to jump out.

In any case, we drove to Brenton's shop for her initial inspection of her 46-foot brigantine. Mimi burst in through the boatshop door and descended upon her half-built vessel, bellowing to her girlfriend, "Tape!" A 50-foot steel-measuring tape was produced and stretched from stern to bow. Mimi read the tape and exclaimed, "This is not my boat, it is two inches too long!" Her appearance and remark occasioned a complete stoppage of all work by the builders as they stared at her in disbelief. From that point on, things went steadily downhill as Mimi criticized everything from the weather, her long trip to Nova Scotia, the perceived discrepancies in her boat, and the general inability of anyone to do anything right. Over the course of several similar visits to the shop, the builders dubbed her "Mimi-the-horrible," as they learned to duck whenever she arrived on the scene.

On one subsequent visit, she complained bitterly that the construction of her boat was being neglected as some of the builders were working on Admiral Black's boat. She ranted and raved until Brenton re-assigned all his builders to her boat alone, at least until she left. She was still there however when Admiral Black arrived for his inspection. He told me confidentially later that Mimi had cornered him with a word of advice. She said he would have to watch those builders as they couldn't be trusted and they had not been working on his boat at all while she was there.

On another occasion, I was in the after cabin with her, discussing furniture layout. By agreement, we were only to rough in plywood furniture and equipment, trim and finish to be done in New Jersey later by Mimi's husband as there was "no one in Nova Scotia that knew anything" or was capable of doing a proper job on her furniture. She swept her arm toward the stern windows and said, "I want a three-quarter bed up there!" "But Mimi," I replied, "a three-quarter bed is not big enough for two," thinking of her husband. "Well, it's big enough for me! Hell! It's only me and the dog that's going to sleep there anyway!" she retorted. Then pointing to the forward corner of the cabin she announced, "And I want a bath tub right there!" I explained to her, as one might to a very small child, that "The cabin wall is rounded and the bath tub is square. In order to install one there, it would have to be away up near the roof." "Well, put it there then, and build me a ladder to climb up to it!" she ordered. I heard muffled sputtering by the builders. Later I asked them what they were laughing at.

"We were just picturing Mimi's great big arse waddling up that ladder into her tub," they replied.

Mimi had named her vessel *Gemini*, after herself of course. Building went along over a frustrating year, never knowing what ultimatum Mimi would order next. On one visit near the end of construction, she arrived in her van, again ensconced in her custom front seat, her girlfriend driving and her husband clinging onto his makeshift box seat with a huge black dog, in the back. The van came to a halt among the rocks, pounding sea and bleak fog of the boatshop yard at Bald Rock. Mimi turned to her husband and ordered, "Alright, get out! Get the tent and the dog. You're going to camp here and watch over those bastard boatbuilders!" Mimi had already reserved a lovely suite of rooms at Halifax's best Nova Scotian Hotel where she and her girlfriend would reside for the duration of the current visit. Every visit occasioned some complaint or derogatory remark, so it was a relief as construction drew to a close.

September 1968 saw *Gemini* completed and ready to launch. The auspicious day arrived as all present awaited Mimi's appearance. Her van pulled into the boatyard and Mimi yelled out, "Don't put that boat into the water until I get back!" The van pulled away again and headed for town. We didn't know what to expect next, but it probably wasn't good. After a while she re-appeared followed by a car from which emerged a priest and two altar boys, all in full clerical regalia. They gathered around the bow of the boat for a serious and formal blessing and Mimi broke a bottle of champagne over the stem in christening. For once, Mimi was smiling, solicitous and very polite to the priest. As he left with his robes, censer, holy water, and altar boys, she followed him to his car, bowing and scraping. Saying, "Yes Father, thank you Father; thank you Father." She opened her purse and handed him a generous offering. As his car left, Mimi turned to the assembled men and bellowed, "Alright you bastards, get that God-damned boat into the water!" The splash took place and *Gemini* was on her way to New Jersey. Dick Shaw had arrived as he had agreed with Mimi to sail the boat to New Jersey. Mimi assumed she would be sailing too, but Dick was adamant. If she was going to be on board, he wasn't. We had all learned a few things from our association with Mimi. Dick left with the boat, and Mimi drove back to the USA in her van.

I learned that Mimi's husband worked on the cabin interior for the next two years and did a beautiful job with teak and rosewood saved for that purpose. I don't think Mimi ever sailed the boat much and she was sold in 1969 to Herb Shriner, a TV personality and movie actor from the 1960s.

Unfortunately, Herb was killed in an airplane crash shortly after her purchase, and when his estate was put up for sale it included his home in Florida, his custom, flying boat seaplane and the yacht. 1970 saw her owned by Murray Laurie of Miami and by 1974, she was owned and operated by Robert Entin, of Fort Lauderdale. He removed her squaresails and yards and sailed her as a staysail schooner, renamed *Compass Rose*. He enjoyed her for a number of years and maintained her in impeccable condition. She had originally been built with all Honduras mahogany hull and trim. Her bulwark rails, railcaps and trim were always maintained bright, and even years later, her varnish work remained sparkling and attractive.

Bob Entin had some interesting experiences with her including a wedding on board when the bride and groom stood on the foremast platform, the minister on the mainmast platform and the gathered guests on her main deck looking aloft to witness the ceremony. This was the first time I had ever heard of an up-the-mast wedding.

Gemini, BUILT FOR "MIMI-THE-HORRIBLE," WAS EVENTUALLY SOLD AND RENAMED *COMPASS ROSE*.

The next yacht out of Brenton Gray's was *Snow Goose*, Hull #106, a 46-foot gaff main with topmast rig Privateer ketch for Dr. Harry Mergler. Harry's wife, Irmgard, was a pleasant lady who took to life afloat with grace and competence. They had three teenaged children, Myra, Marcia, and Harry Jr., who crewed. Harry was a proficient teacher in the computer-engineering department at Case University, Cleveland, Ohio. Although Harry was a soft-spoken and reasonable man, it was easy to see he was a real worrier. He reminded me of a quote I once heard about Mark Twain: "I am a very old man and I have known a great many troubles, most of which never happened." Harry thought they were still all about to happen.

Nevertheless, we did a good job of building and equipping *Snow Goose*, delivering her to Harry in July 1969 for $40,430. Harry and his crew sailed her away to Ohio via Boston, New York and the Hudson River to Buffalo. 1971 and the following year were spent sailing and cruising in local waters. Unfortunately, late in 1971 *Snow Goose* suffered an extensive engineroom fire requiring 1,385 hours of expensive repairs.

In 1975, *Snow Goose* was sold to Rick Newmeister of North Carolina, who found it necessary to replace some of the boat's forward wooden stanchion posts, knightheads, and bow planking. He attributed this rot situation to inadequate ventilation, especially since the yacht was operated in the warm humidity of fresh water sailing. He renamed her *Love Affair* and I expect she was his mistress for years afloat thereafter.

At this time, I had under construction one 65-foot Vagabond barquentine, two 55-foot Aquariuses, three 46-foot Privateer ketches, one 46-foot Distant Star brigantine, two 32-foot Destiny ketches and one R-30 ketch. Altogether, it was an extremely busy time, especially with much other custom design and repair work underway. Nevertheless, I was always glad to hear from previous owners and tried to accommodate their requests for advice and replacement parts.

MORE 46-FOOT YACHTS AT THERIAULT'S

STERN, *MINSTREL*, BUILT FOR THE PUBLISHER OF KINGSTON'S *WHIG STANDARD*.

CHAPTER TWENTY

MEANWHILE, AT A.F.THERIAULT & SONS, several more 46-foot yachts were under construction. They were: #405, *Chebucto*, a Buccaneer schooner for W.D. (Bill) Walker, #406, *Divertiti*, a Privateer ketch for Robert Hordan, #407, *Minstrel*, a Privateer for Michael Davies, #408, *Blackjack*, a Distant Star brigantine for Jack Donahue, and #409, *Gemarama*, a Privateer for Mahlon Teachout.

All were the same hull design although cabin layout and rigs were different.

Bill Walker was one of those rarities in my life, a Canadian customer. Not only that but he was living just up the road from me in Halifax when he came to see about getting his marconi main schooner built. He had seen many of the vessels I had built lying at our wharves in Melville Cove opposite my design office as they waited for delivery. It finally became too much for him to resist.

Bill was a quiet, reserved gentleman who had a career with the Canadian Navy as sailing officer on both the East and West Coasts. In British Columbia, Bill had commanded the sail-training vessel *Oriole*, while on the East Coast he had skippered *Pickle*. *Pickle* was a prize-of-war, formerly the pride of the German sailing Navy during World War Two. She gained the reputation of being Hitler's yacht, although I doubt he ever set foot aboard, as he was deathly afraid of water.

Bill was an excellent sailor and loved the sea. He was patient and calm in decision which made him a successful commander aboard sailing vessels and at sea. He explained to me that he didn't have much money, which was true, but would like a 46-foot Buccaneer schooner to retire aboard in two years. His proposal was for us to build the hull, deck, cabin and masts, which he would then finish himself over time, although he was admittedly not a carpenter or boatbuilder. The deal for *Chebucto* was struck and we began his boat for a complete exterior, tanks, cabin floors, and main bulkheads. Masts were to be rounded and placed on deck. He chose *Chebucto* for her name, as it was the old original name for Halifax, from the Mi'kmaq word "Che-buc-took" meaning Big Harbour.

Bill and his wife Marian were lovely people and they had teenagers in the family who would crew as well. They had a house in Sidney, British Columbia, and it was their plan to sail the boat south, through the Panama Canal, then north to British Columbia, visiting many ports of call en route.

In my discussions with Bill about equipment for his boat, he said he didn't want any complicated electric or electronic items at all, since in his view, they only worked until they were really needed, and then they failed. The most sophisticated equipment he wanted was a bucket and a rope as these always worked. This thinking became known to us as Walker's Law, and I must say it generally worked out the way he described.

Our experience of building *Chebucto* for Bill was pleasant and rewarding. He got along well with the builders, and everyone tried to do the very best they could for him. In order to save money, he had us install a used diesel he had found. Other than that, we completed her exterior including rails and trim. She had an open cockpit amidships over which Bill rigged a temporary awning.

In August 1970, Bill motored her to Halifax and secured her to our floating wharves in the centre of Melville Cove. From here, Bill set to working on her over that fall and through the winter of 1971. Often ice in the Cove was too thick to get his rowboat through, but not solid enough to walk on. Bill persevered with great determination, pushing a long ladder out ahead of him, then crawling over it, until he reached the boat and could go to work in her cold cabin with his simple hand tools. By spring, he had made much progress and proudly took a friend out to see her. The friend looked all about at the apparent confusion aboard and at a loss for something nice to say, commented, "Well Bill, you certainly have something good to start from." Undaunted, Bill continued bravely on until he considered her complete. In August 1971, the family moved aboard, including Bosun the large German shepherd and Clipper the cat.

They headed for Maine, but in the centre of the Gulf of Maine, suddenly encountered a tremendous gale, Hurricane Beth. It was only Bill's superb seamanship that got them through. At one point, a huge wave washed Bosun overboard. Bill told me that he was just able to grab him by the collar as he went by and drag him back aboard. With the usual mishaps and joys, they cruised south, spending Christmas in the Caribbean and then traversed the Panama Canal. Unfortunately, in California Bill's old diesel quit forever and he had to wait in San Diego until we could ship him a new 85 h.p. Perkins and its associated equipment. Underway once again, they reached Sidney, British Columbia, in August 1972. Their initial cruising adventures over, the family moved ashore. Bill continued as a sales agent for us interviewing prospective customers and sending us their names, although none ever materialized. I found we had to process 1,000 enquiries to realize one sale. I maintained a close and pleasant communication with Bill however, and was greatly saddened to learn of his sudden death only a few years later.

Bill was a rarity in this life, a genuinely nice person, and is missed by everyone who knew him.

As an aside to the *Pickle* story, we later had her on our moorings after Norman Gowland of Toronto bought her surplus from Crown Assets. He was a middle-aged eccentric with a pleasant but strange personality. He was an active part of the TV Evangelical station, *100 Huntley Street.* Norman was one of those people who wandered through life buying things. He had a bit of money and just liked collecting everything that struck his fancy.

Pickle was one of those things. He had little nautical knowledge, and having bought the 55-foot vessel for $25,000, didn't know what to do with her. I think he had some vague notion of restoring her to her former glory as a showpiece of sailing, but obviously had no idea of what would be involved in effort, expertise, and money. He asked if he could have her put at our floating wharves for two or three weeks. She was overly large for our facility, but we set a storage fee and agreed.

Not having heard from him for three months, we began to look for him. We tracked him to a motel in Quebec as his last residence. The motel owner said he didn't know where he was now, but requested that we tell him if we found him, as Norman had abandoned two or three surplus army trucks in the motel parking lot.

Weeks stretched into months as winter came, freezing the vessel in 30 inches of ice, requiring tending, pumping and snow shovelling. Finally, Norman replied to registered letters we sent threatening seizure for debt, and sent us some money on account. During this period, our local newspaper got wind of *Pickle* and her history, which soon hit the news wire services. I had letters and phone calls from various places around the world, including one from a man in Texas with a pronounced Southern drawl. He asked, "You-all got Hitler's yacht up theaah? We got us a war museum down heaah with Hitler's car and Hitler's airplane, and we thought we should have Hitler's yacht, too." He asked how heavy it was and if it could be sent by rail. I explained that she was much too large for that and that she would have to be towed by sea. This did not seem to daunt him at all, as he asked how much we wanted for her. I told him $50,000, to which he replied, "Is that all? I thought it would be much more, we'll be back in touch with you."

Time went by, the story faded, and there was little more interest until a man named Rene Renault from Quebec called us. I told him he would have to contact Norman Gowland. He apparently persevered until he found him. He bought *Pickle* from Norman and sent a small tug to tow her to Gaspé where he was going to undertake her restoration. Apparently, he was a determined opportunist who had leased a shipyard, which was no longer in use, near a federal prison. He devised a plan of bussing inmates to the boatyard each day to work on the boat as a make-work-training program for which I suspect he was being paid while getting his work done as well. I do not know what became of *Pickle* after that, and never heard of her sailing anywhere.

Her long and colourful history included being originally designed by well-known naval architect Henry Gruber in 1936 and being built for a wealthy German industrialist to compete in the King of Spain Cup Race from New York to Spain. Her construction was of mahogany plank over iron frames, 12-ton lead keel, teak decks and the finest of rigging, trim and equipment. Then named *Heligoland*, she won the cup and went on to further ocean racing successes. Taken into the Nazi navy, she sailed out of Kiel, captained by Grand Admiral Karl Doenitz, and others. After the end of World War Two, she was taken to England as a prize-of-war and later sent to the Armed Forces Sailing Association at Shearwater, Halifax Harbour. From there, she sailed in many Boston-Halifax and trans-Atlantic ocean races, winning numerous cups en route. Many naval men took pride in her, as she became part of world and Canadian yachting history.

Next, we delivered #406, *Divertiti* to Bob Hordan at Theriault's yard in May 1971, complete sail-away with extras for $36,550. She was a marconi main Privateer with semi-enclosed wheelhouse with an additional 30 items of extras to our standard contract. We heard from him several times over the next five years as he sailed the vessel and undertook the usual repairs dictated by time.

The next Privateer ketch out of Theriault's was *Minstrel*, #407, for Michael Davies of Kingston, Ontario. Michael was owner and publisher of the Kingston Whig-Standard newspaper as well as his local T.V. station. He had a family of young boys and saw the yacht as a training ship for them. Michael was very family and community oriented, funding the arts, and maintaining a respected place among his peers. He saw himself, complete with red hair and red beard, as a strolling *Minstrel* in life, hence the name of his yacht. He was always polite and reasonable through the designing, equipping, and construction of *Minstrel*.

During construction, he sailed south on a voyage of adventure aboard Nova Scotia's sailing ambassador, the schooner *Bluenose II*, and was instrumental in saving one of two men lost overboard in a huge storm they encountered. Michael gave this account of the August 7, 1969 gale:

"By 6:00 A.M. of the third day, the wind was 60 m.p.h. and we were preparing to heave to when we were hit by a huge breaking wave, which swept the ship from aft of the bow right to the stern. Five crew members were washed off the deck, three managed to pull themselves back but two were swimming for their lives in the lee of the ship. We got ropes to them both. To rescue a man at sea is not easy under the best of conditions; we had the worst. Both men were dressed in heavy clothes including foul weather gear and boots; it was 6:30 and pitch dark, the wind was shrieking, gusting to 70 m.p.h., its noise in the sails and rigging was deafening, and the boat was pitching and rolling in the 40-foot waves. It took 15 minutes to haul the first lad up the side of the ship. When we turned to start on the second one, he was gone ..."

I am sure that Michael's voyage aboard *Bluenose II* as well as all his other sailing experiences made him choose and equip *Minstrel* carefully and properly. She was a 45-foot Privateer ketch with open cockpit mid-ships equipped with a folding dodger. Her hull was white with a green wale and mahogany trim kept bright. His no-nonsense extras list was chosen with good sense and care.

Launching day arrived and *Minstrel* was delivered to Michael at the builder's yard after trials, May 29, 1970, for $48,000. She had a competent delivery crew divided into watches for the trip to Kingston via Maine, Long Island Sound, and the Hudson River, a voyage of 1,600 miles. The voyage was well planned, the vessel stout and well founded, so the whole thing went off without a problem.

Michael kept in touch with me as he sailed *Minstrel* around Kingston as well as more extensive cruises to Bermuda, New York, Newfoundland, P.E.I. and eventually back to Russell Theriault in 1977 for repair and refit, with a total of 20,000 nautical miles under her keel. In 1979, he donated *Minstrel* to Brigantine Inc., a non-profit sail training organization in Kingston for young sailors. At that time, she was valued at $75,000.

In his donation address he said, "I think I got the most boat for my money. I had many fine hours aboard, and I'm giving her to Brigantine simply because I want to see her around here and see her put to some good

Nova Scotia, Canada   *Photo Alex Pelan*

use. It's a great boat for kids; there is lots of rigging and lots of ropes to be pulled. She should last many more decades with adequate maintenance and should provide would-be sailors with an excellent opportunity to learn what sailing is all about."

Minstrel's experience with children began early as I visited the builders on one of my inspection trips while she was still in the shop. I had taken my daughter, Lynda, then 13 and sons Kevin, 11, and John Pat, still a baby, all of whom enjoyed playing on the boat and being at the shop.

I had an enquiry from Brigantine Inc. in 1982 concerning maintenance and replied in part:

"Areas requiring repair may be in knightheads, around bulwarks, cabin sills, etc. These places are particularly susceptible to rot from small cracks, which are liable to open, which if subsequently ignored by the owner will allow the penetration of rainwater, festering and rot. Spasmodic attempts at maintenance are not adequate. A wooden boat takes small but constant maintenance. All cracks must be kept filled and all should be kept well painted. Varnish is a dangerous covering, offers very little protection and requires very much more maintenance than paint."

I understand *Minstrel* continued to operate as a sail-training vessel for Brigantine Inc. for many years.

Next was #408, *Blackjack*, a Distant Star Brigantine for Black Jack Donahue of South Essex, Massachusetts. The vessel was built with almost no extras and delivered to Jack in June 1971, for $35,625!

He sailed her off to Massachusetts, but the following year decided on a trans-Atlantic cruise. Jack was a very casual character, so I thought that perhaps he might actually make it. After weeks across the Atlantic, he and his tired crew dropped anchor in a small port in Spain and promptly dropped off to sleep. They were awakened early the next morning by the sound of gunfire, crashes, and splashes in the water around them. Looking shoreward, they could see they were in the middle of a war! Tanks were firing at each other from either side of the harbour. Many of the shells were whizzing by the yacht perilously close, with some landing in the water around them.

Jack hastily assumed that if this was the reception accorded them, it was no place to stay. He hoisted anchor and sailed all the way back to the U.S.A. without ever having gone ashore! He reported some rough weather encountered, but that *Blackjack* performed wonderfully during both crossings.

Next out of Theriault's was *Gemarama*, #409, another Privateer ketch for Mahlon Teachout and his wife, Gena, of Starkboro, Vermont. The Teachouts were a young couple with very little money, but a large dream of living on a yacht with their two little girls, both under ten years old, and cruising. Gena was competent as she organized and cared for Mahlon and the two girls and kept their old car running. They visited our boatshops at Bluewater and Meteghan River, inspecting *Gemjig* and *Minstrel* at Theriault's. They liked Russell Theriault and the efficiency and quality of work they saw there. They told me it would be necessary for them to sell their old Vermont farmhouse with its five acres of land for $52,000 to provide funds for the boat and for them to live aboard for a few years. An optimistic viewpoint caught up in the romance of their dream!

By early spring of 1971 they had obtained funds enough to enter into a building contract for their Privateer, which with extras of $4,600 came in at $40,000.

Gemarama was delivered to Mahlon and Gena in October 1971, carefully built as a topmast Privateer without wheelhouse. They sailed to Florida for the winter, then spent the next few years dividing their cruising between Florida and Shelburne, Vermont. They later sold the vessel in Florida, where her owner was Robert Reis and she was renamed *Yellow Jacket*.

Up for sale again, Paul Fenimore Cooper, Jr. of Cooperstown, New York, bought her for exploration and service work in the Arctic Ocean. P.F. Cooper's nickname was Nick and he was the grandson of Paul Fenimore Cooper, the author of *Last of the Mohicans* and other books. The Coopers owned Cooperstown, and Nick, with his mother and the family fortune, funded many worthwhile causes and institutions. One of their interests was in Arctic research and development.

The vessel was re-named *Ungaluk*, Eskimo for west wind, and loaded on a tractor-trailer to go to the Arctic. She travelled right across the U.S.A. to California, then up the Pacific coast and was launched at Vancouver, British Columbia, where she was re-rigged, commissioned, and began her sea voyage around Alaska to Herschel Island near Inuvik.

Nick's partner in his Northern adventures was Bob MacKenzie, a wild and dauntless sailor of Scottish and Eskimo ancestry. Apparently, nothing was too intimidating for Bob and his Eskimo crew. He re-rigged *Ungaluk* with a longer bowsprit, larger gaff mizzen, and mizzen gaff-topsail. When other men would be reefing and double reefing, Bob was bowling along with every stitch of sail he could get on her. It must have been a wild ride through half-frozen Arctic seas.

Nick Cooper and his mother owned Inuvik Research Laboratories, exploring and testing Northern flora and fauna amid the Arctic tundra. They also had other business interests in Tuktoyaktuk and Herschel Island. July 1979 found Nick and his mother exploring and collecting plants in the northern mountains of the Yukon and conducting sea-ice studies.

The next spring, I had a call from Bob MacKenzie who reported that *Ungaluk* was leaking around the sternpost. I questioned him as to the vessel's location and about ice. He said they had frozen in the vessel over the winter, as haul-out facilities were non-existent. I asked him how thick the ice was. "Nine feet!" he replied. "You mean to say she got frozen in nine feet of ice?" I queried. Even with her super-strong construction, I feared for her safety. "Yes," he replied, "the stern is still firmly caught by the ice, but the bow is trying to float up." A bit more explanation of the situation and I began to see the problem. The heavy ice had tried to pull the sternpost backwards causing the leaking. I told him he would have to somehow get the boat pulled ashore and instructed him how to draw the sternpost back into place with long stud bolts and clamps. He contacted me later and said they had located two bulldozers, and had dragged the vessel up out of the ice, on her side. He said there was no further damage done by this awesome haul-out, and even I was impressed by the vessel's ability to withstand and overcome these most severe conditions.

They re-floated, re-rigged additional sails and were again roaring around the frozen wastes and gales of the Arctic North. The last I heard, *Ungaluk* was living up to her name!

I never had any complaint or criticism's from Nick Cooper or Bob MacKenzie over the years, and in fact, enjoyed consulting with them at length about a proposed 65-foot tern schooner with even more space and sail for their further northern adventures.

BIG, MEDIUM, AND SMALL AT THERIAULT'S

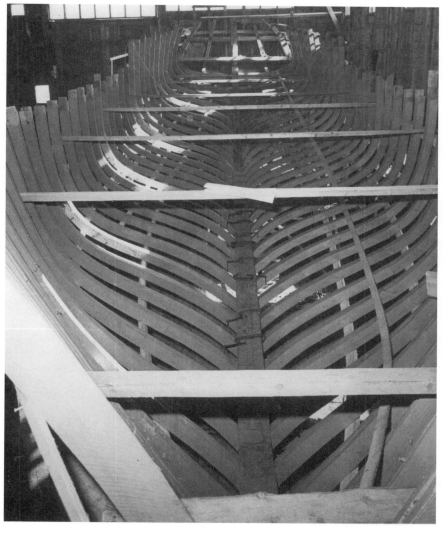

HULL FRAMING FOR A 65' VAGABOND, *SCOTIA MIST*.

CHAPTER TWENTY-ONE

NEXT AT THERIAULT'S YARD WAS a new design, a 65-foot brigantine, #410, for Carleton C. Hitchcock of Minneapolis, Minnesota. Both the boat and her owner offered us problems and challenges we had not encountered before. Carleton named her *Scotia Mist* after her birthplace, and his favourite drink. She was to be a big boat, commensurate with seas to be sailed and her owner's personality.

Carl owned a large manufacturing plant in Minneapolis specializing in making high-stress aluminium parts for the aircraft industry. He had a quick and fertile mind and had always been a dedicated and hard worker in his chosen field. Looking for a larger version of our 45-foot Distant Star, I designed the 65-foot Vagabond for him, with big ship characteristics and feel. His cabin layouts were unique, as they centred on him, with lots of

SCOTIA MIST: BOTH THE BOAT AND OWNER OFFERED CHALLENGES.

space for his own comfort. He designated that his owner's stateroom was to be the entire aft cabin, with a large box mattress and spring set featured. His eating arrangement was a table with one settee—for him. When I asked, "What about room for the crew?" he looked surprised and said, "Oh, yes, I suppose you will have to plan in some space up forward somewhere." This seemed to be a new thought to him, and was really of little consequence.

Carleton liked gadgets, mostly of his own invention. He had his foundry fashion an aluminium spoke ships wheel, taff-rail spindles and other items traditionally made of wood. He designed a system of window blinds and remote controls for all the ship's windows and ports. He also designed a remote stereo-sound system throughout the boat. All the controls were beside his bed, of course. Once on board, he would arise very early, 6:00 A.M. or so, open everyone's curtains, turn on all the stereo speakers and command, "Everybody up! Time to get underway." This was followed by martial music to make sure no one dawdled.

He also designed and built a comprehensive control console to regulate all the various ships systems. He had switches for remote shut-offs on all the tank valves, batteries, chargers, pumps and the like. He became involved in every detail of construction and equipment. Carleton was playing with the planning and building of his ship and it was obvious he was enjoying it all immensely.

Scotia Mist was a big boat of generous proportions, with a 17-foot beam, 7-foot draft and over 2,200 feet of sail. She was powered by twin 6-354 Perkins 130 h.p. diesels shafted through two-quarter logs to 26 x 22 inch four-bladed propellers. Of 55 tons displacement, she maintained 7 feet 6 inches of headroom in five separate cabins plus engine room. Her ballast keel was 10 tons of lead cast into a steel box, affixed with stainless steel keelbolts. A full saloon style deckhouse allowed for an inside control station as well as an aft sailing station when desired.

Carleton took a very active part in planning and supervising construction. It was not unusual for him to arrive at Yarmouth airport in his executive jet accompanied by his plant manager, pilot and chauffeur. They would arrive at the boatyard, disembark from their rented car and march about the yard in formation. Carl marched first with his plant manager on his right. Behind them were the pilot and chauffeur. As he pronounced his decision about what a thing was or where it should go, the plant manager would say, "Yes, certainly Carl." The pilot and chauffeur would echo, "Right, C.C." This scene was repeated over and over, no matter how crazy or inappropriate Carl's idea was. On a few occasions, I said, "You can't do that Carl, that's just crazy." His men looked at me in horror in a manner that said, "You just don't speak that way to C.C.! No one ever does that!" Nevertheless, my relationship with him was mostly pleasant, as I struggled to follow his thoughts.

Sometimes Carl would stay over at the local motel, where it was not unusual to see him walking miles along the highway very early in the morning before breakfast. His numerous lengthy letters and visits during construction were all like well-planned campaigns by a the supreme commander. With long lists of extras, additions and deletions, *Scotia Mist* got built.

She was launched and lay at the wharf for masting, rigging and final equipment. During this period, Carleton stayed nearby. One day, Russell Theriault came to me and said, "We have spotted Carl around the yard before starting time. He is going around picking up small mahogany and oak boards, bolts and nuts, bits of materials and ropes." "What is he doing with them?" I asked. "Why," Russell replied, "he's taking them aboard his boat and hiding them behind lockers and seats. I'm going to say something to him." "No," I said to Russell, "Don't say anything at all, just make a list of everything and give it to me."

Finally, *Scotia Mist* was ready to sail. Nobody could find Carl. I finally found him wistfully looking at his yacht's building berth, the shavings, bits of material and paint pots. Carleton then came to Russell's office to settle up. I handed him the final account, which obviously shocked him. He had been ordering extras without requesting prices. Now it all hit home. He questioned each item, which I had to carefully explain before we went on to the next. When he came to the item billed as miscellaneous boards, nuts, nails, wire, rope, etc., he exclaimed, "What's all this!" I replied, "Carl, those are all the items you put aboard each morning." After a moments silence, he slammed the account closed, took out his chequebook and said, "Well, I am going to give you a cheque for everything, but I want you to know you are no businessman!" I wondered about his remark. He had his boat and I had my cheque. The 65-foot brigantine with many extras had cost him $91,236 in June 1972.

Carl sailed away with his crew as we all waved goodbye. Walking up the yard, I noticed Mrs. Hitchcock still standing there in her furs. She would, of course, be flying home. She walked over to me and said, "I waited to see you. I just wanted to thank you so much for the way you worked with Carl. I have never seen him so happy. It is the first time he ever took time

off from his work to really enjoy himself. But don't be surprised if you see *Scotia Mist* for sale soon, his real pleasure was in building the boat."

I was told later that Carleton came to loggerheads with authorities over his manufacturing business. Apparently, he got on the plant intercom and announced, "This business is moving to Galveston, Texas. All you people who want to go, your move is paid. Any who don't, are fired!" He sailed *Scotia Mist* down the Mississippi River and berthed her at Galveston. En route, one of his propeller shafts unscrewed itself right out of the boat when suddenly put into reverse. The two-inch stream of water coming in almost sank her until the cause was discovered and a replacement shaft and propeller were installed.

Six months later, I saw her advertised for sale and within the year, Carleton had sold her.

Her next owner was William Wikoff Smith, President of Kewanee Oil Co., Bryn Mawr, Pennsylvania. In 1976, Donald E. Washburn of Westminster, California, who planned some world cruising, owned her. We had reports of her in California after that, but then heard nothing further.

In January 1969, I had an enquiry about my Distant Star brigantine design from Harry T. Dolan of Cutchoque, Long Island, New York. He had already been in communication with Admiral Black about revolutionary period ships, guns, and the like. He had visited aboard *Valkyrie* in Virginia and liked what he saw.

Subsequently, Harry came to my design office in Halifax, bringing with him much gathered information about the appearance of the vessel he wanted. In several meetings with him, it became obvious that *Distant Star* wasn't going to be big enough to incorporate all his ideas, and a new, larger design was suggested. The outcome of all this was my 55-foot Aquarius design, a bit of a departure from my previous hull designs in that she was much fuller forward and aft, which was more in keeping with circa 1800 ships.

Harry wanted her to have the appearance of the revolutionary privateer *Rattlesnake*, after which he named her, so I designed her with this flavour in mind. After much discussion and consideration, Harry settled on a brig rig, crossing seven yards, distinctive broad transom with four decorative stern windows and trim, quarter galleries, swivel-stock aft deck rail, deep bulwarks with gunports, channels, walk-around capstan on a flush afterdeck, heavy sweeping bow rails with figurehead and anchor cats. Her longboat was carried in chocks on the trunk cabin, while her smaller ship's gig hung in davits over the stern. Her period rudder was controlled by a rack and pinion steerer aft. Her long, straight keel, and deep forefoot gave her good longitudinal stability even under a press of canvas. Her two-masted brig rig carried 2,400 feet of sail. Final dimensions were L.O.A. of 55 feet 6 inches, 50 feet on the range of the deck, L.W.L.: 45 feet, beam: 15 feet 9 inches, draft: 6 feet 3 inches and with a 38 ton displacement. She carried a cast iron keel of 9,000 pounds, with inside ballast to suit her tankage and equipment.

The building of *Rattlesnake*, #411, at A.F. Theriault & Son, involved a great deal of planning, and a lot of meetings and visits from Harry. We finally drew a building contract in April 1971 and got underway. Her original extras lists totalled 26 items with many others added or deleted over the building period of two years. After lengthy and busy construction, we finally delivered her to Harry at Meteghan River after trials on August 15, 1973, for $80,000. Russell Theriault was very co-operative and helpful throughout the entire planning and construction with a decisive energy that carried the project through to successful completion.

The building period was fraught with delays, changes of specifications, re-arrangements for payments, bank notes and the like. By delivery time, everyone was totally exhausted although relations between us all were still cordial.

BOW FRAMING, *RATTLESNAKE*.

Harry was a worrier and changed visit dates and requests often. Every time I picked him up at the airport, he had an eternal sniffle, a box of Kleenex under his arm and a heavy scarf around his neck. Building the boat put a strain on everyone including Harry and his wife Barbara who was a pleasant, easygoing person with an independent income. It was my impression that Harry had to borrow from her to help meet final billings. It kept me and my small office staff busy revising work lists, prices and drawings over those months, and required a constant awareness of all the hundreds of details and their successful inclusion.

Rattlesnake had been a monumental dream of Harry's over many years as he concentrated all his thoughts, efforts, hopes and finances on the project to the exclusion of everything else in his life. He was absolutely obsessed with her.

Rattlesnake was equipped with bronze swivel guns, carriage guns, boats, anchors, Rodes and hundreds of other items when she sailed away. There were over 200 items on the original standard equipment list and over 90 on subsequent extras lists. Each had to be planned, designed, researched and bought for its specific purpose.

This, combined with the many designs, drawings and revised drawings gives some indication of the vast amount of work involved and exact attention to detail required throughout her construction. The owner's responsibility was seeing that he got what he wanted and funding the entire project. The builder's job was to construct the unusual design with integrity and competence. As the constructor, my job was to design, supply equipment, deal with owner and builder and orches-

BARBARA DOLAN IN GREAT AFT CABIN.

trate the whole undertaking of constructing a revolutionary period brig with all the modern conveniences and methods of operation. It was no small job and owed its success to the patience and understanding of owner, builder and constructor alike.

After the busy time of masting, rigging and sea trials, the day of departure arrived. Harry Dolan boarded the vessel with his amateur crew and they were off for Long Island. Harry entered her through U.S. Customs at Bar Harbour where local officers questioned his purposes severely and extracted U.S. customs duty. Harry told me later one of the questions they had asked him was if he was carrying any rifles or handguns. The vessel was bristling with carriage and swivel guns but they simply ignored all that and marked on their form, "No armament carried." It is strange how one only sees what it is one is expecting to see.

RATTLESNAKE BOW DECORATION.

Harry maintained the vessel meticulously and she was a real showpiece under his ownership. The USA Bicentennial celebrations were approaching in 1976 and *Rattlesnake* was scheduled to lead the small boat parade up New York Harbour. After the parade and festivities, she was berthed at one of New York's piers along with all the many other square-riggers, which were open to the public and crawling with thousands of onlookers. Harry was rushing back and forth along his deck, holding up his arms in protest and calling, "No! No! No visitors here." He didn't want his immaculate vessel soiled by the streaming hordes. *Rattlesnake* was the only vessel in all of New York Harbour not allowing visitors aboard that day.

Some time later Harry was forced to advertise and sell his beautiful dream ship. I suspect financial problems were the cause. Her new owner was Tom Giegerich, a dentist from the mid-west, who prepared her for a Caribbean cruise. His young son, Paul with his friends were to be the delivery crew. Nearing Southern waters, they plotted a 200-mile course to come close to a charted but unmarked island. But their course-made-good was off a bit; they struck a reef projecting from the island, sailed up one side and down the other into 1,000 feet of water. *Rattlesnake* sank immediately. The crew was able to abandon in their life raft and were picked up a few hours later.

Here is an account of the sinking by Herb Stickle, one of her crew on that fateful day:

"What amazed me—what struck all of us as we huddled in the life raft—was how quietly she went under. There was no whirlpool, no explosion, no surging of water. *Rattlesnake* just slowly slipped from view. She settled down level until her deck was awash, then her masts submerged to the yardarms, with the little pirate flag which Tom the owner pinned on her as a joke still fluttering bravely. Then she was gone. It all took less than an hour on a rippling sea in the lee of the treacherous Silver Bank.

There are no buoys marking the Bank, and no lighthouses or markers to warn you off. It lies in the open ocean, 75 miles from the Dominican Republic, and it has snared countless boats and ships over the centuries. In our case, a simple mistake—a failure to allow for the current—brought *Rattlesnake* within the range of coral as strong and sharp as surgical steel."

Next at Theriault's was #412, another gaff-topmast 45-foot Privateer ketch with a full deckhouse, for Dr. George Longbothom of Plainfield, New Jersey. She was to be a family yacht as the Longbothom's children were young adults and would enjoy cruising aboard. George's wife was

Esther, and in the Bible, Esther is the *Witch of Endor*, hence the name of their yacht.

The Longbothoms lived graciously in a well-maintained rambling heritage rural farmhouse and estate in Plainfield and welcomed myself, Russell Theriault and our wives to visit. Our accommodations were in an upstairs wing of the estate house, with its own resident ghost and rich 200-year history. Our association during the building of *Witch of Endor* was very pleasant and cordial. Consequently, her construction went along smoothly to a happy delivery in May 1972 at $51,700. The Longbothoms sailed the vessel for many years thereafter until she was eventually sold to another U.S. owner.

Number 413 at Theriault's was a smaller 32-foot Destiny ketch for young Tommy Modine. Tommy arrived on my doorstep one day in hiking boots and a pack on his back. He was only 20 years old when he walked into my office. He announced that he had seen some of our boats and thought he would like to have one. I did not know who he was but concluded that here was a young adventurer with a dream and no money. As he described his dream, I kept interjecting comments like, "Yes, but these boats are very expensive you know. They cost a lot of money you know." I could see I was not getting my point across. Finally, he said, yes, he would like to order a 32-foot Destiny ketch. I agreed but said we would need a deposit cheque. "Oh, I don't believe in cheques," he replied. I thought, I had better get rid of him as fast as I could until he continued, "Would cash do?" He opened his pack as counted out $20,000 in 20s. It took a moment or two to regain my composure.

Tommy was the grandson and only heir of the Modine dynasty with manufacturing plants and holdings throughout the U.S.A. Among other items, they made all the radiators for International Harvester. They were obviously a wealthy family and Tommy was their favourite son. Early on, he had gotten involved with drugs, as had so many of his age group. A modern musical group called The Who had befriended him and had produced a rock-opera called "Tommy" of which he was the subject. It took a while before Tommy realized he was being used for his privileged lifestyle and money. It all ended in bitter disappointment and Tommy was just getting himself back together as he came to us for his boat. His plan was to live a healthy and adventurous life of cruising, exploring and getting back in touch with real values.

He asked if he could stay aboard one of our yachts, and we accommodated him aboard our 45-foot Privateer ketch, *Wandrian II*. He became friendly with my older children, Bob and Kathy, who were his age. He went to town and bought records of his rock opera "Tommy," for them. It was all very pleasant.

I took him with me to A.F. Theriault's shop, where his boat would be built. He stayed there and was shown the local area by Russell Theriault. Tommy went to the rickety old water-powered sawmill at Meteghan Station where his white oak keel and materials were being sawn out of trees from the millpond. He walked back and forth along his fresh-cut keel and drank it all in happily. It was a really happy time in his life and we all felt his enthusiasm. He visited several times throughout construction, anticipating the completion of his dream yacht.

Building was nearing launching in September 1971 and we attempted to reach Tommy to advise him to come for his boat, which he had named *Raindance*. His family hadn't heard from him in some time but assumed he was staying at his hunting lodge in the mountains of Colorado. Another two weeks went by and still no word was received from him. Eventually we had a grief-stricken phone call from his step-father in Florida, who informed us that Tommy had purchased a .257 Magnum pistol for his twenty-first birthday and that it had gone off by accident, shooting him in the head and killing him instantly. They had found him lying among all his packed boxes and baggage to come for *Raindance*. The coroner said that from the angle of trajectory, it had to be accidental and not intentional. How ironic it was that Tommy's dream ended just as it was about to start!

Next spring, Tommy's uncle and a friend came to take delivery. The uncle was a riverboat pilot on the Mississippi and apparently the only accomplished sailor in the family. Unfortunately, he also liked his cups rather well, as I noticed their sailing supplies included $76.00 from the grocery store and $247.00 from the liquor store. In any case, they set sail as we watched them disappear into the fog of the Bay of Fundy heading for Brier Island.

Many days later, we had a call from the U.S. Coast Guard in Boston enquiring about *Raindance*, as she was reported long overdue. The Canadian Coast Guard had also been alerted, but nobody knew anything. A few days later, we had another call from the U.S. Coast Guard, Boston, who said, "We have located your yacht." I asked where they found her and they replied, "She has been tied up to the Canadian Coast Guard cutter in Saint John, New Brunswick for several days." Apparently, the uncle was sharing his supplies with the Canadian crew and no one thought to call in.

A sister ship to *Raindance* was *Nyeema*, another 32-foot Destiny ketch for Commander Eric S. Purdon of Harwood, Maryland. Eric had distinguished himself as commander of Subchaser 1265 in 1944/45 during the latter part of World War Two. USS PC-1265 was an experimental vessel in that the majority of her crew was black. This was a new concept to the U.S. Navy at the time, and proved that her crew was every bit as competent and valuable as that of any other ship. Eric organized his ship and his crew with honour and efficiency, carrying out all tasks assigned to them with proficiency. In this regard, the assignment was a success and forever changed the role of black sailors in the US Navy. Eric wrote a very good book called *Black Company,* being the annals and successes of PC-1126, which provides informative and interesting reading of the experiment. One of his junior men rose through the ranks to become Rear Admiral, in charge of all the Navy's communications and has proved beyond all doubt what USS PC-1264 set out to demonstrate.

Nyeema was delivered to Eric at Meteghan River June 26, 1972 for $25,000. He and his crew set sail for Maine but it was mostly a power run due to lack of wind. Unfortunately, during her passage across the Gulf of Maine, a lube oil pressure line vibrated off the Perkins diesel. The crew kept adding oil but did not discover the source of the leak. Finally, the engine seized up, making replacements necessary. It surprised me that Perkins Engines made good the work without argument when perhaps blame could have been affixed.

Eric kept *Nyeema* for many years, provided usual maintenance and modifications and sailed her out of Pirates Cove Marina just south of Annapolis, Maryland. In the neighbouring slips were Admiral Black's *Valkyrie* and one of our 45-foot Privateer ketches, *Divertiti*, owned by Bob Hordan. They were often the talk of the area, as they cruised Chesapeake Bay and offered a colourful cross-section of the Rosborough fleet to the eastern U.S.A.

Santa Maria and Operation Sail

Santa Maria: Built for theatrical engagements!

CHAPTER TWENTY-TWO

IN 1973, LOWELL LYTLE of St. Petersburg, Florida approached me about designing and helping to build a replica of Christopher Columbus' galleon, the *Santa Maria*. Lowell was president, organizer and leading light of the Young American Showcase, a group of high-school showmen travelling as a troupe of musicians and actors. Lowell was a fundamentalist Christian with honest exuberance, a creative imagination, a purpose and a drive seldom seen. His project was to build a three-quarter scale replica of the original *Santa Maria* to be used as a hands-on teaching classroom and display-vessel for theatrical engagements. His dream had a practical nature as did the man himself. He required a blend of ancient flavour combined with a more modern practical application for voyaging with a relatively inexperienced crew around crowded harbours.

With these requirements in mind, I set to designing the 65-foot x 19-foot x 7-foot, 6-inch galleon. I had to do a lot of research to keep her as authentic as possible, and much invention to utilize modern materials, equipment and feasible design arrangement. Lowell worked on specifications with me over the drawing board as well as by ongoing letters and telephone discussions.

As his project developed, Lowell found that he could attract some U.S. funding but that the vessel would have to be built in the U.S.A. Consequently, Lowell and his partner, Joe Lathrop, set to willfully and laid her keel in the small community of Snug Harbour, Florida, in May 1974. John Bodden was hired as master carpenter and much amateur help was forthcoming from sons, family and friends of the Young Americans. My plans were detailed and carefully arranged so that inexperienced builders could interpret them. *Santa Maria*'s hull took shape and rose higher and higher among the palm trees. Much of her material was of Florida pine and cypress for frame and planking. The long building process continued as we began to build all her masts, spars, rigging, and boats at A.F. Theriault's yard in Meteghan River. We found antique iron, wooden stock anchors salvaged from old shipwrecks in St. Mary's Bay. We had working iron cannons cast at Lunenburg Foundry while Theriault's made up the carriages and tackle. Pulley blocks, hearts, trucks, parrel and belaying pins were made to order at Dauphinee's Block Shop in Lunenburg while all her Dacron, tan-bark sails were provided by the loft of R.B. Stevens & Sons. When all was made ready, we loaded it on a tractor-trailer and shipped it off to Lowell in Florida.

After the usual delays and problems, she was launched in April 1976, rigged, and commissioned for sea. Lowell travelled to Spain researching authentic furnishings, fixtures, and costumes for his crew. The vessel was scheduled to take part in Operation Sail with the Tall Ships in New York on July 4, 1976 and that date was fast approaching. Lowell's slogan for *Santa Maria* as a living classroom and authentic display vessel was, "Bringing history to life, and life to history!" She had been recreated as a cultural, educational, and historic floating museum.

LOWELL LYTLE, BRINGING HISTORY TO LIFE.

Through all the trials and tribulations, Lowell's indomitable spirit and faith succeeded as his *Santa Maria* joined the host of other tall ships, big and small and formed up for the grand parade of sail. Thousands of hearts beat as one as *Santa Maria* led the flotilla of Class C ships under the Verrazano Bridge and up New York Harbour past the Statue of Liberty and hordes of cheering spectators.

After that glorious day, she continued on with her scheduled tour, hosted by hundreds of cities and towns in the United States and Canada with over 500,000 visitors having gone aboard. Their ongoing guided tours, which included going below deck and then to Columbus' great cabin, offered a chance to relive the past and the experience of life afloat on a Spanish galleon in 1492.

Santa Maria continued with her many engagements for the next two years. On June 11, 1978 on another voyage north, she sailed gallantly into Halifax Harbour. Dozens of welcoming yachts and hundreds of spectators marked her reception as she docked at Privateer's Wharf for a three-day visit.

She proceeded northeast and then down the St. Lawrence River to the Great Lakes, presenting herself en route. Next, it was down the Mississippi, destination Gulf of Mexico. On November 5, 1978 while under power, she caught fire and burned to the waterline. Fortunately, the crew were able to beach and all ten abandoned without injury. Lowell told me later they had re-installed the exhaust from a new generator and although the exact cause of the fire was never determined, it could have been due to the overheated generator exhaust. The next morning they returned to the scene intent on salvaging cannon, rigging, engine shaft, etc. Scavengers had got there first, however, and her bones were picked clean.

All the crew who had served on her over the years had praise for her adventures and capabilities and were greatly saddened by her loss. Undaunted even by this reverse in fortune, Lowell maintained his faith and when I last spoke with him, was planning a new project vessel.

Operation Sail in 1976 with the Tall Ships included most of the world's square-rigged sail training and naval sailing ships then operating, and was planned to be the grandest gathering of all sailing vessels in one parade in the last 100 years.

Invitations had been sent out worldwide, and among all the rest, seven of our vessels responded and attended as part of that magnificent gathering. July 4, 1976 was a pleasant day in New York, but winds were light and contrary making the sail-past up New York Harbour arduous for some underpowered craft. Nevertheless, the fleet sorted itself out and formed up for the grand parade. The U.S. Coast Guard full-rigged ship *Eagle* led all the rest with her cadet crew aloft along each yard's footropes. Class A ships were followed by a myriad of Class B, just as picturesque but slightly smaller. Weaving alongside were innumerable small private power and sail craft, darting about like a horde of mosquitoes. Officials and patrol craft had their hands full that day.

The Class C vessels were led under Verrazano Bridge by Lowell Lytle's *Santa Maria* and her crew of period Spanish soldiers and sailors in full dress, including a brown-robed priest perched on her high bow, holding his large crucifix aloft. *Rattlesnake*, with Harry Dolan in command, followed, taking the honours for best-dressed vessel in Class C, resplendent in her eighteenth-century brig rig, raised aft deck with quarter galleries, bow rails, and seven yards.

I had been invited as a guest for the occasion by *Yachting Magazine,* being a constant advertiser in those days. *Yachting* did themselves proud, and had engaged V.I.P. seating at The Battery in Lower Manhattan for us to view the spectacle. As they all passed by in review, I spotted many of my vessels in parade. Later, we were hosted aboard a large power-yacht for a tour of the Hudson River, East River and all the many docks where the square-rigged flotilla lay, with over 60,000 onlookers boarding for inspection. Thousands upon thousands waited in long line-ups for hours to go aboard each vessel. An estimated 500,000 people were there, all in a merry holiday mood that day in Manhattan. Streets in the Lower End were closed to traffic as brightly coloured parades and many ethnic groups celebrated. I mingled with the crowds and found everyone laughing and friendly, a stark contrast to the cold indifference I had often experienced in New York City.

After the glorious holiday, all the vessels dispersed to other ports of call, displaying themselves on their own schedules. Afterwards, it was back to my drawing board in Halifax and the many yachts being built by various builders.

CUSTOM DESIGNS

DRIVEN BY THEIR OWN DESIRES...

CHAPTER TWENTY-THREE

OVER THE NEXT FEW years, the fame of my yachts spread and various personalities came to me to have a special and specific vessel designed for them. One thing I had learned by now was that each owner was driven by his own particular desires and ideas, which he considered superior. The larger their egos, the more magnificent were their desires. The owners were often very likeable and intelligent men although sometimes their "unique" ideas bordered on the insane. Many came to me over the years but I will mention just a few.

In 1971, Arthur Eisele of El Toro, California came to me for a custom design. He had seen my 50-foot Aquarius similar to *Rattlesnake* and liked the romantic concept and attractive design. Arthur was a multi-millionaire with exacting tastes. He arrived in his own private plane with his wife and children. The interior of the plane was immaculately finished in white and silver with plush white carpet throughout. The family had special airplane shoes, which they donned upon entering. I spent considerable time with Arthur over the drawing board during several visits and eventually came up with a 65-foot version of Aquarius, quoted to Arthur at $275,000 with a shop labour cost of $7.00 per hour at that time. He contacted us again over the years but never did enter a building contract.

Next to contact me was Hugh Downs, the well-known T.V. host of 20/20 and other productions. Many years before, Hugh had sailed a 65-foot ketch with friends from Miami to Tahiti. This romantic adventure had captured his mind and inspired a love of the sea. After the voyage, Hugh wrote a book called, *A Shoal of Stars,* which was the account of his long-distance cruising adventure.

When Hugh came to me, his dream was to re-live that experience and make a movie of it, so he required a boat for the hero of the saga and a chase boat from which to film. We set to work on the drawing board and came up with two 65-foot vessels to suit his specifications. Hugh was a pleasant, smiling and reasonable man, so designing his vessel proved to be a pleasant experience. *Thane II*, his subject boat, was a custom arrangement of my 65-foot Vagabond barquentine design. The design was completed with lists of specifications, hardware and equipment, a building contract drawn and first payment received. The chase vessel, *Delphin II*, was designed as a 65-foot tern schooner featuring accommodations for the film crews, cameramen and directors.

All was ready to begin construction when Hugh put a hold on the project as he had just been offered the 20/20 show. This of course demanded his total time and attention, although he always maintained that someday he would make his movie. The vessels were quoted to Hugh in 1974 at $140,000 each based on a shop-hour of $9.00. The cost in 1999 would be in excess of $700,000, five times as much! Later in 1974, Hugh wrote me from Kathmandu, Nepal, maintaining that the project would still go on, someday.

Also, in 1974, Dieter Grammerstorf of Kiel, Germany, contacted me for a custom designed 80-foot barquentine to be his private yacht. Dieter was a shipbroker and financier of marine and shipping concerns worldwide. His family owned the huge Kiel shipyards in Germany, which supplied and maintained much of the German Navy surface vessels and submarines during World War Two. His imagination was captured by the romance of my designs, consequently he arranged for visits to Halifax to pursue his dream. The result was an 80-foot barquentine named *Blue Viking* to his requirement.

I remember on one visit, Dieter said he would like to purchase something attractive and really representative of Canadian culture to take home to his wife. We walked through the city on the search. At least I walked; Dieter marched. He selected an authentic sealskin, beaded coat made by Eskimos from the North West Territories as being the most representative item he could find to express Canada. I wondered about this choice, but after all, it was his money!

The design was completed and estimated in 1974 at approximately $300,000. Nothing ever came of it, but it was an interesting learning experience for me.

Of course, each new design was a pleasure as well as a challenge, requiring careful consideration and much research. I was paid for each in accordance with the work involved, and there was always the chance that the vessels might someday be built.

One day in 1975 Arthur Godfrey came through my office door. He was in Halifax doing dressage in a horse show. With his red hair and positive, outgoing manner, he put on an impressive display.

My vessels had attracted him and he decided it was time to fulfil a long-held dream of owning and

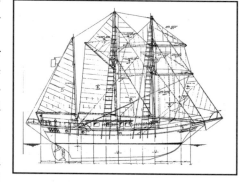

ORIGINAL DESIGN FOR *FLYING G* FOR ARTHUR GODFREY.

cruising a square-rigged vessel. This resulted in a completely new 55-foot barquentine being designed, to be known as *Flying G*, after Arthur's ranch. Some of his custom requirements were a barquentine sail rig with huge winged "G" on the fore topsail, a deckhouse galley-lounge and inside steering station, a sailing station aft, centre and quarter diesel engines plus generator and large tankage, and two private double staterooms forward. The entire large aft cabin was to be Arthur's accommodation with queen bed, seagoing berth, lounge, desk, and two toilet rooms, one featuring a bidet. I went to Arthur's horse shows and discussed building his boat over lengthy and sumptuous dinners. He had a wonderful time with the planning and dreaming, but unfortunately passed away before any of it ever became a reality. Arthur charged through life with his friendly, smiling "Howarya, howarya, howarya!" and an absolutely positive attitude.

In 1975, Capt. Michael Scott of Seaward Adventures Ltd., Calgary, Alberta, approached me for a 130-foot Barquentine to be named *Outward Bound* to be used as a school-training vessel for young cadets. A vessel of this size required a whole new system of design and construction. The project got underway with a society being formed for planning, financing and management. The vessel would accommodate 40 cadets and an afterguard of 14 in 7 private cabins. All was going well until we learned that Canada had just changed the rules through Lloyd's Register, which now maintained that no passenger or cargo carrying vessel could be certified in Canada if constructed of wood! This decision was brought down after over 200 years of service by wooden vessels. Such a vessel must now be built of steel, concrete, fibreglass, or paper maché, but *not wood*! So the project was shelved but was to be resurrected a few years later under slightly different circumstances. Bureaucracy had once again stymied seagoing life in Canada.

Peter Reveen, a well-known hypnotist, came to see me in 1978 while he was in Halifax travelling with his show. Another very engaging yet egotistical man, he knew what he wanted as we custom-designed his 65-foot barquentine, *Impossiblist*. She was named after Peter's stage name and showed his personality throughout. Some of her special features included a 7- x 10-foot relief likeness of Peter's head for the foretopsail insignia, quarter galleries with heavy bow and stern decoration, painted ports, swivel guns, and 62 extra items of equipment. Accommodations included Peter's great-aft cabin with a 7-foot circular bed plus quarter-berths and toilet room with full-sized tub. Forward cabin housed three private double staterooms and large toilet room. Her deckhouse contained galley, lounge and inside steering station. Her aft-deck featured a large U-shaped sailing settee, wheel and engine controls. A comprehensive list of electronics completed her specifications with nothing left to chance. It was great fun following Peter's inventive mind throughout the design process and although she was never built either, Peter always maintained that one day she would be.

Also in 1978 we had an enquiry from a fisherman, Thomas B. Pink from Ramea, Newfoundland for a 28-foot Cape Island style fishing boat. This enquiry initiated a new design based on a traditional type of craft used in the local fishery, called the Cape Island boat. It is generally thought that the famous Cape Islander was developed by the Atkinson family in Cape Sable Island, Nova Scotia, hence its name. In Cape Breton, they were called snapper boats but the meaning of that term seems to have been lost in time. The craft was one of the first to make use of the internal combustion engine after the last days of small sailing fishing craft. In any case, they had been built in hundreds all along the Eastern Seaboard.

Mr. Pink wanted to use his boat in the Newfoundland fishery, and since the coastline and ocean conditions are different there than in Nova Scotia, I modified the hull slightly, making it a bit fuller for the increased power, with a wider beam aft, and greater hull capacity. The boat performed well and later led to many others being built from the same plans.

By 1979, I already had built two yachts from a new 40-foot ketch design called Nomad. She was a more compact version of our popular 46-foot Privateer, arranged with a great aft cabin and mid-ship enclosed deckhouse. Jim Omundson of Lake Oswego, Oregon saw the design, liked it and made an arrangement with us to build her in Oregon under royalty license. His plan was to build several and perhaps a Privateer or two as well. He obtained a large building for a boat shop and set to work. Jim was a fundamentalist Christian, and was sincere, meticulous and hard-working. He was absolutely in love with boats and set to building with a will; his work was the most exact and careful I had ever seen, amateur or professional. However, I doubt that the time invested for such exacting work resulted in a profitable product. His work was museum quality competing in a boatbuilding world of cost consciousness. Although it is wonderful to build to exacting standards, the price factor cannot be maintained.

Jim experienced the usual setbacks of setting up a new shop and a new business but he was always positive. Eventually though, the difficulties got to him and he abandoned the shop and his financial commitments. He simply disappeared. Some of his owners and backers took over to get their boats afloat.

Another home-built amateur boat was a 46-foot Privateer ketch set up by Stan Robertson in Clinton, Connecticut. Stan was a determined builder used to hard work. He decided to build the boat in fibreglass laid up in a plaster female mould in his backyard. This was a one-time production with the mould to be torn away after the hull was laid. She was a huge boat, appearing much larger internally because there were no frames or ceiling. Unfortunately Stan had not used enough parting wax on the mould and it had to be chipped away an inch at a time. Notwithstanding the problems, Stan successfully completed her, she was launched, equipped, and the family left for extended cruising in the Caribbean.

In 1980, I was approached by Major David Letson of Victoria, British Columbia, regarding the design for a proposed 130-foot Barque for cadet sail-training purposes. Major Letson had been a tank man in his former military career, but now was stationed at Esquimalt in charge of cadet training there. He had his own private yacht and was captivated by sailing and the sea. It was his dream to see a wooden sail-training tall ship built for Canada like the other 220 or so in countries around the world. His dream became an obsession and he poured a lot of energy and much of his own money into the project. I showed him my previous design, the 130-foot, 450 ton, *Outward Bound*, which he thought exactly suitable, becoming the basis for the new design. Named *Pacific Petrel*, she was to accommodate 30 cadets with an afterguard of 8 officers, cook and engineer. The barque rig was chosen, crossing eight yards for the opportunity of sail training aloft.

After preliminary discussions with Major Letson, and general decisions regarding dimensions and requirements, I went to work with a will for the largest vessel I had ever designed. No wooden barque had been designed or built in Canada for over 100 years, so a great deal of careful research was required. I pursued my search through Lloyd's specifications and in old designs discovered in our local Maritime Museum and Nova Scotia Archives. As I followed the progression of design at each source, it was somewhat frustrating to discover that each search ended with the words, "For further details on design see James D. Rosborough!" Flattering perhaps, but hardly helpful.

So, drawing on my accumulated experience and employing as much common sense as I could muster, I faced the blank white paper on my drawing board. I already had the entire design laid out mentally, with principal dimensions being as follows:

Length over-all: 130-feet; waterline length: 115 feet 9 inches, draft: 12 feet 6 inches; beam: 27 feet 6 inches, displacement: 450 (long) tons, sail Area: 9,015 sq. ft.

Scantlings were on the heavy side to be rigged for the work intended. Her main keel was 18 x 18 inches over an 18 x 18-inch steel-box ballast keel of 23 tons, 72 foot long. A 12 x 14-inch keelson was affixed over 8 x 10 inch construction floors. Frames were sawn, double-flitched totalling 9 x 9 inches. Also a rider keelson of 12 x 14 inches was employed to stiffen the backbone. Average planking was 3 inches as was ceiling. Clamps, shelves and deckbeams were heavy, to suit. When laid up on the stocks, her stem-head rose 30-feet above the beach.

The drawing took many months while Major Letson began to plan the building site and make overtures to lumber companies in British Columbia for the massive quantities of Douglas fir, Alaskan cedar and hardwoods necessary. I was invited to visit the site on the Forces base at Comox, British Columbia, and advise on set-up of buildings, sheds, and necessary wood-working machinery. It was a monumental undertaking, ably guided by Major Letson and his hired crew of master-builders. Much volunteer work was also employed from other officers and cadets on the base. Lumber, fastenings, and equipment began to flow in as I completed the detailed working drawings. The vessel was up in frame, planking going on, main engines and generators delivered, and other work proceeding well when a major setback occurred.

Apparently, Major Letson in his zeal for the project had been obtaining financing in the only way he could. Since the entire building project was a secret, funds had been requisitioned from Ottawa for a new mess hall, laundry and other bona-fide projects; the money had been channelled into construction of *Pacific Petrel* instead. Eventually, Ottawa got wind of what was going on, and put a stop to work on the project. Major Letson was up on the carpet, investigated and discharged from the service. This must have been heart-wrenching for him, as he had put all his time, energy and personal money into the all-consuming project.

Now Ottawa had a problem. The ship was being built on the Base at Comox, without approval, and in their opinion would not pass Canadian Steamship Inspection for passenger cadet service. Although several private parties wanted to buy her, this would necessitate completing the hull where she stood to be able to be launched and towed away, and military regulations precluded such civilian work. So, in their bureaucratic wisdom they decided to burn the entire vessel as she stood, upon the beach! It must have made a spectacular fire, but Canada was the poorer for not having her wooden barque to join others of the world's sail training vessels.

We were all greatly saddened by this turn of events in light of all the sincere effort, work and hope we had put into the *Pacific Petrel* project.

In 1981 Romeo Cipriani of Charlotte, North Carolina contacted me about an 80-foot schooner for his own use. He planned to have the vessel built in Guyana, South America, since he was in the timber exporting business there. This required a new and completely detailed design with plans to suit foreign builders. She was named *Viking* with principal dimensions of L.O.A.: 80 feet 6 inches, L.W.L.: 67 feet 9 inches, Draft: 9 feet 9 inches, Beam: 21 feet 4 inches, Displacement : 94 (long) tons, Sail area: 2,605 sq. ft., lowers only. Research was done, consultation with my local builders completed and the detailed design and drawings delivered to Romeo some eight months later. I am uncertain as to whether she was ever built or not, but I had a new design to add to my repertoire.

Other custom designs were completed over the years, some built and some not. Of interest were some that were adaptations of 80 to 100 feet wooden side draggers, retired out of the commercial fishery. These vessels all had similar hull shapes that made re-building and re-fitting to appear as square rigged vessels feasible.

One such was the dragger *Flying Cloud* owned by Bob Benson of Yarmouth, Nova Scotia. Bob wanted to convert the 85-foot vessel to be used as a dockside packet as a tourist commercial venture in Yarmouth. I surveyed and measured the vessel with him and concluded a conversion would be feasible. At several meetings with Bob at his period tourist inn, Church-ill Mansion Inn, near Yarmouth, plans were discussed and general specification made for the conversion. Churchill Mansion had been the summer estate of Aaron "Rudder" Churchill, an enterprising shipping and manufacturing magnate of the 1880s, so the new design for *Flying Cloud* felt right at home there.

The conversion plan was completed and work undertaken for the new dockside packet to compliment the romantic sea-going history of Nova Scotia.

FLYING CLOUD REBUILT AS A DOCKSIDE PACKET.

A FINAL TRIO FROM BLUEWATER BOATS

GLAD TIDINGS BEATS TO WINDWARD.

CHAPTER TWENTY-FOUR

DR. BRUCE TREMBLY WAS A busy and competent neurosurgeon from Waterville, Maine. He had a calm, but outgoing personality that made him a pleasure to be around. While his work was in the operating room, his heart was at sea, cruising in sailboats.

Bruce had seen Ken Gifford's brigantine *Sea Queen,* had sailed aboard Garfield Langworthy's *Sea Song,* and had visited aboard Admiral Black's

Valkyrie while she lay berthed at Pirates Cove Marina at Galesville, just south of Annapolis, Maryland. He began a correspondence with me with the idea of owning one of my vessels, a 45-foot brigantine with mid-ship cockpit and custom cabin layout for occasional chartering purposes.

We began correspondence and in August 1971 Bruce, his wife and children visited my wharf in Melville Cove, Halifax, on their return voyage cruising Nova Scotia. Bruce and I got to know each other a bit, and lay the groundwork for his brigantine. Letters and drawings were exchanged and in February 1972 a building contract was entered for *Glad Tidings.*

BRUCE AND MAREN TREMBLY.

With much correspondence and several visits from Bruce, her construction was ongoing at Bluewater Boats yard in DeBaies Cove over the balance of 1972 and 1973 with delivery in Halifax in June 1974 at a total cost of $55,000 including an extensive extras list of some 45 items. Bruce was extremely pleased with her sailing trials and sailed her to his home in Maine.

Later, he cruised the coast of Maine, working out the small problems always inherent in any new yacht, and making custom changes to equipment and rigging that he found beneficial to his own use of her.

In 1975, Bruce sent the following letter about *Glad Tidings* eventful exciting round-trip cruise to Bermuda and return.

Dear Doug,

We arrived back from Bermuda after six and one half days at sea, covering 900 miles on the log. The first thing we saw after leaving

Bermuda was the Portland Light Vessel. The Gulf Stream was boisterous as usual and although we never had seas greater than 12 feet, we were not bothered a bit by them. On one occasion, we were running with the beam sea and a beam wind, actually for several days, with just the two staysails. One night a giant wave came up and crashed right over the boat burying the helmsman in water and heeling us over so that our yard touch the water. One crewman was in the rigging, for some unknown reason, and he felt that the boat had virtually disappeared. This wave generated a fantastic amount of water below and I was sleeping right under the skylight and was drenched, even though the skylight was closed. This didn't seem to hurt anything and didn't even raise the level of the bilge very much but certainly wetted everything inside every drawer and locker. The boat behaved beautifully and on another evening the wind picked up from 40 knots on the anenometer to 70. The last I saw it was 70 and we were too busy at that point getting the staysails off to watch further. She even sailed herself at several knots with the beam wind under bare poles. Seasickness wasn't as much of a problem on the way back and after three days, everybody seemed happy although I was the only one who was able to tolerate cooking below. Hot meals certainly raised the morale of the crew. The entire crew deserted me when we arrived in Portland after clearing customs and I single-handed the boat back to Wiscasset. She certainly is easy enough as long as one is prudent and anticipates sail changes and is conservative about the way the boat is handled. Actually, I had a really good time being alone on her under sail.

With best regards,

Bruce Trembly

Also in 1975, Bruce took *Glad Tidings* to the Newport International-in-the-Water Sailboat Show. We met him there where we used her as our display boat. Hundreds of visitors and prospective buyers were welcomed aboard, notwithstanding a gale of hurricane proportions that came through one day causing considerable confusion and some damage, but fortunately not to *Glad Tidings*. It was a wonderful, hectic, and busy show although no immediate sales were realized from it.

Bruce did intermittent chartering as well as the usual maintenance and local cruising during 1976. During this period several storms and hurricanes were encountered. In one, *Glad Tidings* broke her moorings and went sailing off across the harbor by herself, eventually tangling with a steel bridge. The embarrassment was far worse than the damage.

In 1977, Bruce sailed north once again, cruising the Atlantic waters of Newfoundland and Nova Scotia, including the Gulf of St. Lawrence and Bras D'Or Lakes. By now he was actively chartering when possible, featuring circumnavigations of the islands of Newfoundland, Cape Breton and Prince Edward. It was all very romantic, picturesque and adventurous for those aboard the brigantine.

At the close of the season, Bruce left *Glad Tidings* at our wharves in Halifax. There she attracted much interest and photographs, as she lay nestled in our secluded Melville Cove.

Over the next number of years, Bruce cruised *Glad Tidings* on many adventures, including being the star in a re-enactment of the founding of Port Royal under the command of Samuel de Champlain, in August 1980. Invited guests for the occasion included Prime Minister Pierre Trudeau and his son Sasha, Premier John Buchanan and Mi'kmaq Chief Membertou. It was a grand and glorious day with many speeches, flags, and ceremony as *Glad Tidings* sailed into history.

In April 1972, we signed a building contract, another Privateer ketch, for Stanley Willson of Oshawa, Ontario. Stan was a well-organized businessman who owned and operated a large General Motors dealership. We incorporated a list of some 40 extra items, including Honduras mahogany planking, a semi-enclosed wheelhouse, and dinghy in stern davits, diesel furnace, and an exotic array of equipment. Stan chose her paint and upholstery colours as well as her name, which was to be *Willygon*. I queried Stan about the name and he explained that when his

Typical engine room, 46' ketch.

friends went to the yacht club to look for him and the boat wasn't there, they would say, "Well, Willy's gone."

All went well in her construction, but a few weeks before delivery day, we were advised that Stan had died suddenly of a heart attack. We subsequently advertised and re-sold the boat for Stan's estate, but I thought how ironic her name was—Stan really was gone!

Her new owner was Bill Whittaker who introduced himself as a poor country boy from the mid-west U.S.A. He was a stocky young man whom I suspected was a whole lot smarter than he let on.

Bill had originally contacted us in 1969 for the construction of a Privateer ketch, which he told us he expected to be able to pay for from the proceeds of some forthcoming insurance settlements. Subsequently, he had fallen prey to personal and financial difficulties as he explained to us in a letter of March 17, 1972: "I had a great deal of personal trouble and pressure. My wife, Kate, and I separated and my own family turned against me. I was very unstable (mentally) and did a lot of foolish things." After a series of false starts and N.S.F. cheques to us in 1969, Bill had disappeared until turning up again in January 1974.

Willygon's name changed to *Badu* and though largely complete, Bill wanted a few extra items installed. He and his new wife Sue returned in July to take delivery of the boat, but they did not have the necessary funds. Bill did arrange a bank note with us to pay outstanding balances, but then returned to the U.S.A. to raise funds. Finally, he returned to Halifax on November 26, 1974 to sail away.

I recommended he haul the boat for painting, do necessary maintenance chores and prepare for the unpredictable North Atlantic in December. He had brought a VHF radio with him, but had neither insurance nor life raft, so I convinced him to place insurance which was arranged through my own broker. I made a life raft available to him and asked if he was going to have the VHF installed. He replied that he had run out of time, did not think he would need a radio but that if he did, Sue could stand on the cabin roof and hold the antenna aloft!

His friend, Russell Franklin, joined him for crew, and with great misgivings, I watched *Badu* leave harbor the next day, bound for Plymouth, Massachusetts.

What happened next was pieced together from events told to us by Russell Franklin. He said their voyage from Halifax was uneventful until first landfall in the U.S. about 9:00 P.M. December 1, 1974. Bill and Russell shared the helm; the vessel performed well and sea conditions were favorable.

After midnight, weather conditions began to worsen as the approaching storm moved northwest. They contacted the U.S. Coast Guard at Cape Ann, were warned of the storm and advised to seek shelter, but Bill decided he could make Cohasset and proceeded onwards. He was at the wheel and steering was responding normally given the turbulent sea conditions, until they struck something. Russell took over the wheel while Bill went below to check the vessel. When he came back on deck, he reported it was useless to steer any longer as the steering equipment had sustained damage. Within minutes they grounded firmly although the vessel was lively, being pounded by waves. Bill instructed Russell to inflate the life raft and take himself and Susan the few remaining yards to shore.

In a screaming hurricane and high seas the vessel apparently had struck rocks, carrying away the keel heelpiece and its lower rudder support gudgeon. With nothing to hold it in place and battered by high waves, the rudder un-shipped and sank from the vessel. There was now no steering and Bill reported later the vessel going around in circles until beaching among the jagged Black Rocks off Cohasset.

The early winter storm was severe all right. Winds were over 55 m.p.h., storm-driven tides washed out roads, damaged buildings, closed highways and commuter trains, caused coastal vessel sinkings, airplane crashes, and highway deaths. Much shoreline property was damaged and shipping affected.

Bill stayed aboard with the engine running until coaxed ashore by the police. He said it wasn't until then he shut the engine off! If the rudder with its 1 1/2-inch shaft had been out of the boat for any appreciable time, the inflow of water would have flooded the vessel and engine as well!

Over the next few hours of darkness, *Badu* was unmercifully driven up over the Black Rocks 1,000 yards towards the shore. In the first dim light of dawn, she was beached high with her starboard hull planking stove in; a lesser vessel would have been ground to a pulp. As it was, Bill made two phone calls; one to the insurance company and one to Fairhaven Marine to request salvage. Fairhaven replied that it was useless to salvage as nothing could be left after such a storm. Bill persisted; they came down to look and were amazed at the minimal damage and stoutness of the yacht. Cranes and flatbeds were brought, rigging and masts removed and the boat slung and lifted onto a flatbed trailer.

In his negotiations with the insurance company, Bill maintained that he had lost steerageway well to seaward, that he had not struck before the final grounding and that the whole endeavor was not his fault. To make a long story short, the insurance paid his claim, subrogated, and instructed their lawyers to sue us for faulty design and/or construction. I couldn't believe it!

Photos taken at the time clearly showed the missing heelpiece which could only have occurred by severe grounding. This opinion was later supported by accredited marine surveyors, who stated that, "This heelpiece had evidently been carried away during a grounding incident. That it could be carried away by wave action is simply inconceivable."

A final clincher, of course, was that the rudder could not have carried away while the propeller was turning or it would have jammed and stalled the engine and/or beaten itself to pieces. The propeller was perfect after salvage.

The case dragged on through a long series of discoveries and sworn statements from all concerned. Years went by and thousands of dollars were spent. The insurance company counsel was Vincent Prager of Montreal. By October 1982, all my money was gone. I requested my lawyers to transmit to Vincent Prager that further pursuit would be useless, regardless of who was right or wrong. Our pleas were ignored and Prager bore onward. My lawyers requested that I release them from the case, as they weren't getting paid either. I said, "No, no, you're doing a great job, just keep on going." "But you can't pay us," they replied. "Keep on going anyway," I said. They said that if I wouldn't discharge them, they would have to apply to the Federal Courts to have themselves dismissed. In due course, a weighty document arrived bearing gold seals and blue ribbons resembling a prize from a country fair. The papers advised Prager that my lawyers couldn't get paid and were leaving the case. Prager finally must have gotten the message since we never heard another thing from him. Also our case was pretty strong with expert witnesses and opinions galore which may have affected the outcome.

Bill Whittaker had his yacht repair paid for with oceans of cruising in view. In November 1976, I had a very friendly letter from him, written on his *Badu* letterhead from Titusville, Florida, just as if nothing had ever happened! It confirmed my suspicion that he was not the poor country boy he had first described himself as being.

The last boat we were to build at Bluewater Boats in DeBaies Cove was *Whimsey*, Hull #13, a privateer ketch for Paul Lawrence and Arthur Probasco of Berkeley, California. Paul and Arthur were both building inspectors for the city of Berkeley, had met there, and became friends. They were pleasant, quiet-spoken, and calm. They were a pleasure to build for. *Whimsey* was simply appointed with galley forward, open centre cockpit and marconi sail plan.

She was well built and delivered to Paul and Art in Halifax, July 31, 1975 at a total cost of $70,000 with a few extras. It all went very smoothly and I remember thinking we had finally learned how to do it right.

Paul and Art cruised down the Atlantic seaboard with only minor mishaps, writing the good news to us enroute.

Unfortunately, Art developed very serious arthritis, and so they had to give up a life on the ocean and move to the dryer climate of Arizona. The boat was re-sold in Florida and presumably continues her adventures.

A Quartet from Windjammer

Sailing trials, *Polynya*.

CHAPTER TWENTY-FIVE

BACK AT WINDJAMMER YACHTS in Parrsboro, Osmond Yorke and his men were busily at work on another 45-foot Distant Star brigantine for Lou Tolve of Mamaroneck, New York. Lou was an intelligent and pleasant young man in the amusement park business, running roller coasters and the like, so I thought he should be well conditioned to sailing a cruising yacht over the ocean waves.

The vessel was a typical brigantine except for all teak exterior trim and a few extras. The 6,000 hours of building proceeded without serious incident. Osmond Yorke said the $75,000 vessel took seven months to build with carefully selected local material and all teak exterior trim throughout 1975.

Lou Tolve arrived with his crew and after trials, set sail for his homeport in New York. Lou remarked he was well satisfied with Nova Scotian craftsmanship as he planned for future Caribbean cruising.

The next boat at Windjammer was a completely new design. I planned to offer a compact version of my 45-foot series and so designed the 35-foot Pilgrim. I offered her in either a cutter or ketch rig, although I felt she would handle better as a ketch due to her full under-body and short ends. She still featured a great aft cabin but in addition was flush-decked and carried a fully enclosed deck-house as well as aft sailing station. The principal difference between Pilgrim and Privateer was that there

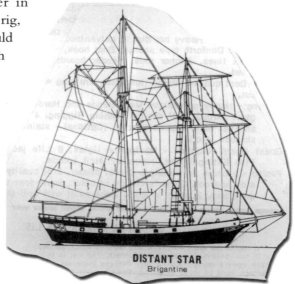

DISTANT STAR
Brigantine

was little storage space and tankage in Pilgrim. She was all accommodations. Nevertheless, she made a fine pocket cruiser and showed a constant cruising speed of 6 knots whether under power with a 35-50 h.p. diesel or sail.

Harold Snyder saw the design, liked it, and contracted for the first, a cutter, to be named *Polynya*. Harold was a scientist and an ocean researcher with Memorial University in St. John's, Newfoundland. He was also project manager and Executive V.P. for directing the construction of the massive Churchill Falls hydroelectric scheme. During our building time with *Polynya*, Harold was Director of the C-Core program, short for Center for Cold Ocean Resources Engineering, based in St. John's. He explained to me that a Polynya was an area of open water in the Arctic ice, which didn't freeze over due to bottom currents moving upwards. It was favored as a safe haven by vessels navigating those areas, hence, her name.

HAROLD SNYDER—A SCIENTIST WHO YEARNED FOR THE OLDEN DAYS OF SAIL.

She was completed at Parrsboro and delivered to Harold at Halifax, June 1977 at a total of $63,000 with $18,000 of extras installed. The shakedown cruise from Parrsboro to Halifax gave us the opportunity to see how she handled at sea, proving sail rig, seakindliness, and power.

Another Pilgrim, *Calluna*, Hull #507, this time rigged as a ketch, was contracted for with yet another Canadian, Albert Ebner of Port Lambton, Ontario in May 1977 and set up on the ways at Windjammer in Parrsboro. She was built to a power away stage of construction, but with exterior and sail rig complete. Albert was a woodworking instructor in Ontario, and planned to complete her interior himself. Consequently, we supplied only the cabin floor and main bulkheads. Albert would do makeshift camping aboard on his delivery sail home.

She left Halifax in July 1978 having cost Albert, $55,000. We heard from him again on his safe arrival in Ontario saying that he was working on and sailing the vessel.

At the same time of building the two 35-foot Pilgrims, a 46-foot Distant Star brigantine was set up for Ken Dorman of Juneau, Alaska, an experienced sailor and competent technician. He had his own ideas of design, construction, and equipment and worked along with us during the vessel's building and commissioning.

Megan D.'s layout was fairly basic in a galley-forward arrangement. Her center cockpit housed the engine controls, and was protected by a folding dodger.

We launched the vessel in Parrsboro in September 1978, rigged, and outfitted her at the new government wharf next to Osmond Yorke's Quonset boat shop. My sons, Bob and Kevin as well as their cousin Martin Trites, a rigger, worked hard putting it all together and we had an interesting and friendly time—almost a party atmosphere for all concerned— builders, riggers and owners. The vessel cost a total of $73,000 by 1978. Prices had risen considerably since our early days of building the same size vessel!

Megan D. departed Parrsboro September 11, 1978 for Alaska via the Caribbean, Panama Canal, and West Coast to Juneau. Credit must be given to Ken for his determination, seamanship, and mechanical ability as they safely reached their destination and continued many years of living aboard and cruising in Northern Latitudes.

FOUR PRIVATEERS FROM THERIAULT'S

A SHIPYARD FULL OF ROSBOROUGH VESSELS NEARING COMPLETION AT
A.F. THERIAULT AND SONS, METEGHAN RIVER.

CHAPTER TWENTY-SIX

IN FEBRUARY 1972, WE HAD AN enquiry from Dean Moburg, Seattle, Washington for a Privateer ketch. Dean operated an office of court reporters in a world of legal debate, lawyers, accusations, and proof. I recognized where he was coming from, and realized I would have to be very careful to dot all the i's and cross all the t's in dealing with him. Consequently, his contract including extras had to be concise, detailed and professionally executed.

A lengthy correspondence of Dean's desires, specifications and equipment, drawings and the like, led to a visit by him and his wife, Karen, in October 1972. As Dean sat in my 10 per cent chair, he introduced Karen, his wife, who sat patiently while Dean described his dream-ship. Her name would be *Golden Girl*. I asked if he was naming her after the former movie star Jean Harlow, and he replied emphatically, "Certainly not! I'm naming her after Karen." Politically, I thought it might be best not to pursue this line of thought, as I stifled a raised eyebrow.

Many details were discussed with custom layout and lengthy extras lists. Finally, building contract #415 was signed in January 1973 for the custom vessel including 42 extra items at $52,000, total. Dean had selected a brilliant signal yellow paint for her hull, decks, and masts. Countertops and upholstery were yellow-gold. Dean certainly carried his obsession to the limit throughout!

Cabin layout was something of a new departure for us in that *Golden Girl* boasted an enclosed deckhouse incorporating settees and berths as well as an inside steering station. Forward cabin was divided into two separate private staterooms and a large toilet room with a shower. Her great aft cabin contained the galley, a washroom, dining table with large squared settee and quarter-berths up in the stern and quarter windows. It was a good and sensible arrangement utilizing available space to the maximum.

Her sail rig was marconi main and mizzen but with a provision for a main yard for square sail and raffee. On the West Coast of North America, the prevailing winds are either from the north or from the south, so these sails could be used to great advantage.

Lengthy and detailed correspondence ensued with Dean throughout construction. He was busy with his legal work, so all reports and decisions had to be carried out by mail. Nevertheless, building went on reasonably well despite all the extras and detailed custom specifications.

Towards the end of construction Dean became very busy and asked his friend and legal counsel, Charles Perry, to represent him for acceptance, payments, guarantees, and the like. It was now time to ship the vessel, which we had agreed with Dean would be by rail from Nova Scotia to British Columbia. There, Dean would accept delivery, launch and rig the vessel and sail her to Seattle. We had previously agreed to a fixed charge of $800 for loading and blocking aboard a rail car.

We began our negotiation with the CNR only to find serious dimensional restrictions due to the route having to go through a series of tunnels in the Rocky Mountains. For a while, it looked as though it would be impossible to ship by rail. This was a serious blow to us as we began detailed enquiry of the railway. I must say they were entirely co-operative, providing us drawings of tunnel measurements for loading. *Golden Girl* would just not fit no matter how we placed her. Finally, it was suggested we angle-load at 45 degrees. Drawings were made, submitted, and accepted. Final tolerances allowed for only three-eights of an inch on one side to the tunnel and three-quarters of an inch on the other! In addition, it would be necessary to slow the train going through eight miles of tunnels, with two railway brakemen walking ahead and behind the car all the way through!

LIFT AND PLACE. LIFT AND PLACE. LOADING *GOLDEN GIRL* AT SIDING, METEGHAN STATION.

Given these restrictions, we took *Golden Girl* to the nearest siding at Meteghan Station on a low bed trailer together with a host of workmen, timbers, tools, and a large crane. We slung the boat and lifted her onto the railcar, then began the tipping process to the necessary 45° angle. Railway inspectors hopped up with their measuring tapes and said, "No, still too high." We lifted and moved her an inch. "Still too wide." We lifted again; now it was down to fractions of an inch. This process continued all that day while the crane lifted and replaced; lifted and replaced. The stress level was intense, especially for Russell Theriault and myself. The inspectors finally said, "She's okay right there, don't move anything!"

The next day we began the blocking, bracing, and cabling down. One taffrail had to be removed and everything securely blocked aboard the rail car. Wooden bunks were provided to carefully cradle the boat throughout her length. It was a monumental exercise in loading and blocking, not to mention stress and patience. Windows were covered, and a tarp rigged for a total cover. She finally left on her trip west.

Dean had become increasingly anxious due to all the delays as delivery time stretched onward. At one point he even threatened to sue us for inability to ship. However, it worked out as we resolved one problem after the other. The loading, which we had contracted to Dean for $800, finally cost us $2,800, plus all our own time and expenses!

Golden Girl finally arrived at her destination. Dean began sailing her and I am sure he enjoyed his pride and joy. He asked our permission to be our West Coast U.S.A. representative and set himself up commercially, which, I am sure, provided him with an economic advantage. He corresponded with a number of prospective buyers, none of which materialized, unfortunately.

I later heard from Dick Mealey in January 1978 that he had bought *Golden Girl* and was fitting her out for his own use. He told us, among other interests, he owned a gold mine in Alaska, which I mused would be a good thing to have for anyone operating a cruising sailboat. I remembered the old quip, owning a wooden boat is like standing in a cold shower tearing up $1,000 bills.

I heard later from Emery McCall who had bought the boat in 1980 but lost it in a divorce settlement. He had renamed her *Destiny* and painted her British green. He said she was beautiful and that he had lived aboard and cruised the U.S.A. west coast and Mexico. Apparently, the vessel was subsequently seized, neglected and had sunk in Mexico. I prepared a summary of replacement costs in 1994, which took into account the fact that she had cost $55,000 to build in 1973 and that we understood another $46,555

U.S. in extra equipment had been subsequently installed. Her fair market value could certainly be between $120,000 and $140,000 as equipped, given her good condition.

During the stressful days of 1973 I received a letter of notice from A.F. Theriault & Son, Ltd., as follows:

Dear Mr. Rosborough;

We regret that we are forced to have to inform you that building contracts from this date on will be subject to revision and re-pricing. Through recent Incentive programs and labour legislation instituted by our Provincial and Federal Governments, we have no choice but to increase our labour and overhead rates. As well, materials have risen more than usual over the last 12 months. Therefore, after serious consultation with all our management staff, we find that it will be necessary to increase our prices to you for future yachts by approximately 15 percent. We are ready to meet with you at any time to discuss contract prices for the various yachts involved and trust that we may be able to co-operate on future yachts as we have in the past.

Sincerely,

J. Russell Theriault

The new progressive changes in labour laws and large expansion grants referred to in the letter were introduced by the government as make-work and benefit programs for general workers. The opinion of the boat builders was, "Why should we work hard for six dollars an hour while Uncle Louie is just leaning on a shovel up the road for ten dollars?" So our boat shops had to increase their wages. But 6,000 hours to build a boat at increased wage rates put final costs beyond the breaking point as prospective customers regretfully headed over the hills and out of sight. The squeeze was now on with the costs of our yachts rising alarmingly, the golden days of wooden boat building were over and we had to struggle for every new contract.

In May 1972, we had contracted with William G. Neill of Ontario for a Privateer ketch with much custom work and numerous extras. Bill, together with his mother, owned a ranch called Flint C, which he told me stood for Flint Creek, so he named his yacht *Flint Sea*, to match. He was a tall man with a wife and young family and had specific ideas of how his boat should be laid out, built, and equipped to accommodate them. Right or wrong, he knew what he wanted. *Flint Sea* had a raised-headroom enclosed centre cabin which eventually housed a small organ and a crystal chandelier, as well as the inside steering station. A large 'thwart-ship owner's double stateroom was installed in the forward cabin, including full toilet room with shower. A normal galley-aft layout was used in the aft cabin and the usual V-berths in her fo'c's'le.

Bill visited the boat shop to witness construction and progress. On one occasion, he was staying at the local motel with his mother, wife, and children. As we adults sat down for supper in the dining room, Bill ordered a normal three-course meal, and had the soup sent down to their room for the children. He and his wife ate the balance of the meal. How strange, I thought, that must be how wealthy people can afford yachts. *Flint Sea* was built and delivered to Bill for a total of $70,000, including $16,000 in extras during the 1973 season, before the new labour costs came into effect.

The third Privateer, Rebel's Chariot (Hull #417) was for Brian Tranter of Newmarket, Ontario. She was largely of standard construction but layout included a fully enclosed centre deckhouse containing galley and dining area. Her aft cabin featured an athwart ship double berth in the stern and quarter windows, while the forward cabin contained lounge and berth areas. She was completed and delivered to Brian at Meteghan in July 1973 at a total cost of $46,500.

Brian's plan was to cruise up the St. Lawrence River to Ontario and then down the Mississippi. Later I heard that the vessel had wintered in Canada, but I lost track of her after that.

In May 1972, Dick Allen resurfaced, this time ready to order a Privateer ketch for himself. As noted earlier, Dick Allen had been Dick Shaw's right-hand man in Simplex Corp., when he was contracting and selling many of our earlier boats. Dick Allen had delivered several yachts and had been instrumental in supplying equipment and completing contracts for their construction. Dick was always in and around the marine scene in New England and Florida. He had a wealth of experience and knowledge and I was glad to hear from him again. We had become friends in those earlier days and I was happy to finally build the boat for which he had waited so long.

I drove to Yarmouth, on May 13, 1972, my 44th birthday, and met him at the Grand Hotel for negotiations. It was his plan to found a yacht brokerage and sales office in East Hampton, Connecticut, to be called Heritage Yachts, where he would act as our New England sales agent. Our meeting was cordial as always and plans were drawn to begin his Privateer ketch, *Privateer*, Hull #418, and our sales partnership.

With this happy beginning, we laid his keel and signed building contract #418 on June 10, 1972 for a standard layout, gaff-topsail ketch to cost $40,000. Construction proceeded in an orderly fashion, and Dick took possession in Meteghan November 28, 1972. He sailed to Connecticut without incident and berthed her there for a number of years. He declared he never had any problems with her which was, I expect, at least partly due to his good maintenance and seamanship. He showed her to prospective buyers although no sales ever materialized. In my experience, you had to talk to one thousand dreamers before one sale was made.

In August 1975, Dick sent us a clipping from Connecticut showing his *Privateer* featured in a sailing pageant of the Manhatten Savoyards who were a singing group performing the Gilbert and Sullivan operetta *H.M.S. Pina-*

fore. They boarded the ketch in full costume and rendered excerpts as she sailed along.

Dick cruised from New England to the Caribbean and Bahamas over the next few years. By August 1978, he berthed in Ft. Lauderdale and had put *Privateer* up for sale, partly because he had bought a marine supply and hardware store. So after six years of sailing, Dick had swallowed the anchor, but planned sailing again when he had recouped his finances. The sea is always in the sailor's blood, and its call cannot be denied for too long.

INGOMAR, HMS DOLPHIN, AND OBSESSION
A SPECIAL TRIO FROM METEGHAN RIVER

RUSSELL THERIAULT ON THE BOWSPRIT OF *INGOMAR* DURING TRIALS.

CHAPTER TWENTY-SEVEN

EARLY IN 1972 WE HAD AN ENQUIRY from Nicholas Phillips of Ft. Lauderdale, Florida for one of our 65-foot vessels. Nick had seen *Wandrian II* and two other Privateer ketches in Florida, liked what he saw and wrote to us. We sent him our brochures and on April 17, 1972 he replied:

Dear Mr. Rosborough:

I have studied the brochures on Bluenose Boats with great interest. Your designs and the construction appear to be the closest approach to what I have been looking for that I have encountered so far.

My requirements, in order of importance, are: seaworthiness and safety, comfort, ease of handling, ease of maintenance, and cost, combined for permanent, year-around living aboard and long-distance cruising in U.S. and European waters, for two to six people, all adults and more likely one to three couples.

I am not interested in speed or windward ability especially, preferring to use power to get to windward. I will cruise and anchor out, and seldom use marinas or docks except for refuelling and provisioning, with an occasional marina stop for friends or a day or two for an excursion ashore. I'll be short-handed much of the time but want the brigantine rig with roller furling, reefing, winches, etc., to make handling her short-handed as easy and safe as possible.

The 65-foot Vagabond design with various additions, alterations and alternatives is what I hope to be able to swing, but the sail-away price given is too general for me to estimate the final cost of what I want. I am enclosing a sketch of the interior layout desired, and a long list of notes, comments, equipment, and ideas which are, of course, quite tentative and subject to change, but which will, I believe, give you a good idea of what I have in mind.

I have had the opportunity to inspect briefly two 45-foot ketches— the Sea Chase and the Wandrian II, so I have some real idea of the construction and finish. Furthermore, I grew up on the New England coast, so I am quite familiar with this type of work. It suits me fine.

What I have set out above is the culmination of a dream of more than 40 years, backed up by the many years of racing, cruising, studying, instructing at yacht clubs, and commanding various small boats, both sail and power, for the U.S. Coast Guard in World War II, from Nova Scotia to Florida, Bermuda, Bahamas, and the South Pacific. I realize that converting my dream to reality may not be possible because of cost or other factors, but it seemed best to set out the entire idea first. It will all take some time, and I am aware that the many questions I have asked, and the many estimates requested will take a lot of your time, but I am quite convinced that your designs, construction, and cost offer my best chance to turn my dream into reality.

Sincerely,

Nicholas Phillips

We replied to his questions and subsequently he and his wife Betty visited us at A.F. Theriault's yard at Meteghan River June 4, 1972. There, they met the builders, examined Carleton C. Hitchcock's 65-foot Vagabond brigantine, *Scotia Mist*, and other 45-foot vessels being built. They then drove with me back to Halifax, saw more vessels at our wharves, and had dinner with us and Edwin Ray Phillips at our local Armdale Yacht Club. We spent a day in our office in Halifax going over plans and specifications for them for their new 65-foot Vagabond barquentine *Ingomar*. Nick left a deposit cheque and I was to forward custom plans, detailed specifications and a building contract to him in Florida.

During his visit, Nick, now 58 years old, had told me he had worked 18 years in Venezuela as manager for Gulf Oil. He and Betty had one daughter just being married and one son still in college in New York. They were currently living in a furnished apartment in Ft. Lauderdale but looking forward to living aboard and cruising their new yacht. As a boy, Nick and his brother lived near Boston and sailed both Tancook and Alden schooners, so he was no stranger to either cruising or wooden boats. He was a Certified Public Accountant, so his lengthy correspondence was accompanied by long detailed lists of everything to do with *Ingomar*, defined and priced in neatly listed columns. I think he derived almost as much pleasure from this phase of planning as he did in taking delivery.

In any case, we signed a building contract on July 15, 1972 for the vessel at $97,000, including $17,000 worth of extras.

Nick was retired in his apartment in Florida, so the building and equipping of the boat became his whole life and work. He spent many long hours re-working plans, lists, specification, guarantees and warranties, all of which had to be carefully scrutinized, amended and noted as they arrived by mail.

Nick and Betty visited several times, and their visits were always cordial as Nick delighted in the impressions of his dream-ship being born. On one occasion nearing the end of construction, he brought a valuable double-barrel Parker shotgun in leather case and a Winchester carbine. He presented the shotgun to me in appreciation of all my hard work, and the Winchester to my draughtsman at that time, Lloyd d'Entrement. Lloyd had carefully drawn all of the plans and revisions for *Ingomar* under my direction.

Delivery time neared as masting, rigging and all the last minute equipment and extras were completed. After launching and sailing trials, *Ingomar* left for her home in Florida on August 27, 1973. All up, she had cost Nick and Betty $113,000.

They cruised the boat to some degree and lived aboard at marinas in New England and Florida until February 1975 when they advised me they planned to offer her for sale as she had become too much work and too expensive for them. She was in Panamanian registry so duties, taxes, and commissions would have to be paid to sell her in either the U.S.A. or Canada. Many attempts were made at a sale, with some prospective buyers dragging on the process for months.

Proper maintenance on the big boat was difficult for Nick. When a prospective buyer, Mr. Millar, ordered a comprehensive survey of the vessel, decay was found in part of her garboard planks, some worm in the rudder and sternpost, some dry rot in the stemhead, knightheads and stanchion posts, and cabin sills. The repair estimate in Florida in 1978 was $20,000. Nick reduced his asking price from $140,000 to $100,000, but there were still no takers.

By 1979, Nick had paid the U.S. Duty and put her in U.S. registry. Her price was further reduced to $90,000. *Ingomar* was finally sold to a buyer from Idaho who took her around to the Seattle area.

In 1994, Nick contacted me for plans for *Ingomar* as he was building a scale model. He later told me that he put almost as many hours in the model—2 years, 8 months and one week—as we did originally in the full-sized vessel. Of course, he was once again re-living his dream, but this time from the comfort of his armchair.

In January 1971, we had an enquiry from Hollis Baker of Grand Rapids, Michigan for a square-rigged vessel similar to our Aquarius design. He liked the appearance and romance of a revolutionary period ship with which he could let his dreams be expressed.

Hollis was a genteel aristocrat, born to position and affluence. He had a keen and decisive mind in a social position of command, used to having his decisions obeyed without question. He was heir to the distinguished Baker Fine Furniture Company and the fortune it had generated. When I first met Hollis, he was funding the arts as well as travelling worldwide. He owned a nice modern 44-foot yacht, but liked the idea of commanding a square-rigger. I asked him what he would name her and he replied, *HMS Dolphin*. "I don't think you can call her that, Hollis," I remarked remembering the restrictions of British law. "*I can!*" he asserted firmly.

In our several forthcoming meetings, he told me that while traveling in England, he had seen a cute little railway with trains, stations, uniforms and all its paraphernalia. He liked it, bought it, and had the entire thing taken apart and shipped to Michigan. There he bought a dis-used 18-mile railroad that ran from Grand Rapids to Boyne City, and over three years, set the whole thing up as a tourist attraction. Hollis sometimes wore a railway engineer's striped cap and distributed advertising folders about his railway as he went from place to place. "You know, I really think that this year we will break even," he once confided to me.

Gradually, I developed some idea who I was dealing with. Hollis always traveled first-class and stayed at the best hotels. Sometimes his wife traveled with him; a gracious lady, immaculately attired and bejewelled, complementing Hollis' own neat and proper appearance and personality.

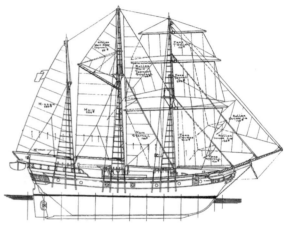

SAIL PLAN, *HMS DOLPHIN*.

We began a correspondence in January 1971, which continued in greater and greater detail as Hollis defined his wishes, and they later made plans to visit us in Halifax for preliminary talks. As it happened, *Rattlesnake* was on the ways at A.F. Theriault's, so Hollis and his wife decided to visit me at Yarmouth and the nearby boat shop to view an Aquarius-sized vessel. It was April 3, 1972 when we first met in person. The meeting went well, and as a result, I began to prepare custom drawings of *HMS Dolphin*. Hollis had sailed yachts all his life, so he knew what he wanted, and more specifically, what he did not want. By September 1972, plans had progressed to a point where we could begin to get contract prices from the builder. Hollis' correspondence now became detailed in earnest requiring much concentrated research and reply on my part. I knew I was dealing with an experienced and demanding man who investigated and defined every detail. Many lists of extras and specifications ensued, leading up to a building contract dated October 25, 1972 at $93,800 for the vessel as then described, built to complete sail-away.

This, of course, did not prevent many other additions and changes which were ongoing over the entire building period. At least we were getting closer to defining *HMS Dolphin*.

Construction was of the very best of materials available to us. Typical was one-and-a-half-inch mahogany plank, all teak exterior and interior trim, lead ballast inside and out and all stainless steel bolts and fastenings. Hollis would have only the best available in everything.

Notwithstanding the exacting work and attention to detail that was required, building went well, with Hollis visiting periodically. At that time, typical wages for boat shop labour was $5.00 an hour. By 1999 costs, *HMS Dolphin* would have cost approximately $720,000.

As Hollis travelled around the world, he kept buying things to go on *HMS Dolphin*, for example a black leather

HMS DOLPHIN: ATTENTION TO DETAIL.

studio couch for his main saloon at $1,500, which arrived by truck from California. Many other custom items arrived and were installed on the yacht.

As construction was drawing to a close, a young man arrived at the yard and introduced himself as Mr. Baker's captain. He had come early to apply seven more coats of high-sheen varnish to the vessels trim and clean her to make her ready for Hollis' arrival. The balance of equipping, rigging and commissioning concluded as delivery day arrived, October 9, 1973. With all due fanfare and excitement, sailing trials and photographs were completed and *HMS Dolphin* left for the U.S.A.

Hollis corresponded often as they cruised from New England to his winter home in Palm Beach, Florida. On May 13, 1974 he wrote:

"The boat seems to continue to be a great success, and we are most pleased with it all the time.

Of course, we have done a great deal to her now, and she is being hauled out this week for a new bottom painting and a complete working over of the topsides—planing, sanding, glazing and painting—so she should be in real yacht condition when we take her north this summer to the Chesapeake."

He always kept her in show-room condition, as he would not tolerate anything less. In later years, I heard she had been sold and made her new homeport in San Diego, California.

In October 1971, Harry R. Carter contacted me from Moscow, Pennsylvania with an enquiry for a custom 36-foot yacht including a set of preliminary drawings he had made as to layout and rig. This vessel was a departure from my usual designs, but Harry was adamant about what he wanted. Firmly convinced that she would be the finest yacht ever built, he later confided in me that everyone should have just such a vessel, and believed that once his was built, a great flood of interest and enquiries would follow.

Due to the press of other business, it was some time before I was able to finalize the custom design, which eventually gelled as a sensible 36-foot marconi main and mizzen ketch rigged motor-sailer to be called *Obsession*, Hull #421, featuring a large deckhouse saloon and spacious cockpit aft. The entire forward cabin was given over to a toiletroom, galley, and owner's centreline double berth. She was a one-man boat built around Harry's ego.

Being a specific custom design, many altered drawings and revisions of specifications were required before we went to a building contract for $37,000 in November 1972. Throughout the year, there was much correspondence and input from Harry. It seemed he liked to imbibe a bit in the evening, giving vent to enthusiastic telephone calls predicting a glowing future for his design. Many ideas were discussed and much correspondence exchanged.

Throughout construction, Harry ordered four detailed pages of extras without quoted contract prices. All the custom design, drawings, etc. as well as engineering and research were included in our contract price. This process went on over three years. Finally, we were nearing completion when Harry began to question almost every item, countering with his own lists of what he thought each item should cost. It became an impossible situation and Harry chose to sue us for incompletion of contract. In the end, the case was forwarded to Irving C. Pink, Q.C., in Yarmouth, Nova Scotia for investigation and settlement.

At his request, Russell Theriault and I attended his offices where Harry was also present. By this time, our files on the boat were extensive. Mr. Pink examined them all in detail, pausing to question Russell, Harry and myself as to definition, execution, and completion.

OBSESSION: A ONE-MAN BOAT, BUILT AROUND ONE MAN'S EGO.

Finally, he closed the files, looked at Harry and said that he could not see any justification for argument, as we had obviously discharged our responsibility as required, completed the necessary work per agreement, and all without excessive charges. "Mr. Carter," he said to Harry, "I can see no reason for further question and suggest you pay these gentlemen their account." Without a word, Harry wrote us a cheque in full for the balance owing.

Harry took delivery and sailed *Obsession* away in 1974. In subsequent months and years Harry would call me many evenings, greet me like a long lost friend, and assure me of the yacht's eventual popularity.

Naturally, this never happened, and I eventually heard *Obsession* had been sold. She certainly lived up to her name as far as Harry was concerned, and swept us all up in his confusing dreams about her.

A Final Quartet of Privateers from A.F. Theriault's

Nan Adele Marie: An exacting building experience.

CHAPTER TWENTY-EIGHT

ERNIE CAMPBELL HAD SEEN BILL WALKER'S *Chebucto* in San Diego and looked over our design information Bill had given him. As a result, Ernie contacted us, and on July 2, 1972 visited me at A.F. Theriault's to discuss a Privateer ketch for himself. He had quite a bit of experience in yachting and cruising and consequently knew what he wanted. It was a relief and a joy to work with such an experienced yachtsman. It is always easier to work with someone who knows what he is doing.

Ernie planned his extras and special requirements including a GM 3-71 diesel, 3 k.w. Onan generator, diesel furnace, porta-potti toilets in lieu of marine heads, higher flush-decked fully enclosed mid-ship wheelhouse, aft deck steering station, plank bowsprit and opening trunk cabin ports in lieu of fixed windows. Ernie was in the heating business, so knew his way around equipment, its installation, and use.

After all the correspondence, custom plans and extras lists of some fifty items, we finally went to building contract #422 in January 1973 for *Royal Scott*, a custom Privateer marconi main ketch at $55,000. Her layout was a standard galley aft but with a custom forward cabin featuring a large fridge-freezer and lots of storage room.

Royal Scott was completed to Ernie's specs and delivered to him at Meteghan River on October 31, 1973. Ernie sailed her away and enjoyed many years of successful cruising on both East and West Coasts of the U.S.A.

In September 1978, we learned she had been bought by Harlan Griffith of Olympia, Washington, who planned some extensive deep-sea cruising.

In January 1973, we had a phone call from James R. Leidgen, President of Wells Fargo in Atlanta, Georgia, enquiring about a Privateer ketch. In response to early data we sent, he visited us in Halifax to discuss the boat. She turned out to be a very sensible galley forward layout with semi-enclosed centre wheelhouse model. He asked for custom aft-deck rails and trim, reminiscent of a revolutionary period cutter. She was to be painted black and white with painted ports. We began planning his lists of extras and eventually went to contract in February 1973.

Jim was an astute businessman exceptionally active in his career. He decided to name the yacht *French Leave* as he saw sailing her as an A.W.O.L. escape from his busy life. His friend and partner in the boating venture was Jack Allen. As they were commissioning the vessel, Jim pulled out a framed picture of a cowboy's tombstone he had seen in Arizona which read, "Here lies laughing Jack Allen—drew first, shot last!" and hung it in a prominent place in their great aft cabin.

Construction proceeded well including the lists of extras. Finally all was ready and Jim, Jack and their crew arrived, completed sea trials and left Meteghan River November 30, 1973. *French Leave* had cost $52,000. They had a successful cruise to Florida, berthed her there, and returned to their busy corporate lives. The next year, Jim decided to bring her back to A.F. Theriault's for maintenance and storage.

Apparently, there were major changes going on for him and his next correspondence listed him as President of Brinks and now living in Chicago, Illinois. I do not pretend to know the ramifications of dealings at

JACK ALLEN (LEFT) AND JIM LEIDGEN ON *FRENCH LEAVE*.

higher corporate levels, but assume it is sometimes necessary to make quick changes of loyalties and location. His next advice was that he had made a quick shift to Caracas, Venezuela, South America, and obviously would not be able to use the yacht in the foreseeable future. He asked us to sell her for him. We advertised, prepared brochures, and after many months and two false offers of purchase, sold her to Paul Kleppinger of Ft. Lauderdale, Florida.

Paul was an experienced yachtsman and boat yard operator who was already familiar with our vessels. After considerable negotiation, reconditioning, and alteration, Paul took delivery of *French Leave* in August 1978 at $55,000 including extras he wanted.

Our next customer was that rarity, a Canadian, John F. Shirriff of Toronto, Ontario. John chose a marconi Privateer to be called *Nan Adele Marie* (Hull #424), but with a completely different cabin layout. John was one of those men who investigated everything, right down to the most minute detail, analyzed it all very carefully, and then made a final choice.

It began with the hull itself, which was to be of mahogany plank, all stainless steel fastenings, and total Burma teak exterior trim. Her rig was complimented with a main yard with square course and triangular raffee, set flying. This was a new departure for Privateer, which worked particularly well on the West Coast of North America. The marconi rig sails better to windward, while the squaresails are great while running or on a broad reach.

The yacht maintained the great aft raised-deck cabin, but John eliminated stern and quarter windows, preferring instead a large sunken-well cockpit with comfortable seating, storage and sailing helm.

CUSTOM FORWARD CABIN, *NAN ADELE MARIE*.

Her cabin layout was also unique with galley aft as well as toiletroom, chart table, and two-quarter berths. Her mid-ship enclosed saloon featured two pair of upper and lower berth-settees flanking the main dining table, but without the usual enclosed helm. The forward cabin housed two berths with settees, lockers, and storage.

The fo'c's'le was given over to storage for long distance cruising, and a marine head.

We began lengthy and detailed meetings and correspondence with John over some months leading to finalizing plans for his yacht. At times, he would write us with ideas, discussions of extras and clippings of equipment and methods almost daily. It was quite a flood to keep track of, especially during the busy months of March and April 1973 when I had thirteen vessels building at A.F. Theriault & Sons alone.

As John's file became thicker and thicker the yacht began to take shape from his building contract #424 signed February 10, 1973. He specified American white oak for main fame as he considered it superior to our local oak, which was really a type of grey oak. The principal difference was that American oak has an isolated cellular structure while Nova Scotian oak is porous from cell to cell. Therefore, once rot begins, progression is slower in the American species. However, this only happens long after the vessel is launched, and generally after she has changed owners many times.

It has been my observation that the average boat owner changes his house every seven years, his car every two years, his boat every four years and his wife every eleven years. Not that there is anything wrong with this, he simply gets tired of them and wants something new. There is only one constant in this life, and that is change.

A customer sometimes asked me what the best materials for construction were. Invariably, he would enquire about stainless steel in place of galvanized iron, bronze in lieu of brass, Kevlar in place of fibreglass. I would reply that it all depends on what he wanted to be holding a handful of after the rest of the vessel had turned to dust. The extra cost of these items was never justified by the expected lifetime of the vessel, and certainly not by the average length of his ownership. What was best was quality that would last for the vessel's expected lifetime. This discussion, generally undertaken at the beginning of a contract, often included the owner's remark that this was to be his last boat and would have to last at least fifty years. As most customers were already at least forty years old, I wondered whether they would be sailing when they were ninety.

I would not press this point, but rather asked, "Well, Mr. X., how many boats have you had?" Perhaps he would reply six over a period of twenty-four years. This, I believe, substantiated my observation of length of ownership and indicated that he would probably not keep the new boat any longer than four years either.

John's contract was written using a base cost for a standard Privateer at $38,000 in 1973, which after his initial extras were added came to $62,000. Eventually, many other changes were made and more extras added resulting in her final cost, as delivered to John in July 1974, to be $72,000, including over 140 separate, distinct, and extra items. It was very taxing for me with many details to be catalogued, priced, and kept track of over the building period.

Another marconi main Privateer ketch was ordered by Fred and Shirley Dygert of Ada, Michigan. They were a happy and pleasant couple full of life and smiles. They were both short, rotund people who originally struck me as most unlikely to own, operate, and enjoy a yacht at sea. However, they were to prove me wrong as their optimistic outlook, and determination resulted in an interesting and busy life afloat. It was their plan to cruise the vessel throughout the Caribbean and other exotic places, making documentary films as they went.

Fred had first contacted us in early 1971 about their plans, and replied in some detail to brochures we sent him. Fred and Shirley subsequently visited Halifax in April 1972, when we had an opportunity to sit with them over the drawing board and plan their vessel. Next, they traveled to Theriault's to see the yachts built there. Fred was pleased with what he saw, many items were discussed, and we proceeded to building contract #425 in November 1973. Custom plans were drawn showing most of the vessel's interesting innovations.

Since the Dygerts planned to voyage up rivers and under bridges, I devised a tabernacled mast that could be lowered and raised again with a steel pipe "A" frame housed along the forward railcaps. Hoisting could be accomplished via the power of the vessels own windlass if a convenient crane was not available.

Fred and Shirley chose a very sensible cabin layout with galley forward and main saloon housing inside piloting station, and settees. Since the normal cabin windows were too high for little Shirley to see out of while seated, Fred had us install another set of smaller windows lower down for her. "It's okay to have some for me," he said, "but we have to have some

for Shirley, too." Other items were also constructed to accommodate Shirley's height, and the vessel's name eventually became *Shirley Too*.

Her great aft cabin became the owner's quarters with pullout double and single berths, settees and toiletroom with a second private shower. An outside aft sailing station was also installed on the raised aft deck.

Construction proceeded smoothly due at least in part to the Dygert's sensible, pleasant, and happy nature. They next visited the shop February

26, 1974 when additional extras were added and an inspection of the vessel, then planked, made. Eventually, all was ready, *Shirley Too* was launched, rigged, commissioned and delivered to Fred at Meteghan River after trials on July 2, 1974 for a total of $64,000 including $6,000 in extras.

Fred wrote March 17, 1977 and said *Shirley Too* had now logged over 10,000 miles, and 1,700 engine hours. She was still cruising the Caribbean and Bahamas but Fred had experienced serious health problems, resulting in expensive surgeries and loss of strength. He reluctantly decided to sell the vessel and return to Michigan. He still sang her praises and expressed his gratitude for the many adventures he and Shirley had had aboard their own dream ship.

Shirley Too—LOW WINDOWS FOR LITTLE SHIRLEY.

THE LAST DAYS OF WINDJAMMER YACHTS

QUEST WAITING AT THE PANAMA CANAL.

Chapter Twenty-Nine

In the years that followed, my eldest son, Bob, returned from sea and took up a position selling office equipment. He had joined Bedford Institute of Oceanography ships earlier, going north to the ice to service outposts there and accommodate scientists doing oceanographic work. He was crewing with older sailors, many of them Newfoundlanders. These were hardy, rough men, living simple lives among the ice, mostly in difficult weather conditions, isolation and privation. It was a learning experience for Bob and opened his eyes to another side of life.

His job in office equipment introduced him to the corporate world, finance, and salesmanship. After those two positions, he came with me full time in our boat design, sales, and building operations. He had a natural and intuitive business sense and was a great help in handling customers and boat shops. Initially he took over ordering equipment, research, and delivery. His experience gained aboard our own yachts plus his B.I.O. tenure provided valuable experience in delivering new yachts coastwise in Nova Scotia and even on some deliveries to the U.S.A.

He also taught himself wire and rope splicing under the watchful eye of Jim Chapman and Snook Caines, our riggers. Bob became proficient at masting and rigging which was a great boon as the riggers were not always available when needed.

We usually hired a very pleasant and capable skipper, Don Webster of Halifax for voyages. Don also owned and operated an electronic and mechanical yacht service business, so he had many talents of value to us. He and Bob made a great team, with lots of their own stories to tell.

As the days of wooden yachts began to wane, Bob could see the necessity for him to cross over into fibreglass motor craft, being now more in demand by fishermen, government patrol and some yachtsmen. Some of my older customers used to say, "If God had wanted us to have fibreglass boats, He would have made fibreglass trees." However, progress is progress and the dye was cast.

Bob began to sell locally made glass boats to his own accounts, as well as his work with us. Even in his early days, he would admonish me for pricing my wooden yachts too low, which precluded me giving any extra services to my customers, and sometimes ended in near financial disaster. There was simply no margin for error. I guess I essentially believed a customer when he told me he had little money. I would set to with a will to provide the best boat I could for the money available.

Bob, Kevin, and I traveled from shop to shop as launching and rigging time arrived and helped put the final work on each vessel. A.F. Theriault & Son had their own riggers, but the smaller shops needed our help and guidance as sail rig was not their forte. One of these was Osmond Yorke's shop in Parrsboro.

Osmond himself was a gentle and hard-working man. He always tried his best to please and never swore, no matter how bad a situation got. He had a nervous disposition and was a chain smoker. I often saw him with one cigarette burning in the ashtray, and another smoking on the desk edge as he reached in his pocket for his pack and lit up another. His casual remark to me always was, "These things are killing me, you know."

During the summer of 1978 when we were at Parrsboro finishing up our work on Albert Ebner's 35-foot Pilgrim ketch *Calluna*, Osmond Yorke introduced to me a gaunt man he brought to the shop; "I want to acquaint you with the new owner of Windjammer Yachts, Don Cameron." For some reason this gave me a sinking feeling in the pit of my stomach. Call it intuition, but I knew that here was trouble. I had known that Osmond was getting tired—his old energy, zest, and sparkle were gone— but I did not know he was desperate enough to bow out of his business.

Osmond had operated a shoe shop, a grocery store, and had once been an industrial arts teacher at the high school in Parrsboro. Eventually his maritime blood was aroused and he came to me in Halifax wanting to build boats. We began our partnership in boatbuilding as I supplied the design for a 30-foot Cape Island fishing boat that he built in his garage at his Greenhill home. After that, he acquired waterfront property in Parrsboro Harbour at the site of the old coal docks where trainloads of Springhill coal had been brought and loaded on waiting wooden sailing vessels. Parrsboro has the highest tides in the world, 50-feet at times twice daily. It is always an experience to see the harbour bottom completely dry with vessels sitting on wooden bunks, and then, only a few hours later the tide at full flood, water everywhere, and a vessel sailing away with her cargo. Great currents also ran with the tides, so it was a dangerous place for an unwary sailor.

At one time, Osmond was looking out of his living room window during a vicious gale and noticed a small fishing boat in difficulty with two men hanging on. Without a thought for his own safety, he ran down the hill to the shore, launched his small rowboat, and struck out for the doomed men. He was able to pull one to safety and brought him to shore. Once again, he braved wind, wave, and current to try and rescue the other man. He almost made it, but lost his grip and the man was lost in the stormy sea. In 1975, the Governor General of Canada decorated Osmond with a medal of bravery, over his protests that it was nothing anyone wouldn't have done.

By March 1984, Osmond's health had deteriorated and it became obvious he was dying of lung cancer. He was terribly emaciated and his eyes were dark and sunken. As I visited him at his home that month, he reached feebly for another cigarette, looked me directly in the eye, and said, "These things are killing me!" He firmly believed his own words.

Osmond died July 9, 1984.

After Windjammer Yachts had been sold to Don Cameron I came to him in October 1978 with building contract #508, which was to repair an existing 41-foot fibreglass hull that belonged to Doug Dicks of Sydney, Nova Scotia. We were to install a 6-354 Perkins diesel, shafting, fuel and water tanks, bulkheads, cabin floors, decks and cabins. The balance of equipment and finishing were to be completed by the owner. Work was to be on a cost-plus basis as no one could foresee end costs.

We measured the hull, since we knew we would have to transport it from Sydney and over the old single-lane steel bridge at Five Islands to get it to Parrsboro. Kevin was driving our old Chev tractor-trailer. We stopped at the bridge and once again measured both bridge and boat; they both measured exactly the same. However, we did not take into account the steel bolt-heads of the bridge, and the hull scraped both sides near the deck all the way through. It was a good thing she was to have a new deck before returning. Months later, the bridge was replaced with a new two-lane so the return trip would be okay.

I thought this contract would be a good introduction for Cameron as I began to realize his lack of experience or expertise in building. It seemed to me that anything that Cameron touched turned into a disaster. Fortunately, some of the former boat builders stayed with the shop, which helped save the day.

As time on the job began to mount far beyond what I considered reasonable, I questioned him about some of the invoiced costs, for instance, "think-tank time." I asked him what it meant. "That's the time I go back to the shop evenings and just sit inside the boat thinking about what to do next," he replied. For once, I was speechless.

Osmond at that time was still hovering in the background, and I hoped he might bolster some of Cameron's inabilities. Somehow we completed the work for Doug Dicks on the cost-plus basis as agreed. In the end, he made a private agreement to finish some basic work with Cameron, came to Parrsboro, completed his work, launched the vessel, and powered it to Cape Breton. Even though costs had been much more than originally anticipated, Doug did get the vessel home, completed her there, and sailed her for many years. Bob remained friendly with Doug Dicks over the years, partying (an acknowledged social accomplishment of Cape Bretoners) with him on several occasions.

In February 1979, we signed a new building contract (#509) with Windjammer for a 46-foot Buccaneer schooner for Kenneth Link of San Diego, California. Ken was a reasonable young man and the vessel was quite basic although her contract included sixty extra items to our standard.

She was to be named *Quest* and was a marconi main schooner with open mid-ship cockpit. Power was to be a G.M. 3-51 diesel. The aft cabin had no stern or quarter windows but was reserved for the owner's stateroom. The forward cabin included galley, settees, dining area, a large toiletroom with shower and berths for five, altogether quite a sensible vessel and easy to construct. Our contract with Ken Link was for $111,000 including his extras.

We got underway but trouble appeared almost instantly. The boat shop had difficulty pouring the lead keel, which had to be re-claimed twice. It seemed that every step of the way there were problems and delays. Eventually the hull was planked, but not without an increased amount of my time and attention.

The weeks turned into months as a job that should have taken ten months turned into sixteen! I was thankful that we were on a fixed cost contract this time, even if it did require much more time, labour, and effort from us than it should have.

In the end, with time dragging on and problems galore, Bob, Kevin, and I along with some of our own workmen, packed up tools and materials and went to Parrsboro to finish the job. We took our three-quarter ton truck with large slide-in camper to live in while there, parked it behind the shop and set to work on the boat.

At 2:00 A.M. a few days later, a bumping and scratching noise outside the truck awakened me. Looking out I discovered two men trying to siphon gas from our truck. This was the last straw. I leaped from the camper with my nightshirt flying, screaming obscenities. I grabbed the shirtfront of one robber who was much taller than I, pulled him down to my height, and swung for his chin. The poor guy was in total shock—they had not expected anyone to be in the camper. His unlit cigarette dropped from his lower lip as I made contact, but Bob's restraining arm had prevented my fist from doing the damage I intended. Bob had taken time to pull on his jeans, and grab his 12-inch sheath knife as he left the door. Kevin was attired in his Fruit of the Loom underwear and L'il Abner boots as he chased the second robber up the road. A third one was waiting in their old car with the engine revving and back door open for his friends to affect a hasty exit. I wondered what the trio of robbers thought as Bob, Kevin, and I gave chase screaming dire warnings of what would happen if we saw them again. Perhaps they thought they had encountered some banshee devils from hell, but in any case, we never saw them again.

Ken Link and his crew had arrived at Parrsboro and patiently waited at the local hotel for three weeks until *Quest* could be at least rudimentally readied for sea. She was launched, masted, ballasted, and rigged. Charlie Murphy and Osmond Yorke, and some of the other former employees had come back to the wharf to assist, as all felt a responsibility for the incomplete vessel. During the last few days Cameron was nowhere in sight. I went looking for him, but he had disappeared.

We did the best we could. Ken and his crew were aboard. I went over the accounts and made adjustments for work not done or done improperly. He graciously agreed to take the vessel "as is" with these allowances made. The tide being high, they went out to adjust the compass, dropped off the adjuster, and kept right on going for Florida.

In the days that followed, there was much confusion between Cameron, his bank manager in Parrsboro, the Federal Business Development Bank (FBDB) that had financed the boat shop, and others. Cameron contacted us, accusing us of sending the yacht away without his permission, and avoiding invoices as well as other ridiculous notions.

On November 8, 1980, we had a very nice letter from Charles Link, Ken's brother who reported on *Quest's* maiden voyage:

Dear Mr. Rosborough:

I had the opportunity to meet Ken in Portland, Maine and sail with him from there to Houston, Texas on *Quest*. Since I was on her for 30 days under all types of weather conditions, I could observe some of her characteristics.

She is balanced perfect and can be steered by the trim of her sails. She has a very pleasant motion in a seaway, smooth and steady.

When we were about 250 miles east of Cape Hatteras we ran into a storm of 60 knot winds with gusts to 90 knots. The sea had a distance of about 25 feet from the bottom of a hole to the top of the swell. When pointing directly into them the bow would hang out into space, then drop into the hole burying her bow almost to the bowsprit.

She lays a-hull at about 80 degrees off the wind. Quite a bit of roll. She lays-to at any angle you choose with the staysail. The farther out you let the boom the farther off the wind she lays.

Quest is a pleasure to sail as she does everything a good sailing vessel should do.

Charles Link
San Diego, California

QUEST IN PARRSBORO.

I also had some pleasant letters from both Ken and his wife Kathy as they sailed coastwise and through the Bahamas heading south to Galveston, Texas, after many storms and repairs along the way. *Quest* was laid up there for the winter pending the balance of delivery to San Diego the following spring.

Meanwhile, I carefully overhauled and assessed all the omissions and shortcomings found with *Quest* as she came out of the Windjammer shop as I was sure that Cameron would question every detail.

Four typewritten pages of itemized and individually priced items either never completed or needing correction adding up to $8,500 was sent to Cameron, but we never received a reply.

As a sequel to the unhappy demise of Windjammer Yachts, we learned that shortly after *Quest* had left Parrsboro, Cameron had attempted to sell contents and materials from the shop, even though, we assume, they were still under assignment to the F.B.D.B. Apparently, Cameron had posted a sign on the shop saying "Everything Must Go." Next, we were told, he rented a large truck, loaded it with everything he could from the shop and the big, old Parrsboro house he had rented, and headed for parts unknown. F.B.D.B. and the Parrsboro bank both contacted us as they attempted to locate anything of value and to release to us our property retained at the shop. As we went to collect our goods, I saw Cameron's sign lying in the front yard. I picked it up with a wry smile as I put it in our truck and thought, "Well, Cameron certainly made good his word because everything is gone!"

It was an ominous epitaph for the last days of wooden boat building in Parrsboro.

Last of Our Wooden Boats at A.F. Theriault & Son

Bridge of the *Mahalo Nui*.

CHAPTER THIRTY

BEFORE THE END, WE HAD a bright flare-up of interest from four different and unlikely quarters.

The first was an enquiry from Michael Riq and Raymond Pallisco of Abidjan, of the Ivory Coast of Africa. Michael, his wife and Raymond visited me in December 1973 in Halifax to contract a vessel for them. Their intention was to make Marseilles, the South Coast of France on the Mediterranean, their homeport, while their residences were elsewhere in France, and their business address in Abidjan, Africa. Although both men corresponded with me, Michael handled most technical arrangements. Raymond visited several times during building, as he seemed to be able to get away more often.

Our building contract #426 was signed with them during their December visit although custom drawings had been completed prior to that time. Due to the distances between us, plans and agreements had to be orchestrated carefully to conclude a successful construction. Our initial contract was signed at $110,000, which became $117,000 with extras by delivery in September 1974. Raymond was a 5-foot Corsican who strutted about with his hat on sideways and his hand stuck in his shirtfront. At the time we met him, they were in the timber exporting business in Abidjan, selling mahogany logs to Brunzeel in Holland to be made into marine mahogany plywood. Naturally, we supposed they would want their yacht planked with mahogany, but Raymond said, "No! No! Pine please, that is the best."

Raymond told me he had never been in North America before and could only speak French. I conjured up my high school and college French as we began to plan his boat. He liked what he saw of *Rattlesnake* and *HMS Dolphin* and settled on that design for themselves. He wanted to call her something typically Canadian and settled on *Belle Province*; I did not tell him the difference.

I asked him what they used to harvest the enormously large (7 to 10 feet in diameter) mahogany logs in Africa. "Le bull-do-zer?" "*Mais non, l'éléphant!*" he replied. I thought he would have no language barrier at Theriaults, but actually their Acadian French was not much closer to Raymond's Paris French than mine was.

In any case, our negotiations were successful and they chose the *Aquarius* barquentine as most suitable to their intended use.

BELLE PROVINCE: NAMED FOR SOMETHING TYPICALLY CANADIAN.

Belle Province was powered by twin 85 h.p. Perkins diesels, quarter shafted. The owners also chose a gaff mizzen rather than the usual marconi. Fifty extra items were added to our original plans and specs but construction went along well with a minimum of confusion and changes. She was very close to *HMS Dolphin* in layout and construction, so we had that recent building experience to guide us.

Raymond visited the shop at Meteghan River a few more times, where he noticed that many of the Acadian workmen wore dark green ball caps. It seemed to be an identifying symbol that they liked. He bought one and would strut about the yard doffing it to every workman he met and greeting them with, "Okay," his one English word.

As delivery time neared, the owners asked us to arrange to have the vessel delivered to Marseilles under her own power by sea. Bill Walker agreed to the delivery and began to assemble his crew and equipment. Mac MacKay of *Arctic Witch* went along as radio operator along with other competent crew Bill selected.

Raymond visited Meteghan River for a final inspection and acceptance. Russell's wife Sylvia recognized the auspicious occasion of having such a distinguished visitor from France, and went all-out to prepare a special dinner in his honour. She sent Russell to the liquor store to purchase the best wine they had available. It was a wonderful and sumptuous dinner— Sylvia had done herself proud. Beaming with satisfaction, she asked Raymond how he liked our wine. After a small pause, Raymond replied, "Madame, if we had this wine in France, we would throw it out the window!" He was certainly honest, if not diplomatic.

Building drew to a close and *Belle Province* was launched, rigged and commissioned for sea. Bill Walker and his crew arrived, provision was completed for the trans-Atlantic passage and sea trials were concluded successfully.

Belle Province's maiden voyage ended happily. Her owners sailed her in the Mediterranean until they sold her to Belgium owners in 1980. They intended to do some chartering with her out of Brussels and we heard later that she was actually engaged in that trade in the North Sea.

Our next enquiry came from Ron Douglas in Victoria, British Columbia who was in real estate investment and wanted a large trawler-type motor yacht for intended cruising to the Polynesian Islands in the Pacific. While not our usual style of designs, I knew A.F. Theriault & Son would be capable of building her based on their wide experience with similar motored vessels. Ron's choice name for her was *Mahalo Nui*, which means thank you in Hawaiian. He was originally going to call her Mahalo Nui Nui, which meant thank you very, very much, but he thought that might be over doing it.

Ron pulled out all the stops on the style, layout and equipment of the vessel. She was patterned after Monk designed trawler-cruisers popular on the West Coast.

Bill Walker told us initially in April 1975, about Ron Douglas and his desire for such a motor cruiser. We wrote him with our brochures and drawings of the Offshore 50-foot cruisers we had previously built in Chester for Dick Shaw. He replied that he wanted a 58-foot boat between a Grand Banks trawler-cruiser and a good quality fish-boat. He was thinking of twin Caterpillar 3160 diesels to deliver 12 knots speed over a 1,000-mile range.

By June 12, we had forwarded him preliminary design drawings, and negotiations for the vessel had progressed far enough that contractual letters were exchanged. Ron made his first payment for construction to us August 4, 1975 on a preliminary estimate of $135,000.

MAHALO NUI: BASED ON TRADITIONAL FISHING VESSELS.

Changes to the drawings, specifications and equipment began almost immediately as Ron discovered new ideas. Changes to equipment lists were ongoing and constant from the start. I was glad I was not on a fixed contract price with him. Additional changed items meant a longer building period was necessary as we went on into 1976.

Ron visited the boat shop again March 6-7, 1976 when two more pages of ordered and changed items were decided upon. Almost every aspect of layout and equipment came into question and it kept me hopping to keep up with added details.

Her original lines drawing was compiled by Bernard Theriault at A.F. Theriault's yard based on traditional Eldridge-MacIsaac lines for 60-foot semi-displacement vessels used in the fisheries on both East and West Coasts. I still had to do all the detail drawings and alterations as we went along.

Ron next visited the yard on April 19, 1976, and again many items were discussed, altered, and defined. Ron was able to view work on the boat and seemed pleased with the quality of construction. He had been complaining about how long it was taking without considering that an additional $40,000 of work had been added.

As delivery time drew nearer, Ron asked us to arrange a captain for the voyage from Nova Scotia to British Columbia. We were able to get Don Webster to agree to at least the first leg to the Caribbean, as he also had his own business commitment to look after. How long he could stay with the boat depended upon how the delivery trip went. Finally it arrived; *Mahalo Nui* was at the dock. Engines were run up and equipment tested. Ron, his crew, and Capt. Don Webster arrived. It was a hectic scene for two or three days as provisions were brought on board, last minute adjustments made

MAHALO NUI: DISASTER TO COME.

and compass swung. Ron, his 15-year-old son Jamie and 30-year-old daughter Charronne were going to sail with the yacht as well as first mate Mark Surette.

At that time in Nova Scotia, one of the local distilleries had just introduced a new wine called Baby Duck. As a promotion, they marketed T-shirts with a little baby duck and of course, the words Baby Duck on the front. Charrone bought one and wore it proudly, displaying the motto to great advantage. The boatyard workers would remark "Look, here comes Baby Duck!" The nickname stuck and she sailed away with it.

After a stormy session with Ron as to final charges and payments between himself, me and Russell Theriault, *Mahalo Nui* headed for sea July 28, 1976 as Russell and I said to the Heavens, "Thank you very much."

The delivery voyage proved difficult from the start. The vessel encountered heavy seas in the Gulf of Maine with 16-foot seas in a strong northeaster. After more bad weather, they took shelter in New York. By then, everyone aboard was exhausted. The additional stress of building and paying for the vessel took its toll on Ron who collapsed from exhaustion. The doctors thought he had had a heart attack, and recommended he return home to British Columbia and allow the yacht to proceed without him.

The next disaster occurred when *Mahalo Nui* collided with a freighter in Delaware Bay. The decks buckled, there was damage above the water line, and severe destruction to the flying bridge. The yacht was repaired only to face Hurricane Belle while moored at Cape May. This time, the only things frayed were already-worn nerves.

Another problem that showed up en route resulted from Theriault's having installed some of the cooling water hoses with plastic pipe. There was no air-conditioning provided in the design to cool the engine room and the combination of warm ocean water, high air temperatures in the Caribbean and heat in the boat caused the plastic pipes to collapse.

We heard later that the vessel, after she had been driven ashore by hurricane winds and abnormally high tides in California, required a canal to be dug with bulldozers to re-float her.

The next tragedy was that one of the pair of Cat 3160 diesels seized up, necessitating the complete replacement of the unit with all the associated work of engine removal.

Underway again, *Mahalo Nui* slid into Canada and was berthed in Victoria. I can well imagine Ron Douglas' relief after almost three-and-a-half months, 8,600 miles, two hurricanes, a mid-sea collision and the long trail of shipyard repair bills, delays, and all the mounting costs of crew and provisions.

The next thing I heard about *Mahalo Nui* was that Canada Customs had seized her for default in the payment of duties and taxes. Ron had provided us with a fishing boat tax license in Nova Scotia, making it unnecessary for us to charge him these monies upon delivery. In addition, there was some intention of keeping the boat out of Canada, although in Canadian Registry, perhaps cruising the U.S.A. and Polynesian Islands. Apparently, Ron's choice to keep her in Canada resulted in Canada Customs' action.

In those days, a Canadian owner had to pay duties on foreign items of manufacture (exclusive of diesel engines) plus federal sales tax on the completed cost plus provincial tax compounded if the vessel were to remain in the province of manufacture. Consequently, most owners arranged export from Canada, foreign registry or other means of deferring taxes.

I presume that in Ron's case, the taxes were eventually paid and he finally began cruising the vessel.

Gilles Rouest was a French Canadian entrepreneur in the field of tourism, as a recreation planning consultant. He originally came to see me in October 1974 when he was interested in an 80- to 90-foot vessel for tourist charter work similar to the Windjammer fleet of cruise ships operated by Mike Burke in the Caribbean. When I told him such a vessel might cost $300,000, he retreated to re-consider his plan.

He appeared again in April 1975, asking about a 46-foot Privateer ketch but with a completely new concept in cabin layout. His plan was still to accommodate as many tourists as possible, but in the smaller vessel. This was actually very sensible for his purpose and would provide a cruise ship within his means. Gilles drew a little sketch of the layout and configuration he wanted, mailing it to me March 9, 1975.

I set about re-designing a Privateer ketch with steam-bent frames and a flush deck at the height of normal bulwark rail caps. This provided enormous room inside the hull, which could be given over to increased accommodations. Her layout consisted of a double great aft cabin with private toilet room and shower; a center mid-ship cockpit with galley to port; a double cabin to starboard; another toiletroom; main saloon with dining area, berths for four and inside helm station; a third toilet room with shower; and a fo'c's'le with four berths, making a total sleeping arrangement for twelve, if necessary.

Her sail rig was to be a simple marconi main and mizzen ketch, stayed all-round with a stern boomkin and plank bowsprit. The new plans were exchanged and we went to building contract #429 for *Nacona*, October 10, 1975 at a base price of $60,000 for the raised-deck Privateer plus $10,000 in extras for a total of $70,000.

Construction went along well at A.F. Theriault's throughout 1975 and into 1976. Gilles visited again March 22, 1976, inspected the vessel, and ordered other extras.

Launching, trials and delivery took place July 24, 1976 at a total of $74,000. Everything went smoothly and we heard from Gilles December 7, 1976 that *Nacona* had finally arrived in the Virgin Islands after four months in transit and waiting along the way.

In short, she provided an interesting and practical departure from our normal Privateer, which performed well at sea and cruising among the islands.

The next unusual contract was when we were approached by Judge Omer H. Chartrand and Jack Grey to do a rebuild on the 70-foot trawler-cruiser called *Sea Gypsy*. *Sea Gypsy* was originally built in 1962 for Don Ellis of Florida Keys as designed by John Atkin, Sr. She was a big ship with at least one-third of her space given over to engine room with twin G.M. 6-71 diesels, two generators, air conditioning, tanks, machinery and all the associated equipment and electrics necessary to run and supply such a mechanical marvel. It required either a full-time engineer or an owner with a definite bent for tinkering with machinery to keep her going. Much equipment had been added over the years as well as new construction such as her flying bridge by Rybovitch in Florida. She bragged accommodation for six plus crew of four and a spacious main-deck saloon with bar, piano, Baldwin organ, galley, dining area and lounge.

GILLES ROUEST: A BOAT FOR THE TOURIST TRADE.

As mentioned earlier, Jack Grey had been an early lifetime chum of mine. Our mothers had been friends before we were born, and each of us being only sons had spent much time together summering in St. Margaret's Bay, southwest of Halifax. I later attended the Nova Scotia College of Art with Jack and his best friend Joseph Purcell as we finished our formal education together.

In 1976, when I was dealing with Jack in the sale, repair, and delivery of *Sea Gypsy*, he was living in a fisherman's house, which he had bought in Blue Rocks, Lunenburg, Nova Scotia. Shortly after, Jack had developed an advanced case of agoraphobia and was confined to his house. He cowered behind the kitchen stove and his fear was so great that a local lad hired as his caretaker had to lead him by the hand even to cross the room to the washroom. This was quite a shock to me after the outgoing and effusive life that Jack had led for so long.

In any case, Omer Chartrand had bought the 70-foot cruiser and planned to voyage long distances. He had just retired from the bench as a federal judge in Quebec, and I wondered about his ability to handle such a craft in large crowded harbors. However, mine was not to reason why.

Sea Gypsy was badly in need of rebuilding around her topside and superstructure so we agreed to the repair. Once *Sea Gypsy* was hauled on the slip at A.F. Theriault & Son, it became obvious just how bad the deterioration was. It was apparent she had been repaired at some previous time when huge amounts of plastic filler had been used to fill areas decayed by dry rot. It was the worst case I had ever seen and must have cost a small fortune in filler, and fibreglass.

In November 1975 in Lunenburg, I surveyed the work necessary with Russell Theriault who estimated approximately $30,000 if the wood was replaced or $20,000 if simply a patch job was done.

Jack Grey was unable to help so it was up to us to make it all happen. Apparently, Jack had moved much of the yacht's furnishings including her piano, couches, tables, and chairs ashore to his house, which caused enquiry from Canada Customs later. The yacht remained in U.S. registry and Omer Chartrand formed a U.S. corporation to own her.

The re-build and overhaul of equipment was finally completed, and Ernest Theriault and his crew steamed the vessel around to Halifax for Omer to pick up. Much of the boat's equipment had to be overhauled or replaced due to its age and length of time unused. Capt. Don Webster became involved with much of the electronics and mechanical repairs and was also scheduled to sail with Omer while in Canada. However, this never happened and Omer took delivery himself in Halifax, June 15, 1977. He changed his plans about leaving Canada immediately and journeyed instead around Nova Scotia, through the Gulf of St. Lawrence and up the St. Lawrence river to Ontario. We were told he endured some scarring en route due to several encounters with wharves.

He also left behind a trail of unpaid bank notes and insurance premiums which were not satisfied until after legal proceedings were instituted against him. This surprised me, but then, after all, he knew his way around payments of debt and legal matters.

His plan became one of cruising with his family to the Gulf of Mexico via U.S. waters. It took until March 1978 for us to realize settlement of our accounts as he cruised *Sea Gypsy* coastwise in the U.S.A. Once again we learned the benefit of the axiom, "No cash–No splash."

Some Last Boats with Donnie Russell

Grey Starling: My own personal dream ship.
Every detail was the best I could manage.

CHAPTER THIRTY-ONE

WORK AT A.F.THERIAULT & SON was over, and the last yard actively building my boats was Donnie Russell at Lower Ship Harbour. Most of our American customers were gone and we were grasping for business wherever we could find it. I made up new brochures, ran ads in several international yachting publications, and sent out scores of letters. Every 1,000 packages of literature cost me five dollars to mail, and resulted in perhaps 100 enquiries, which if we were lucky, resulted in approximately one building contract. I had been sending out 3,000 mailings per year and spending over $1,000 per month on ads, so with customer interest waning, it became useless to keep beating the dead horse. Everyone still loved the boats but no one had the money to buy them.

Nevertheless, in January 1979 we had an enquiry about a ketch rigged 35-foot Pilgrim from Pete Grenier of Beaupre, Quebec. Pete had worked as a technician abroad for many years and was now ready to retire and fulfill a lifetime dream of cruising in his own boat. He was a practical and enquiring man but lacked much nautical experience. He began to research all the myriad of items open to his requirements and finally settled on what seemed best to him.

Pete and his wife Anna (hence *Pitanna*) visited me in Halifax on January 5, 1979 when we discussed his yacht at length and the plans began to take form. After several lengthy and detailed letters, we finally signed building contract #308 for *Pitanna*, on March 16, 1979 including 47 extras for a total of $71,500. Over the building period 80 more detailed extras were added.

Pete and Anna took up residence near me in Halifax, where Pete read avidly and studied navigation, seamanship and, of course, equipment as they waited for the boat. I began to wonder if the vessel would sink from the sheer weight aboard.

Pete had an aggressive nature and he liked to argue. He did not drive a car so drove with me to the boatyard for weekly inspection trips. He was also a chain smoker, making his company doubly disagreeable. My exasperation showed through once and he exclaimed, "You think I'm just an ignorant, dirty French-Canadian, don't you!" " I never thought you were dirty, Pete," I replied calmly.

Pete was a stickler for guarantees and warrantees, both with us and the many suppliers involved. Nevertheless the boat was built, with her many extras and frayed nerves all around. She was launched in Ship Harbour, motored to Halifax, rigged and commissioned and was ready to sail June 20, 1980 at $77,000.

Glenn Plat was hired for delivery skipper as far as Long Island, casting off with Pete and Anna. He wrote as follows:

Dear Doug:

Just a note to let you know that we (Pete, Anna, Pitanna, and yours truly) arrived in Long Island safely. The boat will be off down the waterway soon and I will be back at the Cove in a week or so to get Wind Storm ready for Bermuda.

Will give you full details of the delivery when I see you, but meantime just a few notes. We were all right about Pete, nice guy, but he doesn't know his topping lift from page 58 in the Nautical Almanac. He can't get into too much trouble on the waterway, and hopefully, he will learn enough on the way down to make his way out to the Bahamas.

Pitanna behaved beautifully. We took four-and-a-half days light to light, Sambro to Montauk Point. First couple of days good sailing with Pete and I alternating at the wheel, but the job was made easier by the self steering gear, which worked all right after some fiddling. Poor Anna was sick for the whole trip good weather or bad, but I must hand it to her, she served up the meals, sick or not.

The third day we had a heavy NE blow. I couldn't stay at the helm any longer, didn't trust the Aries because we hadn't worked all the kinks out of it, and of course couldn't trust Pete as he just didn't know enough to handle her in heavy seas. It was blowing about 30-40 knots, so ran her off on the starboard tack under staysail sheeted in hard. All hands stayed below, I ate and slept, owner's party slept and was sick.

While the storm lasted she rolled considerably as you might expect quartering off before the seas, that put the shower outlet under water some of the time. For some reason or other there was no valve on that line so some water got in the shower sump. I know the outlet is high up on the hull but you might make sure there is a seacock on the next boat. When last seen, Pete was busily installing same.

Other than that minor problem, we had a great sail. Things quieted down in about 12 hours. We had sail on but wind dropped off Nantucket Light Vessel so steamed in to New London over the last 24 hours.

When putting the main up, Pete got the end of a batten under something, put his back into it and tore the pocket. These little things will happen, and a guy has to learn, so I explained a little elementary sail design to him, after he confessed he didn't know what a batten was or why they are there.

Which leads me once again into one of my favourite beefs. Pete and Anna Grenier are so typical of the couples today who spend all their time and effort getting a boat, either building it themselves or working like hell to make money to buy one, and the only thing they neglect is learning how to sail.

Means more work for people like me, I guess, but if it wasn't for the fact that the boats are a lot better than the people are, more of them would kill themselves.

See you in a week or two.

Glenn

I had a letter December 15, 1980 from Pete saying that they were in Jensen Beach, Florida and that they had experienced troubles with the Perkins diesel; I replied the same day to the address he gave but never heard from him again. I heard from a Mr. Frank Mosher on another matter September 1981, and he said he helped Pete and Anna sail in the Caribbean but that they were very green and excitable. He wondered if they had come to grief. Again later, we heard that Pete was caught in a blow with the vessel heeling severely. Apparently, he was scared to death, powered back to Florida, stomped up to a broker's office, slammed the boat keys on his desk and

Grey Starling—Hull framing.

PETER DeBAIE GLUE PLUGGING. MY DREAM SHIP TAKES SHAPE.

exclaimed, "Sell the Goddamned thing—I never want to see it again!" I guess Pete's dream had come unravelled, extras, spares, and all.

Because times were slack in the wooden boat building industry, and Donnie's yard was still active and available, I decided that it was a good

AFT CABIN LOOKING FORWARD. ALL THE COMFORTS OF HOME.

time for me to realize a long cherished dream, and build the boat of my own dreams.

I had long thought about a vessel that would combine the very best of all the boats I had built, both in design, materials, equipment, and workmanship.

I called the new design Nomad. She was a marconi main and mizzen ketch rig with very practical plank bowsprit and steel "A" frame stern boomkins. The plank bowsprit made raising her plow anchor easier as well as allowing jib handling in safety. The stern boomkin provided stowage for her 9-foot Del Quay sailing dinghy, which in turn gave stowage for fenders, dock lines, barbeque, and garbage.

Her principal dimensions were 40-foot L.O.A. on the rail, 12-foot beam, 6 foot 2 inch draft, 36,000 pounds displacement, 11,000 pounds ballast and 770 square feet of sail area. She was powered by a 4-236, 85 h.p. Perkins diesel giving a constant speed of 7 knots with fuel tankage for a 1,000-mile range.

Nomad boasted a fully enclosed centre saloon housing inside steering, navigation equipment, chart table and electronics. Full easy access was arranged to her engine room below.

Her galley was forward as well as schooner style settees and table plus sleeping quarters. Her great aft cabin was given over to a main gathering area with very large curved settee, toilet room, Scottish tile fireplace and a fold-out queen sized owner's berth right up in her stern and quarter windows.

Altogether, she was a totally comfortable vessel in port or at sea and was a joy to cruise aboard.

My first Nomad was named *Grey Starling* after my mother's name, Grace Darling. I had saved a lot of antique and exotic marine equipment over the years, imagining it installed on my personal dream ship someday. Here was my chance; so for three years I designed, built, and equipped *Grey Starling*. Donnie Russell built her with skill and grace. Every detail was the best I could manage. She was ready for launching at a cost of $130,000, in 1982.

I had worked long and hard on her and invested in her the best of everything. She was Honduras mahogany planking, Burma teak cabins and outside trim, stainless steel fastenings, mast hardware and rigging. She had a comfortable aft cockpit steering station high on her aft deck and one-inch bore bronze swivel guns mounted on her teak taffrails. Her figurehead was "Blue Belle" patterned from the U.S. coaster Amanda Fenwick. She powered as well as she sailed and was equally comfortable as a motor-sailer.

Launching day was a grand and glorious occasion. We took her from Donnie's boat shop out the highway in a convoy of trucks, trailers, cars, and onlookers. The power and telephone companies sent trucks to raise and lower power and phone lines en route. We arrived at the wharf beach at Owl's Head, put her trailer as far out as we could and waited for the tide. My daughter Lynda broke the champagne as all cheered and a local fishing trawler towed her off to deeper water.

We stepped her masts, rigged her, bent on sail, and did all the dozens of last minute fitting out items by builders, riggers, and crew.

After that, I stood alone on the wharf with my beautiful *Grey Starling*. The sun was shining brightly and glistening off her new varnish. She was perfect—she couldn't be any more perfect. Her flag snapped in the gentle breeze as her dock lines strained to be cast off. All was quiet, peaceful, and perfect. A lifetime of dreaming, three years of concentrated effort and $130,000 later, the dream was accomplished! I looked at the boat; I looked at her key in my hand as a great sadness came over me. It was all perfect, but it wasn't what I wanted! I turned slowly and walked up the wharf, wondering what it all meant.

"I WONDERED WHAT IT WAS ALL ABOUT."

CONFESSIONS OF A BOATBUILDER

A Few More Before The End

OVER THE NEXT FEW YEARS, we sailed *Grey Starling*, and enjoyed her very much. We showed her to many prospective customers and took them for demonstration sails. She was kept as a showpiece at our wharves at Melville Cove, across the road from our design and sales office in Halifax. There, she became a familiar sight to sailors and landlubbers alike, providing a picturesque subject for many a camera.

We advertised her for sale for several years, starting at $120,000 and gradually reducing to $80,000, but no takers. She was finally sold for $60,000 to Ken Saari of Oakville, Ontario in September 1991. Ken and his wife wanted interior cabin changes made, so my son John Patrick and our boat builders removed her large curved settee and foldout queen berth from the aftercabin, and replaced them with conventional quarter-berths and a bench seat. Other modifications and equipment changes were made to his request at a total of some $15,000. She was measured at 20.21 tons for Canadian Registry and eventually sailed away to Ontario in June of 1992.

Subsequent to the building of *Grey Starling*, Eric Hamm of Vancouver Island, British Columbia, contracted for a similar vessel to be named *Shawna Lynn* after his two daughters and to be used by the family for cruising in the Pacific. His wife Ami was postmistress in the small logging town where they lived and Eric was employed in the local logging industry.

Eric had difficulty with finances right from the start, and it seemed he was always waiting for funds to materialize from investments and relatives. Over the building period, his teen-aged children were becoming more adult and making noises about moving away on their own.

Nevertheless, by September 1981 we got on with the boat at Donnie Russell's shop, Hull #314. Her materials were pretty well our standard with oak frame, white pine plank, spruce deck beams, clamps, floors, and masts. Costs had to be watched so there was little chance to use the more exotic materials. After some delays at arranging funds and equipment, she was complete as per our schedule and ready for shipment at $109,000.

We motored her the 50 miles to Halifax, lifted her onto a flatbed rail car at the harbourfront, blocked, cradled and secured her for shipment to the West Coast. This time our load was a slightly smaller overall dimension so we did not have to contend with the earlier problems we had with *Golden Girl* for Dean Moburg. We had Bill Walker meet the vessel in

British Columbia to inspect her and assure us that she arrived in good condition and complete, November 1984.

After some unfortunate theft and damage on the docks, she was launched, rigged, and powered away to Vancouver Island. This, we thought was a successful end to our work for Eric Hamm.

We did not hear from him as he sailed her and learned his way around *Shawna Lynn*, from 1981 to 1984, so we were surprised by a notice of lawsuit claiming that the yacht had sustained premature rotting to her planking due to the incursion of fresh water, particularly in the area of her aft windows, transom and plank. We had often advised Eric that he would have to keep the vessel painted and ventilated, as is standard maintenance for any pine-planked vessel.

The suit proceeded in Halifax with ourselves, our lawyers, and Eric's insurance company's local lawyers in attendance. As the investigation unfolded, we realized that there had been some serious damage to the vessel after it had gone aground on rocks, resulting in her sinking and a subsequent salvage. Apparently, Eric was operating her at the time although he had also rented her out on bare-boat charters.

In any case, the insurance company must have paid his claims, subrogated the claim, and instituted suit against us as her builders to recover anything possible. After all the lawyers had their say, it was my turn to speak. I explained to them that there had been an obvious shipwreck and that we could hardly be blamed for that incompetence. After a pause, the opposing lawyer closed his file, stood up, put away his pen, and said, "Thank you, that will be all for now," as he headed for the door. We never heard another word from them.

Early in 1977, Kevin Young of Cleveland, Ohio, approached us for a Frame Kit for a 30-foot Destiny.

Since our sales of completed boats were decreasing, it seemed sensible to offer kits of our boats made up to various stages by our boatshops for completion by an owner-builder. While we did get some enquiries about this concept, it was not widely accepted, which surprised me. Apparently, most would-be builders were overwhelmed by the immensity of the work ahead of them and decided to forgo the pleasure of building.

Kevin Young, however, seemed to be the exception. He was young, eager, and strong and had the will to succeed. Together with his brothers and father, Kevin had a large commercial construction company putting up K-Mart complexes around the U.S.A. "With his credentials and background this could be just the young man who will succeed," I thought.

Kevin had originally requested our brochures in June 1977 and after studying the material, decided he would like to try to build his own boat, beginning with our Frame Kit #2, which included the keel and main wooden skeleton for the boat. We prepared it all at Donnie Russell's shop and sent it by road freight to Kevin December 21, 1977, a nice Christmas present for him. The kit as shipped consisted of: 1 long box, keel, stems, etc.; 2 bundles; frame molds (open); 1 crate, stern assembly; 1 crate—transom (made up); 4 bundles—oak timbers (strapped).

The total cost was $3,600. A U.S. Customs Duty of $180 was charged upon entry, plus freight of $600.

Kevin had decided to set up the boat to be strip planked, glued, and edge-nailed. He thought this would avoid conventional carvel planking involving planning ahead, spiling and fitting, which is an art in itself. For the next few years he valiantly plugged away at his building job, eventually almost completing the strip planking. At this point, Kevin realized just how much work was going to be involved in completing the boat and decided to enlist our aid. He proposed to ship back the hull with ballast keel attached for us to complete. We made a completion contract #316 with him at $40,000 August 7, 1981. The hull subsequently arrived and was set up at Donnie's shop.

Donnie had the opportunity to examine Kevin's work in detail and reported to me that it would be virtually impossible to continue on with it and guarantee any kind of acceptable result.

Kevin and his father visited in December, had meetings and an inspection at Donnie's. It was then agreed that Donnie would have to cut away the hull Kevin had so laboriously constructed and begin from the frame again. Consequently, we signed a modification contract with him at that time for $7,700 additional work. During the winter of '82, Donnie's shop was heated with cut up epoxy-saturated mahogany, making a lovely hot fire as old planking was removed and new Honduras mahogany carvel applied.

Kevin had now named the vessel *Two Timer*, since it took two stints at the builder's yard to complete her. He may also have felt she was playing a bit of a dirty trick on him. Kevin was a tall young man and requested at least 6 foot 3 inches of headroom and the same for the length of his own berth.

Kevin added many extra items as we went along. *Two Timer's* re-birth took shape as we completed her to Kevin's new desires. We launched her at Ship Harbour, motored her to Halifax, stepped her masts, rigged her, and completed her outfitting at our wharves. Kevin came to Halifax and we all enjoyed sailing trials.

TWO TIMER AND GREY STARLING IN MELVILLE COVE.

Two Timer was then loaded aboard a low-bed for road delivery to Kevin in Cleveland. The date was then September 10, 1982 and she had cost Kevin $60,000 plus his original Kit #2 and all his own labour and expenses along the way. All was forgiven and forgotten as Kevin added his own personal fittings and enjoyed sailing her over the next years.

In June of 1985, we had a letter from Andrew Swiderski enquiring about a Destiny. He was a miner currently working in the Arctic. We mailed him all our material on the boat and he subsequently visited us.

Andrew had a very rough early life. He survived Poland during World War Two, while many of his immediate family perished. Later, when he was married with children, his mining work took him around the world and away from home a lot. In the process, he became an alcoholic which effectively ended his family life. When he came to us, he was older, his children grown and on their own. He was tired and just wanted to have a small yacht to go sailing off into the sunset.

His daughter, Teresa, lived in Windsor, Ontario with her family, and all his financial matters were handled by her. Finances were always tight with him. He made good money while working, but there were always those periods when his devils caught up with him.

Two Timer: IT TOOK TWO STINTS AT THE BUILDER'S YARD TO BUILD HER.

He asked us to build him a Destiny to be called *Teresa*, but as a basic power-away model. He would live aboard and build in cabin furniture, later adding masts, sails and rigging. We signed building contract #318 with him including diesel engine, steering and tank for $59,000.

The work began at Donnie Russell's with payments coming in fairly regularly up to the stage of planking completed by September of 1986. Andrew changed jobs and his payments fell behind. His daughter Teresa apologized and said they would be caught up soon. However, it still dragged on, and we were obliged to begin to charge Andrew interest on the unpaid balances.

Our agreed work on the boat was completed over the winter of 1986 and she was moved out of the boat shop and stored in the yard pending Andrew's next decisions. He owed us $22,000 and was having trouble sending any money at all, although we were told interest charges would be acceptable to him. Through 1987 and 1988, we had the odd payment. In March 1989, we had a visit from Teresa and a payment on account. We also did preventative maintenance work at her request. By May 1990 there was still $4,000 owing on the original account plus another $8,300 on the requested maintenance work and our creditors were threatening seizure of the boat.

Finally, Andrew showed up in September 1991 to take delivery. We allowed the launching in Halifax although some funds were still owing. Andrew was to live on the boat at our wharves and work on her. By this time, Andrew had over $100,000 in the boat including interest, maintenance, launching and storage.

Although he was supposed to be working on the boat, he got two boxes of one-inch brass nails from me, and nailed them all over the interior of his trunk cabin in various designs. Hundreds of them. Unfortunately, the cabin was only three-quarter inch thick which left them sticking out on the outside! We hadn't seen him in a few days when we got a call from Teresa in Windsor, Ontario. Apparently, Andrew had fallen off the boat and almost drowned. Having scared himself half to death, he boarded a train, still soaking wet, to travel back to Windsor. Teresa said he was still wet when he arrived at her front door. His romance with the boat had ended and he asked us to sell it for whatever we could get.

There were no takers even though we advertised her profusely. The following spring, Andrew surfaced again and wanted to know if I or anyone else would buy her. He was willing to sell her for $20,000! No one was interested, but my son Kevin thought he might be able to complete the boat, mast and rig her over time. The deal was struck and the last we saw of Andrew, he was headed for a mountain in Peru where he had friends he mined with.

Kevin worked on the boat, sailing her as he went. He was running the finish shop at our boatyard in Murphy's Cove at that time, and had built himself a house at Gaetz Brook, halfway between Halifax and Murphy's Cove. Shortly after, he contracted a serious leukemia, which almost ended his sailing days on *Teresa*. Persevering through two years of hospitalization, chemotherapy, and on-going treatments, he survived and returned to work on the boat. Perhaps having her to work on and sail helped him keep on going.

David Marye of Ontario, New York had seen a Jay Benford designed 35-foot Pinky schooner, the original of which was sailed by Benford himself with his wife and children. David had purchased the plans and wanted to know if we could build her for him.

David was a 45-year-old confirmed bachelor and planned to finish the boat himself if we built the hull. Consequently, we signed building contract #322 with him in October 1986, at $35,000 for the hull, ballast keel and deck, to become known as *Pinky*.

Over the months that followed, David visited a few times and sent copious amounts of drawings, suggestions, and questions. I did a layout and sail plan for him, first as a ketch, and then as a schooner, which he preferred. David was a clerical worker at an atomic plant and his payments were rather spasmodic, at best. The work proceeded as planned and *Pinky* was moved outside the shop in 1988 pending payment of account and any decisions on further work from David. In June and July of 1989 we went back to work on the boat installing a cabin, cockpit, rails, mouldings and the like at a further $13,000. The work was completed and *Pinky* was ready for the pickup trailer-truck for her delivery to David in New York. Philip Stevens of Sealand Industries in Chester Basin would be the hauler. We were familiar with their work and experience and had every confidence Philip would see her safely to David. She was loaded along with her two masts and declared out of Canada at $60,800, U.S. Funds.

David worked along on the boat doing cabin work and engine installation in his back yard in Ontario, New York. It seemed to take a very long time, but he was a meticulous worker. Eventually, his financial position caught up with him and he was forced to offer the boat for sale before even being launched.

He claimed he had $94,000 in the boat and eventually had to accept a sacrifice sale, which we later heard was $25,000. The dream had ended before it really began and with David's sincerity, I am sure it still gives him sleepless nights.

Fred Spinney of Saint John, New Brunswick approached us first in 1986 and later in 1989 about building the hull of a classic sloop he had designed. Fred made a good hull model and supplied all the lines and construction drawings for the vessel. She was different than mine of course, but of a down-east yacht style that he admired. After discussions and visits from him we went to a building contract in September 1989 at $78,000, including engine, cabins and trim.

Construction went along well. Fred visited from time to time. He was also working on maintaining his own physical fitness, and made the remark that he hoped all the stress didn't kill a man of his age.

As the building proceeded, the stress lessened and Fred looked forward to delivery. She was loaded on a trailer and delivered to him at Saint John in September 1990. He still had work to do on her himself of course, but the last I heard he was happy and content in his project and looking forward to launching day.

FRED SPINNEY'S 39' YAWL, LOADING. HE WAS HAPPY AND CONTENT.

As far as I was concerned, although business was slow, I was fully prepared and ready to go on building more boats. I had my hammer in one hand, and my drawing pencil in the other. I looked around for work to do, but there was none.

I had been retired from the telephone company for some years, my marriage of thirty-five years had ended, and now there were no more boat customers. It was all very mystifying to me; I couldn't understand what was happening in my world. The bottom had dropped out of everything; it was my dark night of the soul, and I didn't know what to do.

Then I heard a very small voice in my mind saying simply, "Go someplace quiet." That certainly was a strange instruction for a man desperately looking for something to do.

The only place I had quiet was a little log cabin I had built in the woods at Lake Charlotte. I packed up, went there, sat down, and said, "Okay, I'm here, what do I do now?" "Nothing," the voice replied, "Just sit there and be quiet." This was a terrible sentence to pronounce on a 40-year-workaholic! How could I possibly do that? Surely, there was something I should be doing. But the voice had gone quiet. I stayed there in the woods for two years before I began to realize that I had gone to my mountaintop, and it was myself I was looking for. Answers began to trickle in, as my life took a new direction with serenity and meaning. But that has been chronicled elsewhere.

My era of wooden boats had ended and all that was left were the memories, photos, plans and stories of all the wonderful yachts and vessels that this book chronicles.

A ROSBOROUGH BARQUENTINE WITH A BONE IN HER TEETH.

APPENDIX

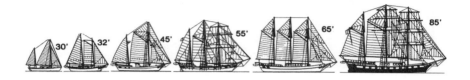

MAINLINE DESIGNS BY ROSBOROUGH:

R-30
Destiny
Pilgrim
Nomad
Privateer
Aquarius
Vagabond

R-30 (30 FEET)

Examples are: *Teredo Verde* and *Sagittarius*
Total built: 4

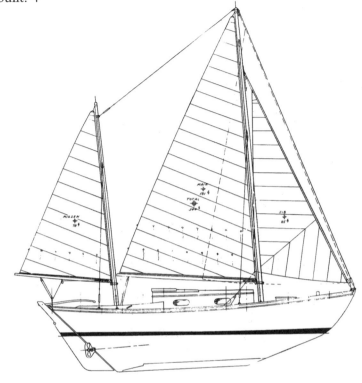

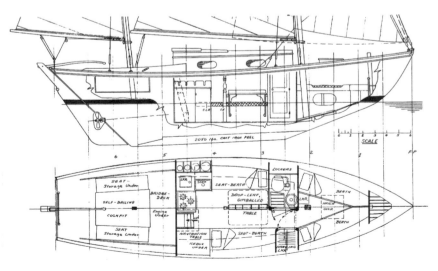

DESTINY (32 FEET)

Examples are: *Nyeema* and *Two Timer*
Total built: 6

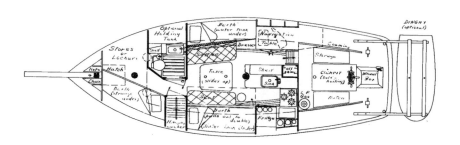

PILGRIM (35 FEET)

Examples are: *Polynya* and *Pitanna*

Total built: 7

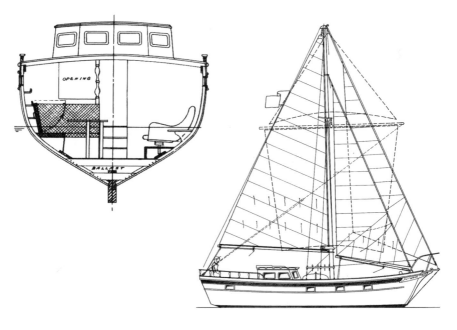

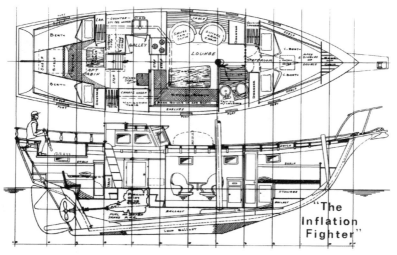

NOMAD (40 FEET)

Examples are: *Grey Starling* and *Shawna Lynn*
Total built: 4

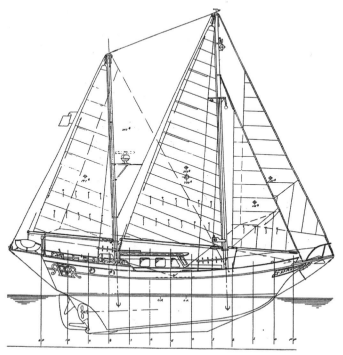

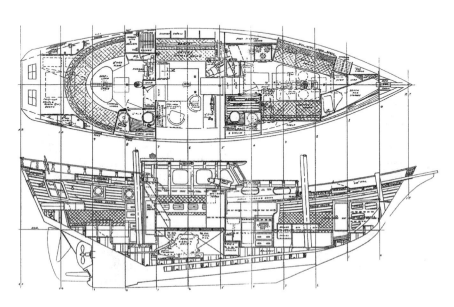

PRIVATEER (45 FEET)

Three different styles of Privateer (same hull):
Ketch, the Buccaneer (schooner), Distant Star (brigantine)
Total built: 65

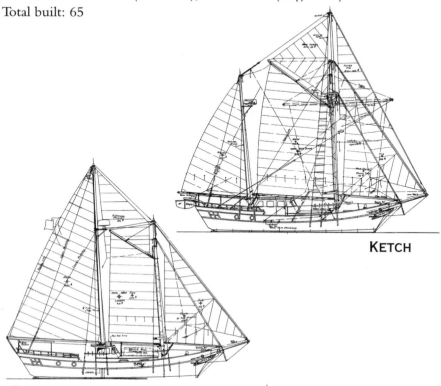

KETCH

BUCCANEER

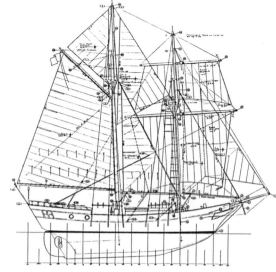

DISTANT STAR